JOSEPH CONRAD AND THE PERFORMING ARTS

Joseph Conrad and the Performing Arts

Edited by

KATHERINE ISOBEL BAXTER
University of Hong Kong, China

and

RICHARD J. HAND
University of Glamorgan, UK

LONDON AND NEW YORK

First published 2009 by Ashgate Publishing

2 Park Square, Milton Park, Abingdon, Oxfordshire OX14 4RN
711 Third Avenue, New York, NY 10017

Routledge is an imprint of the Taylor & Francis Group, an informa business

First issued in paperback 2018

Copyright © 2009 Katherine Isobel Baxter and Richard J. Hand

Katherine Isobel Baxter and Richard J. Hand have asserted their moral right under the Copyright, Designs and Patents Act, 1988, to be identified as the editors of this work.

All rights reserved. No part of this book may be reprinted or reproduced or utilised in any form or by any electronic, mechanical, or other means, now known or hereafter invented, including photocopying and recording, or in any information storage or retrieval system, without permission in writing from the publishers.

Notice:
Product or corporate names may be trademarks or registered trademarks, and are used only for identification and explanation without intent to infringe.

British Library Cataloguing in Publication Data
Joseph Conrad and the performing arts
   1. Conrad, Joseph, 1857–1924 – Knowledge – Performing arts 2. Conrad, Joseph, 1857–1924 – Dramatic works 3. Conrad, Joseph, 1857–1924 – Film and video adaptations 4. Motion pictures and literature 5. English fiction – Film and video adaptations 6. Theater – England 7. Influence (Literary, artistic, etc.)
   I. Baxter, Katherine Isobel II. Hand, Richard J.
   823.9'12

Library of Congress Cataloging-in-Publication Data
   Joseph Conrad and the performing arts / edited by Katherine Isobel Baxter and Richard J. Hand.
     p. cm.
   Includes bibliographical references.
   ISBN 978-0-7546-6490-1 (alk. paper)
   1. Conrad, Joseph, 1857–1924—Knowledge—Performing arts. 2. Conrad, Joseph, 1857–1924—Dramatic works. 3. Conrad, Joseph, 1857–1924—Film and video adaptations. 4. English fiction—Film and video adaptations. 5. Motion pictures and literature. 6. Theater—England. 7. Influence (Literary, artistic, etc.) I. Baxter, Katherine Isobel, 1976– II. Hand, Richard J.

   PR6005.O4Z5435 2009
   823'.912—dc22

                                                                   2008018473

ISBN 978-0-7546-6490-1 (hbk)
ISBN 978-1-138-37627-4 (pbk)

Contents

A Note on Texts		*vi*
List of Contributors		*vii*
Introduction	Joseph Conrad and the Performing Arts: An Introduction *Katherine Isobel Baxter and Richard J. Hand*	1
1	Performing Malaya *Linda Dryden*	11
2	'Sly Civility?': Mrs Almayer's and Mrs Willems's Performances of Colonial Resistance in *Outcast of the Islands* and *Almayer's Folly* *Susan Barras*	29
3	Mixing the Masks of Comedy and Tragedy: The Popular Theatres of Joseph Conrad's Fiction *Richard J. Hand*	45
4	From Stage to Screen: 'The Return,' *Victory*, *The Secret Agent* and *Chance* *Robert Hampson*	59
5	'Post-impressionism' and the Cinema: How We Are 'Made to See' in Conrad's *Victory* *Suzanne Speidel*	77
6	Gorgeous Eloquence: Conrad and Shadowgraphy *Stephen Donovan*	97
7	Comedy and Romance: A New Look at Shakespeare and Conrad *Katherine Isobel Baxter*	111
8	Conrad in the Operatic Mode *Laurence Davies*	127
Bibliography		*147*
Index		*157*

A Note On Texts

The abbreviation *CL* has been used throughout this book for Conrad's letters:

Frederick R. Karl and Laurence Davies, ed., *The Collected Letters of Joseph Conrad Volume 1: 186–97* (1983); *Volume 2: 1898-1902* (1986); *Volume 3: 1903–1907* (1988); *Volume 4: 1908–1911* (1991); *Volume 5: 1912-1916* (1996); *Volume 6: 1917–1919* (2002). Laurence Davies and J. H. Stape, ed., *The Collected Letters of Joseph Conrad Volume 7: 1920–1922* (2005).

Unless stated otherwise, all other citations from Conrad are from Dent's Uniform Standard Edition (London: Dent, 1923–28) which has the same pagination as the Dent Collected Edition (London: Dent, 1946–55) and the Oxford World's Classics edition (Oxford: Oxford University Press, 1983–). The following abbreviations are used for these volumes:

AF	*Almayer's Folly*
C	*Chance*
LE	*Last Essays*
LJ	*Lord Jim*
NN	*The Nigger of the 'Narcissus'*
OI	*An Outcast of the Islands*
PR	*A Personal Record*
Res	*The Rescue*
Ro	*The Rover*
SA	*The Secret Agent*
T	*Typhoon, and Other Stories*
TU	*Tales of Unrest*
WT	*Within the Tides*
Y	*Youth: A Narrative, and Two Other Stories*

Contributors

Susan Barras is currently a teacher of English at the Royal Grammar School in Guildford, Surrey. She holds an MA and PhD in English from Royal Holloway, University of London. She has presented papers at the Edinburgh Robert Louis Stevenson Conference in 2004 and at the International Joseph Conrad Conference in Amsterdam in 2005.

Katherine Isobel Baxter is Research Assistant Professor at Hong Kong University. Her recent publications on Conrad include 'Conrad's Revelations of Solitude' in *Beyond the Roots: The Evolution of Conrad's Ideology and Art*, ed. Wieslaw Krajka (Columbia University Press, 2005); 'Fleshing Out the Bones: Two New Manuscript Leaves of "Falk,"' *The Conradian* 31.2 (2006); 'Conrad: Chronology of Composition and Publication,' in *Conrad in Context*, ed. Allan Simmons (Cambridge University Press, 2008).

Laurence Davies is Professor of English Literature at the University of Glasgow and Visting Professor of Comparative Literature at Dartmouth College. He has co-authored a critical biography of the Scottish traveller, writer and political campaigner R. B. Cunninghame Graham, and has edited all nine volumes of the *Collected Letters of Joseph Conrad* for Cambridge University Press, working with a roster of collaborators including J. H. Stape, Gene M. Moore, Owen Knowles and Frederick R. Karl. In the USA, Davies has won fellowships from the National Endowment for the Humanities and the National Endowment for the Arts, the latter for his work on an opera libretto.

Stephen Donovan is Senior Lecturer in English at Uppsala University, Sweden. He is the author of *Joseph Conrad and Popular Culture* (Palgrave, 2005) and has published numerous articles and book chapters on Conrad and on Robert Louis Stevenson. He is the editor of the new Penguin Modern Classics edition of *Under Western Eyes* (forthcoming 2007)

Linda Dryden is Reader in Literature and Culture at Napier University, Edinburgh. She has published widely on Conrad and is the author of *Joseph Conrad and the Imperial Romance* (Macmillan, 2000) and *The Modern Gothic and Literary Doubles: Stevenson, Wilde and Wells* (Palgrave, 2004). She is co-editor of the *Journal of Stevenson Studies*, and her edited collection of essays, *Stevenson and Conrad*, will be published with Texas Tech University Press in 2008.

Robert Hampson is Professor of Modern Literature and Head of the Department of English at Royal Holloway, University of London. He is the author of *Joseph Conrad: Betrayal and Identity* (Macmillan, 1992), *Cross-Cultural Encounters in Conrad's Malay Fiction* (Palgrave, 2000) and *Conrad's Secrets* (Palgrave, forthcoming 2007). He co-edited *Conrad and Theory* (with Andrew Gibson, 1998), *Ford Madox Ford: A Re-Appraisal* (with Tony Davenport, 2002), and *Ford Madox Ford and Modernity* (with Max Saunders, 2003). He has edited a number of works by Conrad including *Lord Jim* (Penguin), *Victory* (Penguin), *Heart of Darkness* (Penguin), *Nostromo* (Wordsworth) as well as works by Kipling (*Something of Myself, In Black & White* and *Soldiers Three*) and by Rider Haggard (*King Solomon's Mines*) – all for Penguin. He is editing *The Arrow of Gold* for the Cambridge Edition of Conrad.

Richard J. Hand is Professor of Theatre and Media Drama at the University of Glamorgan, Wales, UK. He is the author of *The Theatre of Joseph Conrad: Reconstructed Fictions* (Palgrave, 2005) and editor of the forthcoming critical edition of Basil MacDonald Hastings's *Victory: The Play and Reviews* as part of Rodopi's Conrad Studies series. He has published numerous articles and book chapters on Conrad and has published on other figures from Ambrose Bierce to Frank Zappa. He has published a number of pieces in the area of horror studies and has translated a number of plays by Victor Hugo, Octave Mirbeau and other French dramatists. He is an active theatre director and produced the world premiere of Conrad's *Laughing Anne* in 2000.

Suzanne Speidel is Senior Lecturer in Film Studies at Sheffield Hallam University. Her publications include 'Times of Death in Joseph Conrad's *The Secret Agent* and Alfred Hitchcock's *Sabotage*,' in *The Classic Novel: From Page to Screen*, ed. Robert Giddings and Erica Sheen (Manchester University Press, 2000); 'Film Form and Narrative' in *An Introduction to Film Studies* (Fourth Edition), ed. Jill Nelmes (Routledge, 2007); and 'The Ending Is Out There' in *The X-Files and Literature*, ed. Sharon Yang (Cambridge Scholars Press, 2007)

Joseph Conrad and the Performing Arts: An Introduction

Katherine Isobel Baxter and Richard J. Hand

Joseph Conrad's first novel, *Almayer's Folly*, was published in 1895 and appeared at a time when literary fiction continued to be the pre-eminent art form in contemporary English culture. Certainly, the situation was a stark contrast to the perceived state of the English theatre which had been regarded as being in steady decline for some decades with, for example, Henry James disconsolately proclaiming in the late 1870s that 'it is sufficiently obvious that the poverty of the English theatre is complete' (1949, 123). Perhaps the most famous – and the most damning – indictment of English theatre appeared just four years before Conrad's first novel when Henry Arthur Jones described English drama as 'a "*Slough of Despond*"' in the wide well-tilled field of English literature' (vii). Jones, of course, wrote this in the preface to his own play *Saints and Sinners*, a play which represented the impetus for an 'English Literary Theatre' that obsessed him and other notable figures in British theatre such as William Archer. However, little had changed by 1897 – the same year Conrad published *The Nigger of the 'Narcissus'* – with George Bernard Shaw remarking that 'The nineteenth-century novel, with all its faults, has maintained itself immeasurably above the nineteenth-century drama' (1931, 144). In 1898, the year that saw the publication of Conrad's *Tales of Unrest* and the year that he started to write *Heart of Darkness*, we find Shaw 'praying' that 'contemporary drama might be brought up to the level of contemporary fiction' (1931, 303).

However, despite all the gloomy appraisals of the state of contemporary theatre, it would be a mistake to think that English theatre lacked an audience or profile. The despondency regarding the performing arts was not that they were lacking an audience. Far from it. This was the era when the popular theatres of music hall and melodrama attracted habitual and devoted audiences; the era when concert halls, imported operas and home-grown operettas commanded the attention of the press and the public. It was an era when British actors as diverse as the dramatic actress Ellen Terry or the music hall star Marie Lloyd enjoyed extraordinary cult celebrity. Most illustriously, the year that saw Conrad's first novel also saw Henry Irving become the first actor to be knighted. Meanwhile, in Paris, a revolution was to begin when Auguste and Louis Lumière staged the world's first public film screening on 28 December 1895. Such phenomena may have been 'popular,' but, in the criteria of the time, they were not 'serious'. With regard to the performance of written plays, 1895 was the year that saw the premieres of Oscar Wilde's *An*

Ideal Husband and *The Importance of Being Earnest*, Shaw's *Candida* and Janet Achurch's *Mrs Daintree's Daughter*. These works have only gained their full literary significance in hindsight and were at best perceived as good-willed but faltering steps towards the long overdue inauguration of 'Literary Theatre'.

We have said 'inauguration' but perhaps 'resurrection' would be a more accurate word. In the twilight years of the nineteenth century there was a steady rise of the concept of 'English Literature' as a cultural institution (including as an academic discipline) embodying the values, heritage and identity of the nation. And if one subscribed to the notion of an English 'Literary Tradition,' there could be only one figurehead: William Shakespeare. Shakespeare may have been a poet, but his place as a dramatist was paramount, thus making theatre the keystone of English literary culture. In the mid eighteenth century David Garrick had created the Shakespeare industry with his numerous acclaimed stage performances of the plays from the 1740s onwards as well as erecting a Temple to Shakespeare in the 1750s and launching a high profile Shakespeare 'Jubilee' at Stratford-on-Avon in 1769. Although the 'Jubilee' was severely loss-making, the Shakespeare industry was here to stay. For Algernon Charles Swinburne, writing over a century later, Shakespeare continued to be a fascinating and seemingly limitless sea which despite the noble endeavours of other poets and critics had scarcely begun to be navigated (Swinburne 1880). For the contemporaries of Conrad, however, the legacy of Shakespeare could be oppressive. George Steiner describes the situation as one in which 'the Shakespearean shadow' (150) fell between the knowledge that English drama desperately needed to be rejuvenated and the actual process of writing these new plays. Or, as Edmund Gosse reveals when he writes of the wider Elizabethan tradition: 'It haunts us, it oppresses us, it destroys us' (quoted in Steiner, 150). And while they were tangled in the midst of this cultural soul-searching, the champions of the would-be 'English Literary Theatre' could only gaze across from the shores of Britain to mainland Europe with green-eyed envy. After all, as early as the 1870s in France, Émile Zola had declared in no uncertain terms that drama must become real or die. For the likes of Henry Arthur Jones and William Archer, Zola's plea for *realism* seemed to have come true across Europe – most quintessentially with the rise to prominence of the Norwegian playwright Henrik Ibsen – but had not succeeded in sweeping the English theatre along in the wake of its revolution.

Émile Zola was a novelist, and yet such was his despair at the rotten state of French theatre, he himself turned to writing plays: his 1873 adaptation of his 1868 novel *Thérèse Raquin* is regarded as a key moment in the history of theatrical realism. Zola's fearless endeavour to cross the boundaries of media and write a work of drama explicitly designed to be producible on the stage would be an abiding inspiration for the advocates of the English Literary Theatre and for a fair number of 'men of letters' themselves. For example, an English language writer such as Henry James made numerous ambitious attempts to conquer the stage with his own plays, but the poor and even, on occasion, humiliating reception the works received only succeeded in leaving James defeated and dejected. Zola's decision to dramatise his own work of fiction – the process of self-adaptation – was a technique that was also employed by James several times but perhaps most notably when he adapted *Daisy Miller* (1878) into a play in 1882 and *The American* (1877) in 1891. Other notable writers of the period also practiced self-adaptation: Arthur Conan Doyle dramatised his short story 'A Straggler of "15"' (1891) into *Waterloo* (1894); J. M. Barrie adapted his novel *The Little Minister* (1891) into a play of the same title in 1897; and – once again in Conrad's key year of 1895 – Thomas Hardy completed a stage version of *Tess of the D'Urbervilles* (1891).

Joseph Conrad would himself endeavour to write for the stage with three works of self-adaptation, turning the short story 'To-morrow' (1902) into *One Day More* (1905); dramatising *The Secret Agent* (1907) in 1919; and 'Because of the Dollars' (1915) into *Laughing Anne* in 1920. Furthermore, Conrad also wrote a screenplay, adapting the short story 'Gaspar Ruiz' (1906) into *Gaspar the Strong Man* in 1920. Written twenty-five years after the publication of *Almayer's Folly*, and only twenty-five years after the inauguration of the public screening of film, *Gaspar the Strong Man* indicates the remarkable trajectory of Conrad's writing career, a career which he began very much as a Victorian novelist and yet developed to encompass not only modernist aesthetics but modern technologies.

The fact that – with the exception of *One Day More* (1905) – Conrad's forays into stage and screen dramatisation all come in the last five years of his life has led to the argument that Conrad's self-adaptations were, in Frederick R. Karl's words, a desperate attempt at 'escape from malaise and stagnation' (1979, 838). And, indeed, although *One Day More* was composed at a time when Conrad's writing can hardly be described as 'stagnant' or in a state of 'malaise,' it has continued to be regarded in somewhat cynical terms: John Stape, for example, explains it as a fairly desperate attempt to procure 'hard cash' (2007, 134). Nevertheless, we should not overlook the fact that drama and the performing arts were an extremely important influence on Conrad throughout his career: just as George Steiner perceives a Shakespearean shadow looming large over the English writers of the period, a similar shadow of the performing arts as a whole (including Shakespeare) can be detected across Conrad's oeuvre. As Zdzislaw Najder reveals, as a child Conrad apparently wrote patriotic plays extolling Polish nationalism (2007, 33), and as early as 1897 Conrad admits in his letters: 'I greatly desire to write a play myself. It is my dark and secret ambition' (*CL*1, 419). In 1909 Conrad confesses 'I have a theatrical imagination' (*CL*4, 218). However, in the same letter Conrad admits 'I detest the stage.' Like Henry James and Thomas Hardy who flirted with the idea of becoming a playwright, Conrad can be found to belittle the theatre as an art form but also to have major problems with the concept and presence of theatrical censorship in Britain – stringent legislation which had no equivalent in the freer world of fictional prose – as he unequivocally reveals in 'The Censor of Plays: An Appreciation' (*Daily Mail*, 12 October 1907 and reprinted in *Notes on Life and Letters*). Indeed, for some writers of the time, censorship was cited as a major reason for the poor state of British theatre. Conrad also had a problem –

tantamount to a kind of agoraphobia – with the lived experience of watching a play in the theatre. Nevertheless, Conrad is a paradoxical writer, and such sentiments are at odds with the fact that he did see plays: his visit to London's Grand Guignol at the Little Theatre in 1920 inspired him to write *Laughing Anne* just as visiting a film version of *Les Misérables* in the same year would lead to the *Gaspar the Strong Man* screenplay. Perhaps even more revealing is the enthusiasm with which Conrad advises Basil Macdonald Hastings on the adaptation of *Victory* from 1916 onwards and the gusto with which he attends the subsequent rehearsals prior to the premiere in 1919.

Although Conrad's plays are steadily enjoying a naissance of interest and reappraisal (Hand 2005; Joy; Wheatley 2002 etc.), Conrad's greatest abiding achievement and reputation is inevitably going to remain as a writer of fiction. However, Conrad's novels and other prose fictions are not by definition antitheatrical. On the contrary – and this is the critical impetus that underlies this collection – Conrad is evidently a writer who is inspired by the performing arts as a source for intertextual reference and allusion. Conrad is a writer who composes and orchestrates narratives of disciplined, occasionally operatic, structure. He is also a writer whose works are frequently imbued with theatricality and the strategies of dramatic metaphor, dramatic irony and dramatic actualisation. Since the first screen *Victory* in 1919, Conrad has remained a significant source for screen adaptation, a task undoubtedly facilitated when one recognises how remarkably and consistently cinematic many of Conrad's works are.

The essays in this collection explore Conrad's relationship with the performing arts through various means. Linda Dryden and Susan Barras open the collection with their discussions of the importance of performativity in Conrad's Malay fiction. Whilst considerations of performativity have taken their time to filter into literary scholarship they have been in use rather longer in the fields of cultural studies and anthropology. Explorations of who is performing or acting for whom, why a given performance or act takes place, and how that performance or act is informed by cultural mores can be as interesting for fictional as for real actions. Of course for fiction there are potentially many more layers of interpretation to be had from these questions since the answers given in the fictional realm of the text may conflict with the answers given in the authorial realm.

Linda Dryden takes as her starting point Conrad's imagined breakfasts with characters from his fiction. At the breakfast table all are able to speak, and Dryden suggests this mode of composition is behind Conrad's palpable determination to incorporate Malay voices in his fiction set in the region. However, Conrad also recognises the alienated aspect to those Malay voices, their separation from the world of his European protagonists and readers. His method for representing this separateness is frequently a recourse to theatrical motifs, whereby the actions of the Malays are given an unreal, staged quality. Their actions are dramatised but their motivation to dramatise themselves in such a way remains obscured from view.

As if in response to finding themselves on an exotic stage the Europeans of Conrad's fiction also frequently drift into self-conscious performances, like Josephine Baker's heroine Zouzou who perpetuates her dance in delighted response to seeing her own giant shadow dancing on the back wall of a stage.[1] Finding themselves in an alien environment these Europeans choose to ignore the possibility that it contains a meaningful reality beyond their knowledge. Instead they treat the East as a theatrical space in which to perform their fantasies against a painted backdrop augmented by a troop of silenced local extras. This theatrical space is both liberating and entrapping: it provides a stage for expressions of new emotions but also curtails the expression of others. The risk these Europeans run is that they become as alienated from their European self-identity as they are from their Malayan surroundings. Jim, for example, remains unincorporated into the world of Patusan, existing at its centre by virtue of his difference. And yet his plight is such that his allegiance to his fantasies disallows him from returning to European society. Edith Travers similarly cannot usurp, only ape (albeit beguilingly), the Malays of Lingard's affection. Moreover her theatrical flirtation with the East only disenchants her further from her European culture, embodied by her husband, to which she must inevitably return.

Susan Barras chooses to answer the questions posed by a performative analysis primarily in the fictional realm, applying anthropological and cultural studies theories about *latah* to the performances of women in Conrad's early Malay fiction. Her discussion relates Conrad's fiction to a growing interest, in the late nineteenth century, in racial and cultural psychology. This interest found its way into medical periodicals, publications relating to the colonies, monographs in anthropology, as well as more everyday journals. In some instances the discussions are based on little more than racist conjecture, such as the argument made by T. Duncan Greenlees concerning insanity amongst the indigenous South African population:

> If we consider the theories of those who maintain that while mania represents a loss of the lower developed strata of the mental organism, melancholia indicates an absence of the highest and latest developed strata, then this prevalence of mania among natives of low developed brain-functions goes far to prove this theory. (72)

Elsewhere discussions are based on observation or reported observations of particular behavioural patterns. Once again the interpretation of these behavioural patterns is in no way immune from assumptions of racial superiority on the part of the authors, and the tone of interpretation is predominantly patronizing for all its genuine inquisitiveness.

Whether Conrad followed the debates and accounts of *latah* in any great detail or not he would no doubt have been aware of the phenomenon. In his Malay fiction Conrad was not necessarily straining for a photographic reconstruction of the East

---

[1] *Zouzou* (Marc Allégret, 1934).

nor did he seek to throw a literary glamour over the European imperial experience, but rather, following writers like Louis Becke with his tales of the South Pacific, he explored the frequently destructive relationship between East and West in their imperial and colonial engagement, whilst attempting to withhold moral judgement. He was aware of how people performed differently in different locations whose apparent exoticism could transform them, as if by costume and set, to the point that their actions might even seem strange to themselves. By including scenes of mental breakdown Conrad took this subject to an extreme, whilst also suggesting the cultural barriers to understanding one another's performances of madness.

Returning to the world of the author, Richard J. Hand explores how Conrad drew purposely on theatrical paradigms to structure his fiction. As in *The Rescue* Conrad shows up the insincerity of European bourgeois culture through the stagy behaviour of his protagonists in 'The Return'. But elsewhere Conrad is more playful in his references, drawing attention to the artifice of his own narrative as much as to the artifice of his characters. For all the value that is placed on his veracity, his realism, Conrad was also an arch caricaturist with a satirical bent. Sylvère Monod has enumerated, even alphabetised, the various ways in which Heemskirk, in 'Freya of the Seven Isles,' is disparaged as emphatically Dutch. But Conrad also invoked stock figures of *commedia dell'arte*, loading the horror of Heemskirk with an inflection of stereotype. This use of *commedia dell'arte* invites us to distance ourselves from the protagonists as stock characters in a tale, whilst encouraging us to expect a conventional happy ending. Yet the story veers away from such an ending. This sabotage of readerly expectations is Swiftian in its discomforting satire. We, as readers, have been encouraged to see the protagonists as puppet-like fools who are bound to act in a particular way. And yet that this is our view is a result of our own puppet-like response to the manipulation of literary tropes by the author. As a result the shallowness of our expectations is shown up through our feeble disappointment with an unconventional yet arguably realistic ending. This turn from predetermined expectations, set up by way of reference to traditional theatrical forms, to the performance of unexpected and tragic action leads us into the realm of melodrama. Conrad's own predilection for melodramatic performance is indicated by his operatic taste for Meyerbeer, discussed later by Laurence Davies.

Richard J. Hand, Robert Hampson, and Suzanne Speidel also explore in their respective essays Conrad's use of melodrama drawn from stage and screen. One crucial aspect of the incorporation of melodrama in Conrad's fiction is the increased prominence it gives to the female characters, and our appreciation of them. The debates that have always run concerning the plausibility of Conrad's female protagonists are nuanced here by questions of pose and performance. Just as in the early Malay fiction performativity wove itself into issues of politics and cross-cultural relations, so too in the domestic dramas of 'The Return,' *The Secret Agent*, and *Chance*, as well as in *Victory*, female action is presented as performance, taking its lead from the stage and later the silver screen. In one sense this can be seen as reinforcing the implausibility of Conrad's heroines. They are, we might argue, no more than a conglomeration of clichés of femininity, the Achilles' heel of Conrad's skill in characterization. However, it is also possible to see these clichés as purposeful, adopted either by the Conradian narrator or by his female protagonists themselves, or by both.

In 'The Return' the staginess of the Hervey's house, a Shavian accumulation of aesthetic props, indicates the emptiness of the intellect that those props are intended to vouch for. This emptiness is reinforced by the melodramatic poses which husband and wife adopt in their interactions with each other. These poses are produced unselfconsciously for the most part, and even catch the actors unaware. As the Herveys awaken to the sham of their lives together the reader is encouraged to diagnose their predicament as endemic to the couple's social caste. In this case performance and pose is indicative of sham and insincerity. Thus the implausible characterization referred to before becomes exactly the trait Conrad wishes to identify in his protagonists. Conrad's use of theatrical motifs and devices plays the notion of 'suspension of disbelief' as a metaphor for the operations of bourgeois society.

In *Victory* Lena's various performances elicit a more complex response. She is from the start a performer, one of Zangiacomo's touring ladies' orchestra. Moreover, this early role is itself ambiguous since the ladies of the orchestra appear to be expected to play more lucratively in the intervals than on stage, during their performances at Schomberg's hotel. But Lena is not a good player nor a particularly fine violinist in so far as we can tell (although her failure to respond to Schomberg's overtures only excites him further), and it is only on Heyst's island that she is able to find a role that she can play with gusto. However, like the Hervey's, although with a more tragic outcome, Lena and Heyst are unable to act with full authenticity, and are further plagued by doubt in their own worthiness and each other's honesty. As the novel's denouement approaches Lena adopts a series of postures that seem drawn directly from the melodrama of stage and screen, postures that, ironically, she imagines will realise, in the full meaning of the word, the self-image she aspires to.

Lena's actions may appear contrived, her recourse to the poses of melodrama limited and limiting, and yet this very contrivance indicates the depth of her plight. Her melodramatic performances at the end of the novel are in some sense no more nor less than her musical performances at the beginning. In both cases their result is the semi-satisfaction of male appetites, and their intended outcome is shelter and security. True, Lena's passion for Heyst elevates the terms of her performance in the second half of the novel, yet it remains a performance. What is highlighted here is the lack of freedom in action available to Lena. Even on Heyst's magical island, the boundaries for female action are limited, reaching no further than the conventions of melodrama. No wonder then that Lena has seemed to critics psychologically unconvincing. She is no more so to Heyst or to herself. Nor is Lena alone, for Flora too, in *Chance*, is consumed as the passive object of masculine desire by a series of hungry male gazes. Flora seems less in control of her performance than Lena, particularly in the first half of the novel, and yet her very passivity appears a protective performance through which she breaks occasionally, as with her 'horribly merry' look to Mrs Fyne during her retrieval by her box-making relative (171). Moreover, as Robert Hampson explores, Flora's passivity mirrors the silent heroine of early cinema whose body by virtue of being filmed performed erotically under the thoroughly male lens of the camera. Once again the actions available to the female protagonist are limited, framed on all sides by a masculine gaze that includes, ironically, Mrs Fyne's militant feminism.

If the explorations of theatrical and cinematic melodrama in Conrad illuminate the performances of Conrad's heroines, in particular, Stephen Donovan's discussion of shadowgraphy animates the very shadows of nature. Whilst Conrad rarely attempts to mimic an extended performance of shadowgraphy, as he might with melodrama, he draws upon shadowgraphy's play of light and darkness quite specifically at times to recreate the impression of glimpsed action, and decontextualised movement. Of course shadows are in themselves a familiar Conradian motif extending far beyond specific allusions to nineteenth-century entertainments. However, the very familiarity of the language of shadows in Conrad's work, and in Western culture more generally, can often blind us to particularised references which recall mechanical rather than numinous actions.

Conrad's use of such references is both retrospective and at the same time historically accurate, in that his stories and their narrators are set in a Victorian past contemporary with the popularity of amusements such as shadowgraphy. Yet their use also acts as a retrogressive counterpoint to the cinematic stylistics discussed previously. In one light we can see these references as part of Conrad's production of his self-image, whereby the early twentieth-century author nostalgically displays his roots in the previous century: here is one whose old fashioned values of honour and duty are to be indulged sympathetically because he is not really of this century but of the last. And yet it is also possible to see these references as thoroughly modernist, combining old and new technologies in a mosaic of allusions, fusing memory and the contemporary to create surprising new images.

Conrad's engagement with Shakespeare – explored in this collection by Katherine Baxter – proves to be similarly Janus-faced. On many levels Shakespeare represented the past, or rather a variety of pasts, for Conrad. Shakespeare links at least three of Conrad's several lives together: his childhood, his sea career, and his life as a writer. It is Shakespeare whom Conrad recalls, in *A Personal Record*, as his first acquaintance in English letters, through the translations of his father, a childhood memory associated with 'the first year of our bereavement [following the death of Conrad's mother], the last I spent with my father in exile' (PR 73). And it is Shakespeare who accompanies Conrad during his early years in the British Merchant Navy, in a 'five-shilling one-volume edition … read … at odd moments of the day, to the noisy accompaniment of caulkers' mallets' (PR 72). Finally Shakespeare provides a wealth of motifs, structural, linguistic and thematic, to the author Conrad throughout his oeuvre. Moreover, Shakespeare in all these lives stands as a totemic figure of English culture. He is one of the significant West-European writers to whom his father turned as an exemplar of national culture during his years of exile. As Conrad developed his language skills as a mariner, Shakespeare proved a useful and absorbing literary primer. And in his years of authorship Conrad turned to Shakespeare, as his father had before him, as a touchstone of cultural order and belonging.

However, what Conrad chooses to do with Shakespeare is as often modernist as it is traditionalist. Shakespeare becomes one of any number of sources, literary, performative, technological, to which Conrad alludes in the pursuit of his art. At times these allusions are unstructured, called upon as and when necessary to illuminate a point. Elsewhere Conrad manipulates his Shakespearian references to expose new visions of the world, particularly of the imperial and colonial world, through careful, and sometimes subverting, plotting. In this respect Conrad lights the way that others such as Eliot and Joyce were to follow.

The unlikely juxtapositions and subversions of genre and form that characterise so much of Conrad's use of the performing arts are particularly notable in his relationship with opera. As Laurence Davies shows, Conrad adapts opera both to characterise his own work and to stylise his prose. Opera is yet another performative mode on which Conrad draws in the patterning of his fiction. And yet it is more than this and stands as a metaphor for Conrad's allusive method as a whole. For opera's polyphonic quality is perhaps the closest we can get to describing the orchestration of multiple voices that characterises so much of Conrad's work, sending us back to our initial image of Conrad entertaining his protagonists at the breakfast table. Allowing each a voice Conrad hears them all, individually, or in duets, trios, even choruses.

Desmond MacCarthy, in a review of Joyce's *Exiles* in 1918, notes that for the dramatist and the novelist it is crucial to find characters who thoroughly embody their theme, so that in exploring the characters these themes come to the fore quite naturally: 'for nothing *happens* at all unless it happens to a particular person, and action is dependent on character' (208). In opera this takes on a further dimension in that the musical themes must also be convincingly embedded in the protagonists and their actions. As Davies shows Conrad's adapts this musical aspect by allowing his themes to percolate through the leitmotifs of his characters' speech. Returning finally to Conrad's external allusions, the ways in which he incorporates elements of the performing arts into his fiction, we might push the musical metaphor a little further and hear these as bass notes and polyvocal harmonies that enrich the melodic themes of his protagonists and their actions. Whilst they do not carry the plots they provide a framework for them, nuancing the themes through counterpoint and resolution.

Just as the voices that emerge from Conrad's fiction are polyphonic and heterogeneous so too there is no single line we can take on the influence of the performing arts on his work. What the essays that follow demonstrate however is that despite his general dislike for much that was on the British stage in his time Conrad was influenced by the performing arts and incorporated its tropes and structures into his work in imaginative ways. More importantly, these essays show that an investigation of this influence can shed new light on Conrad's oeuvre.

Recognition of this influence allows us to approach his work again from a different angle and emerge with new insight, not only into the texts themselves but also into Conrad's authorial methods as a whole. The eight essays in this collection do not offer a definitive account of Joseph Conrad and the performing arts but collectively offer an exciting and engaging forum for one of the most interesting and nascent areas of Conrad studies: one which will continue to grow and develop for years to come.

Chapter 1
Performing Malaya

Linda Dryden

Fictions, and photographic images, of the East were the primary means through which late nineteenth-century Westerners who had never travelled beyond the European continent were able to access Eastern culture. Readers of fiction were reliant on the writer's interpretation, or the photographer's composed image, and this usually involved the Eastern stereotype. However, for those who had travelled to Eastern territories, other possibilities were available: writers with an intimate knowledge of the geography and peoples of Eastern nations could choose to challenge the stereotype and present other realities. Joseph Conrad was one who chose to take issue with the traditional stereotyping of the East. In his 'Author's Note' to his first novel, *Almayer's Folly* (1895), he complained: 'The critic and the judge seems to think that in those distant lands all joy is a yell and a war dance, all pathos is a howl and a ghastly grin of filed teeth, and that the solution of all problems is found in the barrel of a revolver or on the point of an assegai.' 'And yet,' says Conrad, 'it is not so' (*Almayer's Folly* vii); and he proceeds to outline a more radical manifesto for his own writing:[1]

> And there is a bond between us and that humanity so far away. I am speaking of men and women – not of the charming and graceful phantoms that move about in our mud and smoke and are softly luminous with the radiance of all our virtues; that are possessed of all refinements, of all sensibilities, of all wisdom – but, being only phantoms, possess no heart. (AF viii)

The fact that he contests the stereotype of Eastern peoples here positions Conrad within the anthropological zeitgeist of the *fin de siècle*. Robert Hampson has outlined the Conradian project thus: 'Conrad repeatedly confronts the issue that was to become so important in twentieth-century anthropology: how to describe another culture' (2000, 1). 'In particular,' says Hampson, 'Conrad's exploitation of the "dialogic possibilities" of multiple viewpoints and competing narratives anticipates the "dialogic modes" of modern anthropology' (2000, 25). James Clifford charts the emergence of ethnography as a reaction against the notion of

---

[1] Robert Hampson notes that this 'Author's Note' is a response to Alice Meynall's criticism of 'colonial literature as "decivilsed"' literature. See Hampson 2000, 112.

the 'European bourgeois ideal of autonomous individuality' and the notion of culture as 'a single evolutionary process':

> By the turn of the century ... evolutionist confidence began to falter, and a new ethnographic conception of culture became possible. The word began to be used in the plural, suggesting a world of separate, distinctive, and equally meaningful ways of life. The ideal of an autonomous, cultivated subject could appear as a local project, not a *telos* for all humanity. (1988, 92–3)

Although Conrad sometimes conforms to the Enlightenment view, what Clifford Geertz calls the 'uniformitarian view' of man, the fact that he employs 'multiple viewpoints and competing narratives' is a sign of his modernity, of his attempt to break away from the nineteenth-century binaries of 'savage' and 'civilized' (35). From the beginning of his writing career Conrad set out to challenge the romance and adventure genre and its simplistic, reductive assumptions about Eastern peoples, representations that for Edward Said constitute 'Orientalism'.[2] Conrad's purpose is comparable to Geertz's stated objective of anthropology: 'the enlargement of the universe of human discourse' (14). Conrad wants to illuminate the 'bond between us and that humanity so far away,' and in endeavouring to do so he anticipates Geertz's expansive project for ethnography: 'Understanding a people's culture exposes their normalness without reducing their particularity ... It renders them accessible: setting them in the frame of their own banalities, it dissolves their opacity' (14). Thus as Said observes, Geertz's 'interest in Islam is discrete and concrete enough to be animated by the specific societies and problems he studies and not by the rituals, preconceptions, and doctrines of Orientalism' (326).

Geertz and James Clifford both see culture as performance: for Geertz 'our formulations of other people's symbol systems must be actor-oriented' (14). Geertz argues that anthropological writings are interpretations and as such they are not all that different from literary fiction. They are '"something made," "something fashioned"—the original meaning of *fictio*—' (15). For James Clifford, taking his cue from Stephen Greenblatt, even individual identity is a performance: 'The fashioned, fictional self is always located with reference to its *culture* and coded modes of expression, its *language*,' and 'cultural symbols and performances take shape in situations of power and dominance' (1988, 94; Clifford's italics).

Situations of power and dominance exactly describe the literary imperial encounter within which 'self-fashioned' imperial Westerners enact their cultural roles and occasionally adopt the dress or idiom of the 'other' for purposes of the performance of domination. As Geertz asserts, culture should not be regarded as a set of 'concrete behavior patterns' but rather as a set of 'control mechanisms—plans,

---

[2] Said speaks of 'orientalism' as presenting Eastern peoples and landscapes as 'a spectacle, or *tableau vivant*' for the benefit of the Western gaze (158). For Said, Western discourse posits the Orient as static and unchanging, fixed in time as an infinitely romantic space and people and thus denied any autonomy or historical specificity.

recipes, rules, instructions ... for the governing of behavior'. The performance aspect of culture thus becomes clear because 'man is precisely the animal most dependent upon such extragenetic, outside-the-skin control mechanisms, such cultural programs, for ordering his behavior' (Geertz 44). As such, cultural programs are contingent on place, nation, politics, beliefs, for their performance by the self-fashioned individual.

The notion of performance, then, is crucial to understanding cultural specificity: Conrad's Malay fictions express cultural difference through the way his characters 'act out' cultural codes of behaviour. The essay that follows will thus concentrate on Conrad's representation of Malays and Europeans, their behaviour, appearance, and their environment. In his early Malay fiction Conrad's characters perform their given cultural roles within a complex matrix of political and cultural conflict. Hence, in *Almayer's Folly* (1895), the enactment of Malay culture by Nina and Dain reveals the programming of their culture, while the 'performance' of a character like Mrs Travers in *The Rescue* (1920) reveals an attempt to appropriate Malay behaviour and dress for purposes of power and deliberate fictional self-fashioning as a means of exploiting her femininity. Furthermore, it will be shown that for Conrad even the act of writing itself is essentially a performance by the author, and by the cast of characters conjured up to perform the fictional narrative.

Writing Malaya

Conrad's first successful attempt at writing fiction was *Almayer's Folly*, followed closely by *An Outcast of the Islands* (1896).[3] Other pieces of Malay fiction ensued, 'The Lagoon' (1896), 'Karain' (1897), *Lord Jim* (1900), *Victory* (1912), and much later, *The Rescue*. In the earliest of these fictions Conrad's intent was to 'sympathize with common mortals, no matter where they live; in houses or in tents, in the streets under a fog, or in the forests behind the dark line of dismal mangroves that fringe the vast solitude of the sea' (AF viii).[4] Conrad was attempting to portray the reality of lives in the Far East, to bring to his readers an exposition of their shared humanity with Eastern peoples. This is a direct challenge to the popular late nineteenth-century imperial romance characterised by the fictions of G. A Henty, H. Rider Haggard, and Captain Mayne Reid. Conrad, aware of such fiction, sought to exploit its appeal in the literary marketplace, but at the same time to contest its assumptions about the otherness of the peoples of the Empire.

In *A Personal Record* (1912) Conrad claims that the fictional characters for his first novel were regular visitors to his imagination: first Almayer, then 'as was only proper, his wife and daughter joined him round my table, and then the rest of that

---

[3] 'The Black Mate' was, according to Conrad, written in 1886, but he never regarded it as a serious piece of fiction and always maintained that *Almayer* was his first piece. See Knowles and Moore, 41–2.

[4] However, Conrad did have some disputes with his good friend Sir Hugh Clifford over the authenticity of his fictional Malaya. See Dryden 1998.

Pantai band came full of words and gestures.' He declares wryly that, unknown to his landlady, it was his 'practice directly after [his] breakfast to hold animated receptions of Malays, Arabs and half-castes.' (PR 33–4). The impression is that of Conrad conjuring up his 'cast,' creating the illusion of theatre, as though the characters are actors in debate with their director. The act of writing thus results from the performance that Conrad initiates when fashioning his exotic cast and its narrative. *A Personal Record* was completed many years later, and his affectionate, nostalgic evocation of those early days of writing may have been influenced by the intervening years. Nonetheless, these reminiscences reveal Conrad's imaginative processes at work, how he imagined his art as performance.

What is also evident here is that Conrad's breakfast 'receptions' allow for equality of races and persons by representing all the voices in the 'debate'. His narratives are particularly suitable for performance analogies because they reproduce the theatrical experience of all the cast being equally present before us. Conrad's theatrical method of composition, as outlined above, thus gives the native Malay voices the same validity as those of the Europeans. In so doing, Conrad makes a significant departure from earlier imperial fictions: his multivocal narratives ultimately privilege neither the European nor the Malay. With Conrad, therefore, we enter a new imperial arena for fiction, where racial conflict and racial tensions are acted out within fictions that do not assume dominant European voices and perspectives. As in the theatre, we hear the voices of all the 'actors,' and our response is more conditioned by the force of the argument than in earlier imperial fiction.

Conrad began *Almayer's Folly* 'in the front sitting-room of furnished apartments in a Pimlico square'; his characters 'came with a silent and irresistible appeal' (PR 33–4). Later, Conrad recalls, the tenth chapter of the novel was begun aboard a steamer 'gripped by the inclement winter alongside a quay in Rouen' (PR 23). Here he speaks of the 'hallucination of the Eastern Archipelago' that had gripped his imagination, but which was put away for no apparent reason except that the crew were 'leading just then a contemplative life': 'I will not say anything of my privileged position. I was there "just to oblige," as an actor of standing may take a small part in the benefit performance of a friend' (PR 27). Underlying this theatrical imagery is a sense of life as a continuous performance of self, in James Clifford's sense, where the power relations govern roles of dominance and subordination; and Geertz's notion of culture as performance is suggested in Conrad's self-awareness of his role. Reflecting back on his writing, Conrad proposes that writing is the conscious performance of concretising the imagination in written narrative: 'I had given myself up to the idleness of a haunted man who looks for nothing but words wherein to capture his visions' (PR 32). His choice of words – 'hallucination,' 'haunted,' 'visions' – suggests an unreality akin to the suspension of disbelief necessary for the spectator in a theatre.

For Conrad, making his readers *see* his meaning was important, as famously outlined in his 'Preface' to *The Nigger of the 'Narcissus'*: 'My task which I am trying to achieve is, by the power of the written word to make you hear, to make you feel – it is, before all, to make you *see.*' If he achieves this, then Conrad feels he has achieved 'everything' (NN 5). The emphasis on *see*-ing foregrounds how Conrad perceives his art as a visual performance. He makes much of the notion of art in this Preface, allying the writerly act with the arts of painting and music: art is performance in its widest sense. He argues that the 'light of magic suggestiveness' can be attained in writing 'only through complete, unswerving devotion to the perfect blending of form and substance.' It is 'only through an unremitting never-discouraged care for the shape and ring of sentences' that writing can achieve its goal of bringing the imagined world to life (NN 5). Reflecting thus on the act and effects of writing, Conrad is formulating what Allan Simmons calls an 'artistic manifesto' on how to achieve perfection in writing (Knowles and Moore 2000, 280). In 1912 Conrad called *The Nigger of the 'Narcissus'* a 'landmark in literature,' clearly feeling that he had achieved his goal (*CL5* 145).

In writing about the sea Conrad was writing from lived experience; in his earlier writings about the Malay Archipelago he had not yet perfected his art. In a review of Conrad's fiction in 1898 Sir Hugh Clifford even felt that despite his evident literary powers, Conrad had failed to capture the true Malay character: 'Mr Conrad's Malays are only creatures of Mr Conrad, very vividly described, very powerfully drawn, but not Malays'.[5] Hugh Clifford was conscious of fiction, in James Clifford's sense, as 'salvage' ethnography, where cultural practice that has been lost is forever preserved in the text.[6] Hugh Clifford was for many years a colonial official in Malaya: his love, and deep knowledge of the country and its people is reflected in his writing. In 1927, long after he finished writing fiction, he averred: 'Today my tales are to be valued, not only as historical, but as archaeological studies' (1989, 219). Christopher Gogwilt recognises Hugh Clifford's efforts at 'salvage' ethnography, but sees Conrad's Malay fictions as a deliberate act of misrepresentation: 'Conrad adjusted the "Malay" subject of his early work to participate in this problem of representation, omitting the array of ethnographic detail one finds in Clifford's text, to create a carefully misrepresented Malay fiction' (72).[7] Thus, in response to Hugh Clifford's criticisms, Conrad had grumbled to William Blackwood: 'Well I never did set up as an authority on Malaysia' (13 December 1898; *CL2* 129–30). His intention was not ethnography,

---

[5] Hugh Clifford 1898. However, Laurence Davies questions the value of accepting Clifford's opinion over Conrad's: 'Clifford's main objection is to the informality of Conrad's 'Malays,' but Clifford saw people under much more formal – often ceremonial circumstances'. Davies, private correspondence.

[6] James Clifford explains this further: 'Ethnography's disappearing object is ... a rhetorical construct legitimating a representational practice: 'salvage' ethnography in its widest sense. The other is lost, in disintegrating time and space, but saved in the text.' (1986, 112–13)

[7] See Gogwilt's chapter 'Rescue Work: Conrad's Malay Archipelago' (69–87) for further discussion.

but the art of representation; and years later Hugh Clifford graciously acknowledged Conrad as the greater artist.[8]

Hampson has carefully explored how much of an authority on Malaysia Conrad actually was;[9] others have looked at Conrad's Malay fiction as a response to, and subversion of, the adventure and romance tradition (see Dryden 2000, and White). The point of the rest of this essay will be to chart how far Conrad moves from the mere performance of exoticism to the truth of *lived* lives in the Malay Archipelago. The fact that his characters are performing their culture, in Geertz's sense of responding to cultural programming, allows Conrad access to a greater authenticity. His characters, as we have seen, were imagined as actors, and as such Conrad's method accords with Geertz's notion that the performance of a programmed culture is *the* truth and *the* reality. Conrad's awareness of writing as performance is also close to James Clifford's sense of culture as performance: what Conrad's Malay fictions reveal is how far he saw Malay culture as performance by both Malays and Europeans, and how far he saw imperialist adventurers as performing individual 'self-fashionings' in accordance with their perception of their culture as superior.

Performing Malaya

The choice of the Malay Archipelago offered Conrad relatively uncharted literary territory for his narratives, and for his literary 'actors'. Writers like Rider Haggard were making imperial fiction about Africa popular; Kipling was making India his own; R. M. Ballantyne had written about Polynesia; but Malaya remained a relative mystery. Hugh Clifford was writing of his experiences as an official in the Malay provinces and meeting with some success, but it was Conrad, who with the publication of *Almayer's Folly*, was to be hailed by a reviewer for the *Spectator* as a future 'Kipling of the Malay archipelago' (Sherry 61).

In the imperial romance the reader is a mere onlooker, with the East paraded as a spectacle, in Edward Said's sense of 'Orientalist' fictions; in the emergent modernist sensibility of some of Conrad's early fiction, we become intimately

---

[8] Writing to Conrad from Lagos in 1921 Clifford generously withdrew his complaint:

> I have often, during the years that have supervened, told the story you tell – tho' in rather different fashion: – How I had the temerity to deplore the fact that you did not know more about Malays, & how *you* (with only too much justification) deplored the fetters imposed upon my knowledge finding any adequate expression by my woefully imperfect mastery over my own language. No man can doubt upon whose side the balance of the advantage lay.

In *A Portrait in Letters: Correspondence To and About Conrad*, ed. J. H. Stape and Owen Knowles, *The Conradian* 19.1–2 (1995): 179.

[9] See Hampson 2000, in general, but in particular, 6–30.

involved with the lives and hopes of all the protagonists. It is Conrad's purpose, as he states in *A Personal Record*, not simply to watch, but to empathise: 'I would not like to be left standing as a mere spectator on the bank of the great stream carrying onwards so many lives. I would fain claim for myself the faculty of so much insight as can be expressed in a voice of sympathy and compassion' (PR 12). Conrad's intention is not to inscribe within his fiction the ethnographic 'accuracy' of Hugh Clifford, but to imprint the sensation of actual lives.

In place of the stereotypes and frozen tableaux of the fictions that represented the East as an adventure playground for intrepid Europeans is a will-to-authentic experience and a deliberate exposition of disillusion and loss that is at odds with the simplicities of earlier imperial modes. Striving to establish his own unique voice, Conrad was writing against a tradition of literature and culture that had informed generations of readers of imperial literature. *Almayer's Folly* establishes from the outset the alien environment and broken dreams that will be the hallmark of his Malay fiction. The opening words, 'Kaspar! Makan!' jolt Almayer out of a reverie where he acts the role of hero of his own daydream, a reverie based on the promise of the imperial romance that untold wealth is to be easily acquired in the exotic East (AF 3).

Reaching thus for new modes of expressing the Empire distinguishes Conrad from those other writers of imperial fiction and establishes the earliest traces of his modernist sensibilities. The immediate juxtaposition of Malay and European voices as the opening for the novel inaugurates new conditions within which the imperial narrative will be enacted. It problematises the quest motif of imperial romance that assumes a European perspective and reduces the Empire to an exotic backdrop for intrepid explorers. The multiple viewpoints and conflicting voices in Conrad's early imperial fiction fragment the narrative, and remind us of his breakfast 'receptions' where his assembled 'cast' first voiced their differing opinions. The mulitvocal nature of this narrative suggests, too, alternative conditions for fictional discourse that are at odds with the unity of vision and controlling narrative voice of much high Victorian literature. In Geertz's sense of enlarging the 'universe of human discourse,' Conrad often attempts to permit each culture to speak for itself, and thus denies the European an autonomous perspective on the Empire and its peoples. At other times he presents us with unreliable narrators whose prejudiced views skew the narrative perspective in ways that invoke the imperial romance viewpoint. This allows Conrad to offer us ironic and radical readings of the motives of his European narrators.

It was perhaps Robert Louis Stevenson who, with *The Beach of Falesá* (1893) and *The Ebb-Tide* (1894), had first experimented with what Conrad was trying to achieve in terms of bringing a greater realism, and an element of scepticism, to imperial fiction. However, with his more sustained narratives of empire and large body of work on the Malay Archipelago, Conrad developed a distinctive voice. His fiction cut across earlier imperial literature in its attempt to convey the reality of *living* humanity in the East. In many ways this is a bold step: the peoples of the Empire were largely known through the stereotypes of the romance and adventure genre – the noble savage, the villainous degenerate, the simple child-like native, the exotic temptress, or the submissive native girl. They were, in Said's sense, fixed in time, and representative of a perceived immutable East. As figures in a '*tableaux vivant*' they were available to the Western gaze, but devoid of sustained psychological development, culturally alien and visually often splendid, but always 'other' (Said 158).

Conrad attempts to eradicate the ideological boundaries that 'fixed' and confined indigenous peoples in the Western imagination. The effort is at least partially successful through his efforts at understanding how Malay culture would influence behaviour. For example, Mrs Almayer's dreams are allied to her cultural heritage. After her capture by Lingard she passively capitulates, harbouring dreams of becoming his wife, as, we are told, a captured Malay woman would expect:

> She called Lingard father, gently and caressingly, at each of his short and noisy visits, under the clear impression that he was a great and dangerous power it was good to propitiate. Was he not now her master? And during those long four years she nourished a hope of finding favour in his eyes and ultimately becoming his wife, counsellor, and guide. (AF 22)

Her hopes are governed by her culture in the form of the 'recipes' and 'programs' posited by Geertz: her treatment of Lingard enacts the performance of her cultural programming. In turn, the impression she gains of Lingard's great power is the result of his self-fashioning as the imperial conqueror, according to the rules of his own culture. Yet, in attempting to portray the authentic Malay female, Conrad can slip into conventional stereotyping, reducing Mrs Almayer to a simple 'native'. When she is seen as being quick-witted at the Samarang convent, her cultural background seems to limit her potential: 'She learned the new language very easily, yet understood but little of the new faith the good sisters taught her, assimilating quickly only the superstitious elements of the religion' (AF 22). Eastern beliefs are reduced to superstition by association with Mrs Almayer's selective learning, and by contrast Christianity is afforded a superior role through the implication that it is composed of more than superstitious ritual. It is not language that is an insurmountable cultural barrier, but the 'control mechanisms' of religion.

Usually, though, Mrs Almayer demonstrates the 'common' humanity Conrad speaks of in his 'Author's Note'. Watching Nina elope with Dain, she gives way to a sigh, and 'two tears wandered slowly down her withered cheeks.' She washes these away with her hair 'as if ashamed of herself,' but gives way to another sigh 'for her heart was heavy and she suffered much, being unused to tender emotions' (AF 154). This lack of emotional life is expected of the 'native' stereotype, and thus we may be tempted to dismiss this woman as performing true to type, but Conrad has already detailed the hardships of Mrs Almayer's early existence: stifling her emotions is a survival strategy. Here her motherly love is the stuff of human experience, her suffering expressed as the condition of a woman of a subjugated people.

Speaking of the East in his 'Author's Note' to this novel, Conrad's intention to contest the stereotype becomes evident:

> The picture of life, there as here, is drawn with the same elaboration of detail, coloured with the same tints. Only in the cruel serenity of the sky, under the merciless brilliance of the sun, the dazzled eye misses the delicate detail, sees only the strong outlines, while the colours, in the steady light, seem crude and without shadow. Nevertheless it is the same picture. (AF vii)

The parallels that Conrad draws here are designed to strip away our expectations of the East as a romantic stage set for the performance of a predictably superficial romantic melodrama. He insists instead that what we will be witnessing is not an Eastern spectacle, but the unfolding of a recognisable human drama in an unfamiliar environment. This is a challenge to his readers to put aside their preconceptions of dazzling, colourful exoticism and stock characters in favour of embracing the reality and complexity of the lives of people in foreign lands. It is almost as if Conrad had anticipated Said's notion of 'Orientalism,' and was contesting the perception of the East-as-spectacle, as a glamorous stage set where inscrutable Orientals perform exotic roles. In creating Sambir and its inhabitants Conrad seeks to problematize the one-dimensional stereotype of previous literature: the lives of his Malays are bound to the lives of his Europeans, and the intricate interweaving of the fates of all of his characters approximates to the performance of real lives, not the fictional stereotypes of the melodrama of romance and adventure.

Conrad departs from these stereotypes by putting his native subjects nearer the centre stage, allowing them a greater dramatic part in the action and an audible, compelling voice. The trials of the domestic situation of the Almayer household, the emotional conflicts between family members, the very fact that a central white character is married to a Malay woman and that his daughter is of mixed race are evidence of new roles, and new voices, for non-white characters. The 'performance' of native Malays within the dramatic unfolding of events is no longer peripheral or limited to the villainous or subordinate roles of the imperial romance genre: they are central to narrative development, reminding us of how Conrad gathered them around his breakfast table as equals.

In *Almayer's Folly* a half-Malay woman, Nina, can gaze on a Balinese prince, Dain Maroola, and we see him, largely, as she does:

> Under the folds of a blue turban, whose fringed ends hung gracefully over the left shoulder, was a face full of determination and expressing a reckless good-humour, not devoid, however, of some dignity. The squareness of the lower jaw, the full red lips, the mobile nostrils, and the proud carriage of the head gave the impression of a being half-savage, untamed, perhaps cruel, and corrected the liquid softness of the almost feminine eye, that general characteristic of the race. (AF 55)

Just occasionally, however, the authorial voice betrays a hint of the stereotype: the fact that Dain's posture 'corrected' an impression of feminine gentleness controls our response and repositions him as a romantic, but still half-civilised 'native'. Dain's black silk jacket, luxuriant red sarong and bejewelled fingers and kriss are carefully detailed cultural signifiers, marking him out as romantic and exotic. At the sight of Nina, he joins his hands above his head 'in a sign of respect accorded by Malays only to the great of this earth' (AF 54). The programmes and codes governing Dain's cultural performance are thus displayed; and for her part Nina adopts the role of the modest Malay woman when she draws the 'lower part of the curtain across her face, leaving only half a rounded cheek, a stray tress, and one eye exposed, wherewith to contemplate the gorgeous and bold being' (AF 55).

Conrad sustains a more complex perception of the native subject than is available in the simplistic imperial romance. Simmons has argued that in *Almayer's Folly* Conrad varies the narrative focus in order to present shifting cultural perspectives: 'The resultant *heteroglossia*, or blend of voices speaking in the novel, might be said to recreate, at the level of narrative discourse, the cultural conflicts that form the novel's social and historical background' (163). It is Simmons's contention that despite the narrator's early favouring of European cultural perspectives, the novel ends by privileging the Malay: 'The erstwhile Occidental narrating consciousness has come full circle: it has come to reflect, to empathise with, and to champion the plight of the Orientals' (172). This is crucial in perceiving the shift that Conrad makes from earlier imperial romance fiction towards the emerging modernist approach that is sceptical about dominant truths and reliable narrative voices. The subtle shifts in narrative perspective allow us access to an apparently authentic Malay voice, and an authentic Malay vision of the world. It is through such shifts that Conrad seeks to achieve his aim of representing the 'bond between us and that humanity so far away' (AF viii).

In *Lord Jim* Marlow is complicit in Jim's heroic imperial fantasy by perpetuating a perception of the East as an unchanging and permanent spectacle. Leaving Patusan, he opposes what he regards as the progressive West against the static East which, with its 'colour, its design, and its meaning' is like 'a picture created by fancy on a canvas, upon which, after long contemplation, you turn your back for the last time' (LJ 330). Against an elaborate, but *seemingly* uncomplicated Patusan, Marlow finds a positive affirmation of progress and life in the West: 'I had turned away from the picture and was going back to the world where events move, men change, light flickers, life flows in a clear stream, no matter whether over mud or over stones' (LJ 330). For Marlow, the East is in the imagination, never altering, like a stage set; the West is vigorous and life affirming. His vision clouded by Jim's romantic yearnings, Marlow forgets that the politics of Patusan are complex and real, that those vying for power in the region come from a variety of cultural and political backgrounds. In his desire to see Jim fulfil his romantic dream, Marlow ignores Patusan's cultural complexities and fails to anticipate the very real tragedy that could ensue. The betrayal of Dain Waris by Brown and the subsequent political instability are beyond the control of Orientalist discourse and romantic narratives. They are the authentic events of the real world of imperial power struggles; but Marlow, seduced by Jim's romantic vision, is determined to see Patusan as a static stage backdrop and its inhabitants as performing true to fictional stereotypes.

Marlow's clouded vision is manifest too in his perception of the various people who he imagines exist only in Jim's orbit:

> But as to what I was leaving behind, I cannot imagine any alteration. The immense and magnanimous Doramin and his little motherly witch of wife, gazing together upon the land and nursing secretly their dreams of parental ambition; Tunju Allang, wizened and greatly perplexed; Dain Waris, intelligent and brave, with his faith in Jim, with his firm glance and his ironic friendliness; the girl, absorbed in her frightened, suspicious adoration; Tamb' Itam, surly and faithful; Cornelius, leaning his forehead against the fence under the moonlight— I am certain of them. They exist as if under an enchanter's wand. (LJ 330)

This is again Said's *tableau vivant*, a parade of Eastern stereotypes who are knowable because they are one-dimensional actors set against an exotic and theatrical backdrop, almost like stock characters in a pantomime. Cornelius plays the role of aggrieved wicked stepfather with such passion that even Marlow remarks that it 'was an inexpressibly grotesque and vile performance' (LJ 329). Jim's reality is emphasised for Marlow in contrast to the 'native' stereotypes amongst whom he moves. Marlow can be 'certain of them' because he imagines these people rehearsing the established and familiar roles of romance and adventure.

As Marlow prepares to leave Patusan he endows it with a transience that is reminiscent of the ephemeral nature of a stage performance: 'This was, indeed, one of the lost, forgotten, unknown places of the earth; I had looked under its obscure surface; and I felt that when to-morrow I had left it forever, it would slip out of existence, to live only in my memory till I myself passed into oblivion' (LJ 323). Only Jim exists and cannot be reduced to a mere stage actor: 'But the figure round which all these are grouped–that one lives, and I am not certain of him. No magician's wand can immobilise him under my eyes. He is one of us' (LJ 330–31). It is Jim's status as one of us, a Westerner, or perhaps a seafarer, which for Marlow affords him reality.

Yet, despite Marlow's conviction, Jim plays a role too, and in his tragic, violent demise he performs an ideal role that he had self-fashioned from the childish fiction of romance that he read as a youth. Jim's choice of remaining in Patusan is a decision to reject Marlow's 'real' Western society, and therefore to evade the responsibilities entailed in his transgression. In so doing, Jim opts for a fantasy version of Patusan. Preferring to adopt his self-fashioned role as the tragic hero of his own narrative of imperial adventure, Jim performs a specific cultural role whose rules, in Geertz's sense, are prescribed by the culture of imperial romance where honour is everything. For Jim, and thus for Marlow, performing the romance is paramount. The ensuing tragedy, like the deaths of Hassim and Immada in

The Rescue, is the consequence of white men in the tropics performing their cultural roles in which loyalty to their fellow Europeans overrides their loyalty to indigenous peoples.

Mis-performing the 'Other'

The language and imagery of Marlow's narration of the Patusan episodes of *Lord Jim* invokes a theatrical melodrama consistent with his determination to believe in the superficial simplicity of Jim's romantic fantasy. He reduces Malays to pantomime actors and ignores their cultural specificities. In 'Karain' we find an earlier unreliable storyteller whose narration assumes a similar exotic cultural performance from another Malay. Here the narrator endows Karain's story with a romantic, mythic status that belies the Malay's genuinely complex and tragic dilemma. Like Marlow, this narrator interprets cultural difference as exotic otherness and thus weaves a narrative of theatrical imagery and Malay performances to create an entertaining, enigmatic tale for his listeners. Karain's very Malay-ness becomes, in this way, the means by which the narrator reduces him to a cultural stereotype.

Karain's performance of his culture is denoted by his un-English idiom and large gestures:

> He snatched the sword from the old man, whizzed it out of the scabbard, and thrust the point into the earth. Upon the thin, upright blade the silver hilt, released, swayed before him like something alive. He stepped back a pace, and in a deadened tone spoke fiercely to the vibrating steel: 'If there is virtue in the fire, in the iron, in the hand that forged thee, in the words spoken over thee, in the desire of my heart, and in the wisdom of thy makers, – then we shall be victorious together!' He drew it out, looked along the edge. 'Take,' he said over his shoulder to the old sword-bearer. (TU 18–19)

This may approximate to an accurate rendering of spoken Malay, but for this narrator, committed to stereotyping Karain, it is testimony to the fact that he is 'absurd and unanswerable' (TU 18). After this episode the narrator and his companions 'gave up remonstrating' and 'let him go his way to an honourable disaster' (TU 19). This dismissive, mocking tone is not that of a Conrad who wanted to 'sympathise with common mortals': this is the attitude of an unreliable narrator who conflates cultural difference with cultural inferiority and simplicity.

The British sailors are gunrunners who provide a 'trusting native' with the superior technology of the white man, a trope common to the romance and adventure mode: 'All we could do for him was to see to it that the powder was good for the money and the rifles serviceable, if old' (TU 19). Like Jim, this narrator believes himself to be participating in a stereotypical imperial romance, performing his role as 'superior' white adventurer. When the gunrunners confer on Karain the Jubilee sixpenny piece they regard his pleasure and satisfaction as evidence of 'native' simplicity; but, ironically, this silver gilt token is at least as much a fetish of Englishness: it is a fetish of the 'Great Queen' with a punched hole so that it can be worn as a token (TU 49). Conrad's irony lies in the fact that Hollis, too, has his lucky charms and fetishes. His small leather box contains 'Amulets of white men! Charms and talismans': 'All the ghosts driven out of the unbelieving West by men who pretend to be wise and alone and at peace – all the homeless ghosts of an unbelieving world – appeared suddenly round the figure of Hollis bending over the box' (TU 48). For a moment the narrator catches a brief glimpse of the humanity he shares with Karain, and Conrad's purpose to 'sympathize with common mortals' is revealed: in their cultural performances Europeans and Malay reveal their common bonds of superstition.

On his return to London the narrator, like Marlow, sees a positive affirmation of the 'reality' of the West against the 'unreal theatricality' of the East. Yet it fails to convince Jackson:

> 'Yes; I see it,' said Jackson, slowly. 'It is there; it pants, it runs, it rolls; it is strong and alive; it would smash you if you didn't look out; but I'll be hanged if it is yet as real to me as ... as the other thing ... say, Karain's story.' (TU 55)

For Jackson the dazzle and glamour of Karain and his kingdom are just as real as the grime and aggressive chaos that they witness in London. If we recall Conrad's assertion in his 'Author's Note' to *Almayer's Folly* that the brilliance of the sun in Eastern lands dazzles the eye, causing the viewer to miss the 'delicate detail,' we must conclude that it is Jackson's opinion, and not that of the narrator, that Conrad shares, for it is, nevertheless, 'the same picture'. Throughout the story the narrator is at pains to stress Karain's theatricality and the 'staginess' of his environment because he has been dazzled into missing the 'delicate detail': but Jackson speaks for Conrad when he affirms its reality.[10]

As Hampson notes, Conrad explores the 'stage metaphor in relation to the Malay world in 'Karain' and *The Rescue*' (2000, 113). Thus, for example, Karain's village is a 'stage where, dressed splendidly for his part, he strutted' (TU 6). In *The Rescue* performance of culture takes on even more significance through the opposition between genuine Malays and Edith Travers's conscious and cynical adoption of splendid Malay dress in order to perform a role she has uniquely fashioned for herself.

Hassim, who is dressed like a 'poor fisherman,' nevertheless wears the cultural markers of his status as a nephew of a great Wajo ruler:

> From the twist of a threadbare *sarong* wound tightly on the hips protruded outward to the left the ivory hilt, ringed with six bands of gold, of a weapon that would not have disgraced a ruler. Silver glittered about the flintlock and the

---

[10] For this discussion of 'Karain' I am greatly indebted to Laurence Davies for his generous and perceptive insights.

hard-wood stock of his gun. The red and gold handkerchief folded around his head was of costly stuff, such as is worn by high-born women in the households of chiefs, only the gold threads were tarnished and the silk frayed in the folds. (Res 64–5)

Hampson observes that in Conrad's fiction the 'introduction of Malay characters is often the verbal equivalent of the plates used to illustrate Raffles's *History of Java*.' The introduction of Hassim can thus be read as 'grounded in the material culture of the Bugis' (2000, 177). Conrad pays close attention to the detail of dress where it signifies cultural or social status and role-playing. Hassim's sister, Immada, is therefore similarly richly attired in a black silk jacket with 'exceedingly tight sleeves slit a little way up from the wrist, gold-braided and with a row of small gold buttons' (Res 65). These Malays are of noble birth: like Maroola, they are beautiful, aloof, and infinitely exotic. Yet, despite the apparent 'fixing' of a Malay stereotype through a dress code, Conrad individualises these characters by giving them an idiosyncratic costume, in Hassim's case a jaded former splendour, and in Immada's the very lack of the belt, scarves and head wrappings of the traditional Malay woman.[11] In doing so, Conrad implies a life of hardship that is at odds with the stereotypical role of haughty splendour normally assigned to 'native' nobility in imperial fiction.

By contrast, when a white character dons native dress, they are consciously acting a role, and usually compromising themselves. Mrs Travers adopts some of the gorgeous clothing that was destined for Immada:

> She was wearing a Malay thin cotton jacket, cut low in the neck without a collar and fastened with wrought silver clasps from the throat down. She had replaced her yachting skirt by a blue check sarong embroidered with threads of gold. Mr Travers' eyes travelling slowly down attached themselves to the gleaming instep of an agitated foot from which hung a light, leather sandal. (Res 238)

Mrs Travers explains her native attire as a response to the oppressive heat, but her husband regards it with distaste: '"You should ... try to get yourself presented with some bangles for your ankles so that you may jingle as you walk."' The attention to the missing detail, the anklets, betrays his awareness of Mrs Travers performance: drawing attention to the cultural inaccuracy of her costume highlights her role-playing as a Malay. Indeed, repulsed by the thought that his wife's fellow Europeans may see her dressed in this manner, Travers regards their whole situation as a theatrical performance for which she is appropriately, if provocatively, dressed. Her outfit, he declares is a '"most appropriate costume for this farce"' (Res 239). His outrage underlines his cultural performance as a European male who perceives his wife acting out the sexual desirability of the native Malay woman, and openly flaunting it.

---

[11] See Hampson 2000, 178 for further discussion of this.

What is notable here, however, is the fact that while Immada's clothing, as described above, emphasises a chaste Malay femininity, Mrs Travers's 'dressing up' has overt sexual connotations, as emphasised by her husband's slow glance that rests on her sandalled foot. The sandals force her to 'alter her usual gait and move with quick, short steps very much like Immada.' She is acutely conscious of the effect, admitting to herself that no 'part of her costume made her feel so exotic,' a sensation that belies her excuse that the heat necessitated this attire (Res 256). She is fully aware of the sexual frisson that her appearance will produce, and the effect on her gait emphasises the fact that she is 'performing' a version of Malay femininity. In fact Katherine Baxter draws parallels between Mrs Travers's Malay performance and the Cinderella fable by noting that when she loses one of the sandals it is like the 'dropping of a prop that reveals the show's unreality' (72).[12]

Until the end of the novel, when she once again dons her white hat and yachting skirt, the signifiers of a return to her natural European role, Mrs Travers parades her Malay costume before the men about her. Lingard is aware of the 'mysterious rustle' (Res 291) made by her draperies; he feels that she is 'dimly splendid' in the 'gay silks, cottons and muslins of her outlandish dress' (Res 288); and D'Alcacer is awestruck at the sight of her: 'In the dim gleam of jewelled clasps, the faint sheen of gold embroideries and the shimmer of silks, she was like a figure in a faded painting' (Res 283). Her husband, however, declares disgustedly that she looks '"heathenish in this costume"' (Res 248). Mrs Travers, though, revels in the performance because of the admiration it attracts, because it gives her a sexual power, and because 'dressing up' as a Malay has its own inherent glamour.

In donning Malay dress, Mrs Travers engages in a conscious cultural, and possibly sexual, rivalry with Immada: '"I am robbing that girl of her clothes," she had thought to herself, "besides other things." She knew by this time that a girl of such high rank would never dream of wearing anything that had been worn by somebody else' (Res 256). She may adopt Malay costume, but Mrs Travers does not identify with Malays: rather, she does this as a means of 'aestheticising the other and then appropriating an aestheticised version of the Other through role-playing' (Hampson 2000, 180). Performing the role of a Malay as *she* constructs that role, Mrs Travers effectively creates a distance between her own performance of Malay-ness and the authentic Malay: hers equates to a stage act in which she takes the starring role. Indeed the whole of her experience of Malay culture is reduced in her eyes to a theatrical spectacle:

> 'I mean the morning when I walked out of Belarab's stockade on your arm, Captain Lingard, at the head of the procession. It seemed to me that I was walking on a splendid stage in a scene from an opera, in a gorgeous show fit to make an audience hold its breath. You can't possibly guess how unreal all this seemed, and how artificial I felt myself. An opera, you know ...'. (Res 269–70)

---

[12] Baxter's article offers a detailed analysis of the extended theatrical tropes in *The Rescue*. See Baxter 64–83.

Opera is a dominant motif in Mrs Travers's assessment of her Malay experience, and it is symptomatic of the aloofness that she preserves throughout the story towards any person or experience that threatens her cultural superiority. Her dominance is secured by appropriating the dress of Malay culture and then depriving it of its 'subjectivity and substantiality' (Hampson 2000, 180).

Although Mrs Travers participates in the action of the story, she equates it in her imagination to a stage performance, one that takes place within the 'situations of power and dominance' described by James Clifford. Without recognising or heeding the particularities of Malay culture, Mrs Travers equates it with an operatic spectacle so that she can dominate the 'stage' and reduce the real political struggle taking place around her to an exotic sub-plot. White domination is thus inscribed upon a genuine Malay situation, and the European woman, by virtue of her splendid cultural cross-dressing, assumes domination of 'centre stage'. For her the very substance of the narrative in which she partakes is subordinate to the spectacle she presents. Malay power politics are reduced to a backdrop for her performance and hence deprived of their cultural significance.

Other characters in Conrad's Malay fiction choose to use European cultural signifiers to mark their choice of roles. Jim, for example, resolutely dresses in the white uniform of the imperial adventurer. White is the preferred colour of dress in the tropics for other cultures too because of its coolness; but in Jim's case a white uniform reinforces his role as imperial adventurer. Its 'very neatness' irritates Brown because it 'seemed to belong to things he had in the very shaping of his life contemned and flouted' (LJ 380). In other words, Jim's uniform denotes his performance as a culturally, and morally, superior being: it is a dazzling and dogged statement of European cultural difference and superiority. Mrs Travers enjoys performing the 'other'; Jim needs to perform the imperial adventurer. In both cases characters are adopting roles and performing fictions of their own fashioning; in both cases the arrogance of European performances in the East results in the destruction of young Malays who had a pivotal role to play in their own, very real, local political struggles.

Conclusion

Conrad's Europeans treat Malaya as a personal stage on which they imagine they can perform idealised roles according to the rules of a romanticized European imperial culture: they resemble the readers of imperial adventure fiction, expecting fixed roles for themselves, and for the Malays with whom they interact. Hence, Almayer assumes that Malaya will be the scene of his triumph, where he rises effortlessly to his 'natural' position of wealth and authority by virtue of his European descent. For Jim, Patusan is a country of romance where he performs the role of powerful Prince and benefactor of grateful locals, shedding the reality of his human weakness to perform the simpler, less troubled role of adventure hero. The narrator of 'Karain,' so assured of his own cultural superiority, regards a genuine Malay torment as a colourful melodrama against an exotic theatrical backdrop.

In so doing, he fails to register the negative impact of the squalor and aggression of his own reality in the West. Mrs Travers rises to the adversity of her situation by donning Malay dress and imagining herself in an exotic opera playing the *femme fatale*, thus distilling an authentic human drama into an adjunct to her own vanity and desires. In each case Conrad's Europeans are, in Geertz and James Clifford's sense, self-fashioned individuals choosing to perform roles that their imperial culture has made available to them.

Yet, Conrad undercuts his characters' assumptions by allowing Oriental voices to compete with those of his Europeans: his breakfast 'receptions' with his 'cast' once again come to mind. The heteroglossia that Simmons identifies in *Almayer's Folly* articulates irreconcilable cultural conflicts in Conrad's Malay fictions, conflicts that highlight cultural difference at the same time as they are intended to illustrate common passions. In *As You Like It* Jacques declares that 'All the world's a stage/And all the men and women merely players' (II.vii.139–40). It is a notion that Geertz concurs with when speaking of Lovejoy's analysis of the writings of 'an Enlightenment historian, Mascou':

> There is, there can be, no backstage where we can go to catch a glimpse of Mascou's actors as 'real persons' lounging about in street clothes, disengaged from their profession, displaying with artless candor their spontaneous desires and unprompted passions. They may change their roles, their style of acting, even the dramas in which they play; but—as Shakespeare himself of course remarked—they are always performing. (35–6)[13]

In his Malay fictions Conrad seems to have been striving towards a way of reconciling his recognition of cultural difference with his desire to expose what he saw as common human experiences and passions. Perhaps the route to understanding culture as performance in Geertz's terms could not have been available to Conrad, but what is still remarkable is how much of that journey he actually managed to achieve.

---

[13] This is a point that Hampson also addresses in connection with Geertz and Conrad, (see Hampson 2000, 111–13).

Chapter 2
'Sly Civility?':
Mrs Almayer's and Mrs Willems's Performances of Colonial Resistance in *Outcast of the Islands* and *Almayer's Folly*

Susan Barras

In Victorian England, the taste for spectacle emerged in virtually all areas of Victorian culture: from public ceremonies, architecture, music and paintings to military parades, theatre and pantomime (MacKenzie 46). The enthusiasm for dressing-up, spectacle and performance even pervaded the public schools where boys put on plays and other theatrical entertainments.[1] Elsewhere, less privileged boys could fulfil this need by joining one of the many uniformed youth organisations which began to emerge in the 1880s (MacKenzie 5). Events like the Eglington Tournament gave the British aristocracy a chance to indulge in this enthusiasm in a spectacular fashion, whilst parlour games like 'charades' enabled the less affluent members of the middle classes to dress-up and perform, albeit in the privacy of the home, and in a more modest manner. Meanwhile, stories of the heroes of Britain's rapidly expanding empire fired the British public's imagination and were often translated into spectacular theatrical performances, such as 'The Great Mogul,' 'The Zulu Chief' and 'Khartoum' (MacKenzie 49). Elsewhere in Europe, adventure stories set in 'darkest Africa' and other exotic locations may also have inspired their young readers to re-enact, or stage, their own performances of mastery, both in the familiar surroundings of the childhood home and, later on as adults, in their country's colonies.

It might be argued, therefore, that performance became the medium through which the British, and other European nations, attempted to create for their colonised subjects the illusion of stability and power. By controlling the public stage they were able to give performances which approximated to what they wanted their colonised subjects to see whilst concealing anything which detracted from their grandeur and authority. The use of public rituals, ceremonies, parades and processions not only provided a 'living tableau of centralized discipline and control,' which helped to 'economize on the actual use of violence,' but also gave

---

[1] See Money 46 and Mangan 103–4.

the appearance of unanimity among the colonisers, as well as implying that the colonised consented to colonial rule (Scott 66).

It would appear then, that what Erving Goffman calls 'impression management,' played a central role in the maintenance of colonial power. In *The Presentation of Self in Everyday Life*, Goffman likens everyday human behaviour to a theatrical performance. Goffman observes that a person's capacity for what he terms 'impression management' concerns two kinds of activity: the first involves 'verbal symbols or their substitutes' which the individual uses 'to convey the information that he and others are known to attach to these subjects'; the second involves a wide range of actions akin to acting, so as to give a performance which, amongst other things, disguises the true reason for these actions (14). Goffman states that the first of these activities involves 'feigning' while the second involves 'deceit,' and a person can use either or both to intentionally misinform others in order to control their conduct and elicit from them 'a specific response he is concerned to obtain' (14–15, 17). Goffman calls this kind of activity a 'front,' which he defines as 'that part of the individual's performance which regularly functions ... to define the situation for those who observe the performance' (32). In order to maintain this front, Goffman continues, a person must ensure that he conceals certain things about himself which may be inconsistent with his current performance (50). He must also ensure that the audience 'before whom he plays one of his parts will not be the same individuals before whom he plays a different part in another setting' (57). However, since nobody can maintain a frontstage performance indefinitely, he needs a place – a 'backstage' – where he can relax and step out of his role (115). This 'backstage' is also the place where an actor learns his role, rehearses his part and prepares for his next performance.

James C. Scott takes up Goffman's idea of frontstage and backstage performance to argue that, where there is a dominant controlling power, those subordinated to that power 'offer a performance of deference and consent' (Scott 3–4). At the same time, the power figure 'produces a performance of mastery and command while attempting to peer behind the mask of subordinates to read their real intentions,' and I have discussed elsewhere how, during the late nineteenth and early twentieth centuries, the British and other European colonisers used similar theatrical performances firstly to acquire, and then to maintain, their colonies.[2] According to Scott's argument, however, subordinate groups also employ 'impression management' to stage a public performance designed to 'appeal to the expectations of the powerful' (2). Much of the public life of these subordinated groups is devoted to 'command performances' (29). This means that they must be prepared to give a performance at any moment, whenever they are called into the presence of the dominant power. Thus, subordinate groups are forced to become skilled actors in order to survive.

---

[2] See also Barras, A. H. Susan, *The Great Game: Games-playing & Imperial Romance*, unpublished PhD thesis, Royal Holloway College, University of London, 2001.

However, this does not mean that these subordinated groups (or peoples, or nations) actually agree with the public transcript which has been forced upon them by a dominant elite. Scott acknowledges that what 'may look from above like the extraction of a required performance can easily look from below like the artful manipulation of deference and flattery to achieve its own ends' (34).[3] Furthermore Scott argues that, 'the practices of domination and exploitation typically generate the insults and slights to human dignity that in turn foster a hidden transcript of indignation' (7). In situations where the expression of this indignation would result in severe punishment, subordinated groups have to find safer outlets for their anger. Scott suggests some of the ways these groups can achieve this through, for example, the use of deferential acts as well as, 'gossip, folk-tales, songs, rituals, codes and euphemisms,' all of which allow a 'partly sanitized, ambiguous and coded version of the hidden transcript' (24). As a result, these subversive performances may be seen as the colonised's way of playing games against white men or, in some cases, of playing the white man at his own game. It is clear, then, that Europeans were not the only ones to stage performances in their colonies, and that the colonised also used 'impression management' to stage public performances designed to appeal to the expectations of their colonial rulers.

In *An Outcast of the Islands* and *Almayer's Folly* performance also provides the colonised with a means of expressing an ambiguous and coded version of their hidden transcript of hostility. In both novels, it is Babalatchi, with his covert and complex schemes to undermine all Europeans, who provides the clearest example of such a performance. However, in these two novels, it is not only 'native' men who stage ambiguous performances in order to play the colonisers at their own game. In fact, both Joanna Willems and Mrs Almayer also protest at their treatment by Europeans by staging socially acceptable performances of rage.

This paper considers how, in *An Outcast of the Islands* and *Almayers Folly*, Mrs Willems and Mrs Almayer stage their own ambiguous performances to protest at their treatment by their 'white masters,' their husbands, Willems and Almayer. It will propose that another of the ways that Mrs Almayer achieves her aim of undermining her husband is through the use of the Malay phenomenon called *latah* (a form of spirit possession), which she utilises to express a coded version of her hostility and indignation whilst simultaneously appearing to conform with the (Malay) public transcript. It continues by examining the nature of Aïssa's performance in *An Outcast of the Islands* and ends by suggesting that Aïssa's own performance is less successful in obtaining mastery than that of the other two women.

J. M. Gullick states that, during the late nineteenth century, women in Malay society were considered to be 'different in social status and role' to men (210).

---

[3] Scott adds the caveat, however, that even where such manipulation is successfully productive that victory 'is won on a stage on which the roles have been largely scripted from above and on which the usual performances, no matter how artful, must reinforce the appearances approved by the dominant' (35).

On reaching puberty, a young woman was usually segregated from men and not allowed to talk to them or enter their presence without veiling herself (Gullick 215).[4] Most women had their marriages arranged for them by their parents and often never saw their husbands until the wedding day. This is precisely what happens in *Almayer's Folly*, when Mrs Almayer's marriage to a European husband (Almayer) is arranged by her English foster-father, Lingard. Once married, these women had 'no culturally sanctioned means of going on journeys' and spent much of their time inside the house in the *bilik* or family room – which, in Malay culture, was 'associated with femaleness' (Moshman 150). Vinson H. Sutlive has suggested that the Malay house's divisions into male and female areas represents the social divisions in Malay society between male and female, and the public and private spheres (55). The *bilik* was therefore the female and private domain whilst the *ruai* or veranda and the *tanju* (porch) of the house marked the beginning of the male and public sphere.

In *An Outcast of the Islands*, Willems recalls how Joanna rebelled 'only once' at the beginning of their marriage (OI 9). Following what Willems euphemistically calls this 'first difference of theirs,' Joanna 'did not complain, she did not rebel' because Willems 'had frightened the soul out of her body' (OI 9). It seems strange, therefore, that on learning that Willems has been dismissed from his job, Joanna immediately launches into a violent outburst against her husband. This behaviour is less contradictory than it initially appears. After all, accepted European thinking was that women were 'unstable' and, as a consequence of their physiology, prone to hysteria.[5] As Willems tells Joanna to prepare to leave their home, he notices Joanna 'staring at him with her big slanting eyes, that seemed to him twice their natural size' (OI 26). Joanna's upper lip is 'drawn up on one side, giving to her ... face a vicious expression' (OI 26). Joanna then begins to speak to Willems; first in a whisper, then slightly louder, and finally shouts and screams 'shrilly' torrents of abuse at Willems, followed by cries for help (OI 27). Following this outburst, Joanna collapses into a chair where she 'drummed insanely with her heels on the resounding floor of the verandah' (OI 29).

Until this moment, Joanna has maintained a frontstage performance of 'deference and consent'. However, Scott observes that the necessity 'of "acting a mask" in the presence of power' over a prolonged period of time creates such an unbearable strain that, finally, the subordinate actor's feelings explode out into the open (Scott 9). This may well be what has happened to Joanna Willems. Joanna notably stages this performance on the veranda, the most public part of their home: a place where their neighbours will hear the cries for help she never dared

---

[4] This is seen in the novels when both the Malay Aïssa and the Malay-European, Nina Almayer, veil themselves in front of men.

[5] See Elaine Showalter's detailed discussion of the theories concerning the nature of hysteria around the time that Conrad was writing *Outcast of the Islands*. Showalter, *The Female Malady: Women, Madness & English Culture, 1830–1980* (London: Virago, 1995).

utter at the time of her first 'difference' with Willems. That this is a performance – and not madness or hysteria – is made clear by the way Joanna insults Willems whilst simultaneously 'glancing right and left as if meditating a sudden escape' (OI 27). Ultimately, Joanna's frontstage performance has the desired effect of drawing attention to Willems's brutality – so 'unbecoming' in a white man – whilst providing her with an excuse for her transgression of social expectations. She is, after all, the product of a mixed racial marriage, and thus, in accordance with the gendered racial typologies of the contemporary literature, even more prone to hysterical outbursts than her wholly white, European counterparts.[6]

Playing the hysterical 'half-caste' is only one of the performances Joanna Willems stages as a means of protest. Instead of dressing herself in Western day clothes and imitating a European lady, Joanna is also described as 'trail[ing] through life in [a] red dressing-gown, with its rows of dirty blue bows down the front, stained and hooked on awry; a torn flounce at the bottom' (OI 25). It can be argued that Joanna's performance here is an example of failed mimicry in which Joanna's attempts to dress like a European woman result in her getting it, in Homi K. Bhabha's terms, not quite/not right, because of her own not quite/not white status as one of 'those degenerate descendants of Portuguese conquerors' from 'the outskirts of Macassar' (OI 4).[7] Indeed, following her outburst at Willems, Joanna goes onto the verandah of their home (the male, public domain) still wearing the red dressing gown and, at the end of the novel, she appears in Sambir still wearing the same 'red gown' (OI 29, 243).

These incidences indeed imply that Joanna's performance is one of 'a flawed colonial mimesis,' in which her attempts to be a European lady render her '*emphatically* not to be' a European (Bhabha 87). However, Bhabha also argues that the ambivalence inherent in the image of someone 'not quite/not white' is disturbing for the coloniser because mimicry is simultaneously both resemblance and '*menace*' (92, 91). Bhabha's use of the word 'menace' here suggests that Joanna's performance is not failed mimicry but a form of resistance. By openly wearing dirty clothes designed for the private domain, Joanna is able to express her resentment at being beaten and insulted by her European husband without her breaking both European and Malay societies' rules that she, as a woman, should remain silent in public.

This expression of resentment is sharpened by the irony of her choice of cloth. For it was, of course, through the trade of Indian cloth that the Dutch and British were finally able to make inroads into the far eastern spice trade. European coinage was used to buy Indian cloth which was then traded by the Europeans for spices in the Far East. These spices were then sold back in Europe generating

---

[6] In the novel, Joanna's brother, Leonard, tells Willems to restrain his 'improper violence' because 'It is unbecoming ... with all those natives looking on' (OI 29). This may be seen as an example of the coloniser being forced to stage a performance of mastery in front of the colonised.

[7] See Homi K. Bhabha, *The Location of Culture* (London: Routledge, 1995), 85–92.

further coinage with which to buy fresh supplies of cloth. Whilst the trade of cloth eastward included a huge range in quality, providing for a wide variety of uses, it was the more luxurious cloths that were most highly prized. These cloths might even 'enter the realm of sacred heirloom objects (pusaka)' (Guy 10). Moreover the colours of the cloth were variously significant, green favoured by warriors as the holy colour of Mohammad, red believed to have talismanic properties (Guy 10, 75). The cloth market collapsed in the nineteenth century, partly as a result of the increased production of cotton fabrics in Europe. However, as late as 1883 travellers to Malaysia reported how they were required to present items of clothing such as jackets and head cloths to each local ruler they met (Guy 72). Joanna's choice of a filthy red dressing gown, of clearly European design, indicates on a broad level the demise of the triangulated cloth trade as a result of Europe's colonisation of India and the Far East. European design (and we might presume fabric) replaces the former prized textiles of India and is, moreover, itself allowed to lapse into disrepair. At the individual level the dressing gown signifies the neglect of Joanna's European husband who fails to provide her with high quality cloth according to the old traditions of exchange and gift which governed the protocols of European-Malay relationships. As a result her garment, chosen as dramatic costume, itself performs the degraded economic and personal relationships that characterize Joanna's marriage.

In *Almayer's Folly*, Mrs Almayer also utilises clothes to express her contempt of her European husband. Once a 'pretty Malay girl,' her grief following Almayer's removal of their daughter to Singapore causes her to age rapidly, so that she takes on a 'witch-like appearance' (AF 23, 25, 33). Despite her convent school education and her marriage to a European, Mrs Almayer only wears the 'hateful finery of Europe' at her wedding (AF 23). Now, she dresses in a 'soiled robe wound tightly under the armpits across her lean bosom' (AF 39). Even when she appears from behind the curtain that marks off the private from the public part of Almayer's house, Mrs Almayer makes no effort to veil herself or to dress differently. The theatricality inherent in Mrs Almayer's appearances from behind this dividing red curtain suggests that the public domain occupied by Almayer constitutes the place where Mrs Almayer gives a frontstage performance. Meanwhile, behind the curtain is the backstage area where she is free to indulge in those 'offstage speeches, gestures and practices that ... contradict, or inflect what appears in the public transcript' (Scott 4).[8] It is here, beyond the direct observation of her husband, that Mrs Almayer acts out her feelings of hatred and anger which she barely manages to conceal frontstage.

Early in her marriage to Almayer, Mrs Almayer has an extra-marital affair with Lakamba, the man whom the narrator describes as exercising 'all his influence towards the help of the white man's enemies' (AF 24). At nights, Lakamba comes down the creek in his canoe to 'the back of the white man's house' (AF 25). Even after this affair has ended, Mrs Almayer maintains contact with Lakamba through

---

[8] Note that in the theatre, the stage curtain is traditionally red.

Babalatchi, with whom she carries 'on long conversations in Sulu language' close to 'the great iron boiler, where the family daily rice was being cooked'. Cooking may also be considered as a 'backstage activity since, in a traditional Malay house, it would take place at the back of the house, in the area that is traditionally the private or female sphere (AF 38). Backstage, behind the curtain, is also the place where Mrs Almayer encourages her daughter to marry Dain Maroola, and where she extracts from Dain a substantial bride-price which she keeps hidden in a chest (see AF 66). Although Malay social customs restricted a woman's ability to play an active role in public life, Mrs Almayer uses the backstage domain to great advantage. Her backstage activities empower her, allowing her to influence the affairs of Sambir in a manner that would be impossible for a woman in the male fronstage domain. Here too, Mrs Almayer instructs her daughter on how to take advantage of her position as a rajah's wife in this private, feminine sphere by giving a frontstage performance backstage: 'Hide your anger, and do not let him see on your face the pain. ... Meet him with joy in your eyes and wisdom on your lips, for to you he will turn in sadness or in doubt' (AF 153).

Mrs Almayer also seems to have succumbed to the unbearable strain of '"acting a mask" in the presence of power' over a prolonged period of time. This may explain why she takes what should be a backstage performance onto the frontstage of the public domain. Almayer recalls how, soon after their marriage, his wife began to treat him 'with a savage contempt, expressed by sulky silence, only occasionally varied by outbursts of savage invective' (AF 25). If such behaviour makes it seem that Mrs Almayer has always had difficulty in sustaining a deferential frontstage performance, it should be remembered that she had hoped to marry a rajah (Lingard), but this dream was shattered when Lingard gave her in marriage to 'an unknown and sulky-looking white man' who was evidently 'disgusted' by the idea of marrying a 'native' (AF 23). Therefore, it is not surprising that Mrs Almayer displays traces of her hidden transcript so early on in her marriage. Her resentment culminates with her burning of the furniture and tearing down of the curtains in Almayer's house in an explosive act of rage. This act of rage not only demonstrates her loathing of her European husband but also symbolises her long-standing hatred of Europeans generally, and the way they have ruined her life.

In his footnote to this incident, Jacques Berthoud suggests that this apparently gratuitous act may be a 'gesture of cultural vandalism,' because European furnishings would have been considered luxury items by the majority of Malays whose homes had few items of furniture (AF 220). It is also an instance of cultural appropriation or – in Mrs Almayer's case – *mis*appropriation, since she uses the curtains to make sarongs for the female servants. Moreover it can also be interpreted as a contrastingly silent protest by Mrs Almayer, using the medium of costume to express contempt not only for her European husband but also for European culture in general. Mrs Almayer's frontstage behaviour leaves her husband in no doubt about her feelings towards him – 'He felt she hated him' (AF 25). Why Mrs Almayer should feel confident enough to bring her backstage anger frontstage may be explained by the fact that, on her marriage day, she realises that 'she was going to be Almayer's companion and not his slave and promised to herself to act accordingly' (AF 23).[9] Mrs Almayer knows that, according to European custom, a wife is not treated like a slave: she should not be beaten, and cannot be given away to another (perhaps crueller) master. Therefore, Mrs Almayer assumes that she does not need to offer her husband 'a performance of deference or consent,' because she fears no reprisal (Scott 3).

Mrs Almayer's outbursts suggest that she may be deploying two more culturally sanctioned methods of bringing hidden transcripts of anger and indignation onto the public stage without incurring reprisals. These are through the rather dramatic and exotic behaviour pattern known as *latah* and through spirit possession. Robert L. Winzeler observes that 'Upon being startled or otherwise provoked, persons who are slightly *latah* will typically exclaim an obscenity, strike out or throw an object,' whilst those who are more strongly *latah* 'will enter a state of altered consciousness and mimic words or sounds, imitate gestures or patterns of movement' (317). Whilst Mrs Almayer's actions are not characterised by mimicry, which was the most commonly commented on aspect of *latah* in contemporary accounts, the inappropriateness and violence of those actions may be intended to echo other notable traits in incidents of *latah*.[10] *Latah* is prevalent among adult women, especially where the male-female relationship within a marriage is 'marked by tension and conflict' (Winzeler 325). It is not necessarily genuine behaviour and is sometimes used by Malay women 'who lack other means of doing so' to 'call attention to themselves and express aggression in socially acceptable or excusable ways, especially, if not only, regarding men' (Winzeler 328). Since Mrs Almayer's outburst does not conform to the most commonly noted characteristics of *latah*, it is unclear whether Almayer himself would have interpreted it as such, but it is likely that their neighbours might do so. In any event these scenes, performed frontstage, are clearly aimed at a dual audience: Almayer and their neighbours. Moreover, her performance for that latter audience, under cover of socially sanctioned disruptive patterns of behaviour, provides a hidden transcript of protest which can be read as aimed more generally at colonial domination.[11]

Winzeler suggests that *latah* appears to be related to another pattern of behaviour which Malay women use to 'draw attention to their problems, express otherwise unacceptable wishes, [and] behave aggressively towards men' – spirit possession (329). Spirits were believed to attack women after childbirth, when they were at their most vulnerable.[12] Often taking the form of pole-cats, banshees and screech owls, these spirits endowed those whom they entered with the same

---

[9] In a quite different context this resolve recalls the theatrical potential of Ibsen's Nora.

[10] For examples of contemporary descriptions of *latah* see, amongst others, O'Brien; Hammond; and Hugh Clifford 1927.

[11] Scott notes that women's 'apolitical status' often makes them able to voice stronger dissent to the dominant public transcript than men (149–50).

[12] See Skeat 320ff.

animal characteristics. It may be that Conrad either saw, heard, or read about models of the Penaggalan (a banshee) and Langsuir (a screech owl) spirits during his travels. in the Malay archipelago because their characteristics are remarkably similar to those of Mrs Almayer and Mrs Willems when they give their frontstage performances. The integral part that belief in spirit possession played in Malay culture was already a stock motif in Victorian travel literature of the region. Hugh Low, for example, refers to this phenomenon at various places in his mid-century account of his sojourn with Rajah Brooke (126, 175). Furthermore, by 1900, Walter Skeat had catalogued at some length, in his volume *Malay Magic*, the various spirits of the Malay cultural pantheon.

The intermittent nature of spirit possession meant that Malay women like Mrs Almayer could use it to express their backstage frustrations frontstage in the public domain in what amounted to an impromptu performance given at any time a woman felt she could no longer maintain the mask of deference that her society demanded she should wear frontstage. Of course, this performance, whilst apparently giving women freedom, was itself still circumscribed by male power, by maintaining the female voice as irrational. A woman's voice could still not be heard on a par with a man's in this frontstage domain, but was marginalized in the very moment it attempted to enter centre stage.

Both Mrs Almayer and Mrs Willems live in Malay society. However, whilst Mrs Almayer is a Malay woman, Mrs Willems is of mixed race. Both women are neglected by their husbands and disappointed in their marriages, and both women have given birth to a child. It is possible, therefore, to read their more overt outbursts in the novels as their staging of performances in which they are pretending either to be *latah* or possessed by spirits. Whilst this reading is tentative in Joanna Willems's case, in Mrs Almayer's case such an interpretation is more than plausible.[13] Her extreme mood swings seem to have started around the time she gave birth to Nina and become far worse when Almayer sends the young Nina away to receive a European education. Thus, the first incident would allow Mrs Almayer to begin a performance of being possessed by spirits whilst the surprise nature of the second might allow her to pretend to be or be *latah* as well. Both incidents allow Mrs Almayer to vent her outrage and distress frontstage whilst appearing not to infringe upon the cultural norms of her society.

In *Almayer's Folly*, Mrs Almayer's 'rapid rush of scathing remarks and bitter cursings ... concluded by a piercing shriek' suggest that she is using spirit possession in order to express her anger in the public arena (AF 40). Like Joanna Willems's cries for help, Mrs Almayer's shrieks can be heard 'far away' from the house, leaving nobody in doubt about her husband's shortcomings (AF 40). The narrator describes how, following these outbursts, Mrs Almayer reminisces about her violent childhood 'in a kind of monotonous recitative' (AF 41). Such

---

[13] Joanna may have been aware of these phenomena, so it is possible that she was using either or both of these during her outburst at Willems.

muttering is a typical feature of spirit possessions.[14] Therefore, Mrs Almayer may be pretending to be possessed by spirits in order to disown her transgression of speaking in the public domain.

Scott states that subordinates often utilise story-telling to express their violent intentions by making the story's protagonist carry out the violence they themselves wish to inflict on the dominant group (19). Thus, Mrs Almayer's tales of 'swift piratical praus' may be her way of expressing her fantasy of revenge under circumstances which render it impossible for her to implement the real thing (AF 41). As a woman who once fought with and against men, Mrs Almayer's new life in a society where women are forbidden entry into the masculine world of action and debate must have been particularly stressful for her (see AF 21). However, through her adroit handling of both the backstage and the frontstage, she successfully utilises this society's customs to express her rage in a manner which avoids incurring danger to herself.

There is another female character in *An Outcast of the Islands* who manages, albeit temporarily, to reverse the colonial tradition of the passive, colonised female acknowledging the authority of the white, European male. This is Aïssa, the Malay woman whom Willems meets in Sambir. Although Aïssa's performance does not provide her with lasting success, it is nevertheless interesting to examine exactly what she does achieve and how this may be viewed as a form of colonial resistance.

The origin of Aïssa's performance may be traced to that of a character with the same name (but different spelling) in H. Rider Haggard's *She* (1886). The narrator Holly's first sight of Ayesha is when she appears from out of 'a recess, draped with curtains, through which shone rays of light' (*She* 140). Ayesha is veiled, and her body's curves are silhouetted against the light of flaming torches as she steps into full view. The curtained recess and lights are reminiscent of a stage that is designed to create the maximum dramatic impact for the audience when the principal actor emerges onto it, and this set has the desired effect: 'the curtain agitated itself a little, then suddenly between its folds there appeared a most beautiful white hand ... . The hand drew the curtain, and drew it aside' (*She* 142). What follows is tantamount to a striptease show, as Ayesha stands in front of Holly and his companions in wrappings that are 'so thin that one could distinctly see the gleam of the pink flesh beneath them,' before she finally lets them fall to the ground to reveal herself in her full glory, 'robed in a garb of clinging white' (*She* 142, 155). This performance has the desired effect. This non-European woman, this 'Venus Victrix' as Holly describes her, succeeds in enslaving her audience of European men. Holly sums up the effect these appearances have on himself and the other men in his party when he 'curses ... the fatal curiosity that is ever prompting man to draw the veil from woman, and curses ... the natural impulse that begets it!' (*She* 155). There is an obvious, Freudian undercurrent to Holly's

---

[14] See Lewis 54, 58; and Hugh Clifford's description of the mutterings of a woman in the throws of spirit-possession in his *Sally: A Study and other Tales*, 11.

words; however, they may also be read as a diatribe against the folly of exploring 'virgin' territories full of strange diseases that proved fatal for so many European explorers and settlers. This can be substantiated by the fact that Holly continually associates Ayesha with evil and death: 'this beauty, with all its awful loveliness, was *evil*' (*She* 155).

Ayesha's performance is one of mastery, a mastery that is achieved without violence; and it elicits from her audience a reciprocal performance of 'deference and consent'. It reverses expectations by reversing the typical, 'first meeting' scene between the European, male explorer/conqueror and the ignorant, non-European. Instead of Ayesha bowing down and worshipping Holly and his party, it is they who, on their hands and knees, worship at her feet.

Another, perhaps more important part of Ayesha's performance is her use of the 'look' that not only makes the men capitulate to her will but also is capable of 'blasting' any dissenter into submission or, failing that, to death. The idea of women's performances being associated with death is echoed in *Almayer's Folly*, where the female gaze – or 'look' – is described as 'a woman's most terrible weapon' and, in *An Outcast of the Islands*, it is this performance of the 'look' that Aïssa enacts in her attempts to attract Willems (AF 171).

In *Outcast*, the narrator describes how Willems felt 'charmed with a charm' when Aïssa first looked at him, and how his body tingled 'with that feeling which begins like a caress and ends in a blow' (OI 69). It is obvious here that Aïssa is using the same script as her predecessor since it has the same effect on Willems as it did on Holly. Following this first meeting, Aïssa's actions seem to take on a semi-ritualistic character as 'day after day, when they met ... she stood ... holding him with her look' (OI 75). The repetitive nature of Aïssa's alluring glances firstly entice Willems to her, then her later sexual capitulation serves to bind him even closer. Aïssa's daily trysts with Willems suggest that she is staging repeat performances of their first meeting. The fact that her actions and her 'look' are exactly the same at each meeting emphasises the idea of a certain artificiality that is congruent with her playing a role rather than acting spontaneously. Aïssa's repetition of the same 'look' and the same, seemingly staged, poses have an accumulative effect upon Willems who, like his own European male counterparts in *She*, finds himself falling at Aïssa's feet. Moreover, like Ayesha, Aïssa plays this role in order to achieve mastery, for, as the novel's ending makes clear, Aïssa hopes that her performance will end with her marriage to Willems – a representative of the dominant elite European men who currently hold power in Sambir. For Aïssa, however, the very performance that she uses to win the object of her affections is also the one that leads to her losing Willems. Ultimately, Willems comes to regard Aïssa with disgust, and her final fate is to live out the remainder of her days as 'That doubled-up crone' who has become one of Almayer's 'serving girls' (OI 366).

Aïssa's performance also concerns a different kind of conquest that is more closely related to colonial resistance and power. For Aïssa, Willems is one of 'those victorious men' who look with 'hard blue eyes at their enemies' (OI 75). Thus, to make 'those eyes look tenderly at her face' and to see such a man 'ready to be enslaved' gives Aïssa an almost sadistic thrill: the thrill of a Malay *woman* conquering one of the conquering race of European *men* (OI 75). As Willems lies 'stretched at her feet without moving ... like death itself,' the nature of Aïssa's performance becomes clear (OI 76). It is a sadomasochistic performance in which the 'native' woman becomes the conqueror whilst the European coloniser is transformed into the conquered. As such, it reverses the typical *Robinson Crusoe* scene, found in illustrated editions of the novel at the time Conrad was writing his novel, in which the 'native' is depicted prostrating himself at the feet of the European man, in acknowledgement of his superiority and in gratefulness for his benevolence.

Sadomasochism is popularly believed to involve violent sexual acts with the purpose of inflicting or receiving pain. The use of costumes and props in the performance of these acts attest to its theatricality, even if no spectators other than the participants are present. Bill Thompson argues that this is not the case however, and that the acts involved in sadomasochism 'are experienced mentally and physically as a form of pleasurable arousal-enhancement rather than pain' (4). If Thompson is correct, then Aïssa's game with Willems amounts to a form of erotic arousal prior to full sexual intercourse. In his *Psychopathia Sexualis*, R. von Krafft-Ebing advanced the now outdated notion that, in Sadomasochism, it is men who delight in inflicting pain and women who enjoy suffering it (77, 79). In *An Outcast of the Islands*, however, Willems is the one lying on the ground as if dead whilst Aïssa stands over him, and it is Willems who – following his first meeting with Aïssa – finds himself drinking river water and shuddering 'with a depraved sense of pleasure at the after-taste of slime in the water' (OI 73). Later in the novel, he tries to explain to Lingard how there 'was something in me [Aïssa] could get hold of. She, a savage. I, a civilized European, and clever!' (OI 269). It is obvious that Willems wants to imagine himself the passive partner in a perverted game with a savage woman because this enables him to deny responsibility for his actions. In this respect Willems resembles what Mary Louise Pratt has termed 'the non-hero of an anti-conquest'. That is, the European, middle class male who is 'constructed as a non-interventionist European presence. Things happen to him and ... his innocence lies ... in submissiveness and vulnerability' (Pratt 78). Up until now, playing the role of 'victim' has enabled Willems to blame others for his failures.[15] Thus, it is not surprising that Willems wishes to play the role of the passive partner here. Gilles Deleuze's psychoanalytical analysis of male masochism substantiates this when he discusses how masochists (like Willems) project the desire to punish their father onto themselves so that 'what the subject atones for is his resemblance to the father and the father's likeness in him' (Deleuze 60). In Willems's case, this might be his way of punishing Lingard – whom he regards as a father-figure – for bringing him to his present predicament in Sambir.

---

[15] He even exculpates himself for stealing money from his employer by blaming this not only on Hudig but also on his wife and her family's constant demands for money.

Thompson asserts that, rather than its being a game in which there is always an active, sadistic player and another, more passive and masochistic one, sadomasochism is actually a consensual game in which partners often exchange roles (5). This can be seen in *Outcast* when, near the end of the novel, Aïssa mockingly bows down to Willems, telling him that 'I sit in the dust at your feet' (OI 357). Although Conrad appears to share Krafft-Ebing's view that sadomasochism is about inflicting and receiving pain, he does not seem to agree with Krafft-Ebing that men are always the dominant players in this game.[16] Bernard C. Meyer argues that, in his depiction of Aïssa as the dominant player in her sadomasochistic performance with Willems, Conrad may have been influenced by Leopold von Sacher-Masoch's pornographic novel, *Venus in Furs* (1870), which Meyer describes as being a 'primer of male masochism' (308). Meyer substantiates this by pointing out how Conrad's image of Willems prostrating himself at Aïssa's feet closely resembles the scene in *Venus in Furs* in which the central male character, Severin von Kusiemski, throws himself before the feet of his lover, the wealthy, aristocratic widow, Wanda (310). Given Willems's behaviour towards the two women he is associated with in *Outcast* (Aïssa and his wife, Joanna), it certainly seems as though he shares Severin's view that, as far as women are concerned, 'Man has only one choice: to be a slave or to be a tyrant' (Sacher-Masoch 150).

If, following Krafft-Ebing's view, the more general consensus at the time was that men were the dominant players in sadomasochism, then Conrad's depiction of Willems as the passive player in this performance may also have an important implication in the context of colonialism. 'Looking' or 'gazing' at a feminised land was often the European explorer's (or conqueror's) prelude to the conquest and appropriation of 'virgin land'.[17] Here, however, the roles are reversed, and it is Aïssa who gazes upon Willems as a prelude to conquest and possession. This sadomasochistic performance, in which the stereotypical roles are reversed, also reverses the trope of the feminised non-European land submitting to the European male explorer, a reversal made even more ambiguous at the beginning and end of the British empire when the monarch was also female. Reversing this trope positions the European man as the victim of the non-European land-as-woman. This was how those European men who 'went native' at the periphery were regarded by those back in the metropolis. Unwilling to believe that a European man would willingly abandon his country and its ways, Europeans who remained in Europe preferred to imagine that he had either been forced to do this on pain of death or that he had been enslaved – or 'seduced' – by some exotic female like Aïssa.

---

[16] Havelock Ellis also shared Krafft-Ebing's views on sadomasochism (see volume III of his *Studies in the Psychology of Sex* [1903]).

[17] See Pratt 7; Craig ch.7; and Greenblatt 60 ('It is as if from the instant of landfall Colombus imagines that everything he sees is already the possession of one of the monarchies he has offered to serve').

Aïssa's initial domination and control of Willems is achieved through a performance of submission that approximates what is expected of her not only as a member of a subordinate race but also as a woman. Unlike Mrs Almayer and Mrs Willems, however, Aïssa is only able to achieve a partial, or temporary, success. Ultimately, she is unable to vary or change her role when it is required of her, and her inability to do so foregrounds the futility of her performance. Willems's initial fascination is replaced by repulsion and, like Holly before him, he comes to associate Aïssa with death: 'To-morrow she may want my life. How can I know what's in her? She may want to kill me next!'

Repetition of the same performance, however well it is performed, eventually results in satiation, boredom and finally even disgust. Aïssa's inability to vary her original performance, or to create a new one, suggests that she is not as proficient a performer as Mrs Almayer, or even Joanna Willems, and this is the reason that she is unable to sustain her original victory over white men. Whilst Mrs Willems retains the marital home, and Mrs Almayer achieves independence and a certain fearful respect from others, Aïssa ends her days in obscurity as one of Almayer's serving girls, who is viewed as 'disgusting' by other European men.

Both Mrs Almayer's and Mrs Willems's performances reveal that 'native' women are as capable as men of staging ambiguous performances as a type of resistance to colonial rule. Both Joanna Willems and Mrs Almayer protest at the way they are treated by their European husbands by staging socially acceptable performances of rage. Since nineteenth-century Malay – and to a certain extent, nineteenth-century European – culture restricted women to the private domain and forbade them to publicly express their anger, these two women succeed in complying with this public transcript of silence whilst simultaneously expressing their contempt for their European husbands – and Europeans in general – by wearing dirty and/or inappropriate clothing in inappropriate places. Mrs Almayer also takes advantage of the Malay customs of *latah* and spirit-possession that give her the opportunity to voice her protest whilst simultaneously disclaiming responsibility for her words and actions. Both women's ambiguous and socially-sanctioned performances leave their European husbands (and their Malay neighbours) in no doubt about their real feelings, yet powerless to silence them.

Unlike her two counterparts, however, Aïssa is unable to vary her performance sufficiently in order to retain her audience, so its success is only temporary. Aïssa is, of course, not directly protesting against her treatment by a white man, although she may well have had reason to do so by the end of the novel. Whilst her performance brings only partial success in obtaining mastery over one of the representatives of the European colonisers who have invaded her land, she does succeed, for a while, in reversing the expected roles and transforming Willems into one who is subjugated.

Nevertheless, regardless of the qualified success of Aïssa's performance, there is no doubt that both Mrs Willems and Mrs Almayer's performances achieve what Bhabha has described as 'the refusal to return and restore the image of authority to the eye of power.' Instead, their performances hint at an 'implacable aggression' that their European husbands can never fully suppress or contain. Willems's and Almayer's desire that their wives, if not 'love,' at least 'respect' them mirrors the colonist's own desire for respect. However, the two women's ambiguous performances reveal the impossibility of this desire, and the absurdity of the European coloniser's illusion that it is *he* who has the mastery.

Chapter 3
Mixing the Masks of Comedy and Tragedy: The Popular Theatres of Joseph Conrad's Fiction

Richard J. Hand

Although Joseph Conrad's works are rendered into a terminally 'literary' status, it is important to remember that many examples of his fiction emerge from antecedents in popular prose: frequently, Conrad responds to, utilises or parodies the adventure yarn, the romance novel and even pulp journalism. To give but one example in existing criticism, Lawrence Graver contends that all the stories in *A Set of Six* are a concerted – albeit unsuccessful – attempt to exploit different genres and 'conventions of popular fiction' (125). There is a case to argue that the parameters of popular culture can be drawn more widely and that Conrad's fiction includes significant allusions to, and uses of, popular performance including, as this essay will explore, melodrama, Grand-Guignol and *commedia dell'arte*. After all, even as an English 'man of letters,' Conrad is an extremely *dramatic* writer, a novelist who is able to admit 'I have a theatrical imagination' (*CL4* 218). Novels such as *Victory*, for example, have struck critics such as Yves Hervouet (1990) and Daphna Erdinast-Vulcan (1998) with its sophisticated intertextual schema. The intertextuality of this novel is further defined by Robert Hampson who finds in *Victory* a "theatrical" novel with a complex construction, featuring 'the dramatic handling of dialogue and the use of a Shakespearean intertext' (2000, 160). Even the novel's detractors, such as Douglas Hewitt, can be seen to condemn the novel in terms which reveal its inherent theatricality: Hewitt objects to the novel's melodramatic characterisation and its 'simplified black and white distinction of good and evil' (107), a moral worldview that, we should note, is wholly the stock-in-trade of melodrama.

Melodrama abounds in Conrad. The themes of love and sacrifice in 'Gaspar Ruiz' and intrigue in 'The Informer' are unquestionably melodramatic even in the way they are handled stylistically. The Napoleonic backgrounds to 'The Warrior's Soul' and 'The Duel' would make familiar crowd-pleasing settings in Victorian melodrama as would the themes of honour, conflict and masculinity, even though Conrad would explore these to very different ends. The moral dilemmas in popular Victorian melodramas such as Leopold Lewis's *The Bells* (1871) and the archetypal characters in popular nautical melodramas such as Douglas Jerrold's *Black-Ey'd Susan* (1829) provide surprising templates to the ironic dramas enacted in *Victory*,

Lord Jim and others. While the presence of music hall allusion in *The Secret Agent* (not dissimilar to Conrad's use of circus allusion in *Under Western Eyes*) is a key point of reference within the novel, the overall work represents a sophisticated exploration of melodrama: as the dedication Conrad inscribes in Richard Curle's copy of *The Secret Agent* makes clear, 'the book is an attempt to treat consistently a melodramatic subject ironically' (Curle, 100). Not only does Winnie Verloc represent an ironic exploration of the archetypal melodramatic heroine, Adolf Verloc's name serves as an ironic allusion to Eugène François Vidocq, 'the French double agent and spy' (Knowles and Moore 2001, 433). Vidocq was an immensely popular figure for Victorian melodrama in such plays as *Vidocq, the French Police Spy*; *Vidocq, the French Jonathan Wild*; and *Vidocq, the French Thief Taker* (Chance Newton 184).

Just as melodrama can throw light on Conrad's work, the spectacular moments of violence and 'realistic' horror throughout Conrad's fiction are akin to the explicit displays of the taboo in the morally complex Grand-Guignol, a form which itself could be aptly described as 'ironic melodrama.' The Grand-Guignol was alluded to overtly in *Laughing Anne* and informs the stage productions of *The Secret Agent* and Basil Macdonald Hastings's *Victory*; but it can also throw light on the content and structure of a number of Conrad's short stories and novels. The themes of 'ghosts' and revenge in 'Karain: A Memory' and 'ghosts' and guilt in 'The Planter of Malata' are classic stock-in-trade material of the Grand-Guignol. Likewise, the displays of violence in the novels (including *The Secret Agent* and *Victory*) and sensationalistic short stories such as 'The Inn of the Two Witches: A Find' and 'Because of the Dollars' can be elucidated through reference to the Grand-Guignol. The Grand-Guignol also comes some way in explaining a problematic short story such as 'The Idiots'.

'The Idiots' is typically regarded as a flawed attempt at post-Maupassant style and theme. Jocelyn Baines describes it as a 'savage tale' (173), and Lawrence Graver is upset by a short story which seems to be 'a drama of idiocy, delirium, and murder' which descends into 'pretentious and implausible melodrama' (10, 8). Graver's descriptions can be easily applied to Grand-Guignol, a form which is obsessed with mental degeneracy, slaughter and melodramatic technique. Daphna Erdinast-Vulcan describes 'The Idiots' as 'one of Conrad's most pointless stories ... a narrative without a proper ending, without a moral' (83). Once again, this is a comment which seems extremely apt in relation to the Grand-Guignol, a form of theatre in which sensationalistic spectacle is everything and the comforting moral justice of melodrama is sacrificed for a disconcerting amorality. If we consider the end of the short story:

> 'I want to live. To live alone – for a week – for a day. I must explain to them... I would tear you to pieces, I would kill you twenty times over rather than let you touch me while I live. How many times must I kill you – you blasphemer! Satan sends you here. I am damned too!'

'Come,' said Millot, alarmed and conciliating. 'I'm perfectly alive!... Oh, my God!'

She had screamed, 'Alive!' and at once vanished before his eyes, as if the islet had swerved aside from under her feet. Millot rushed forward, and fell flat with his chin over the edge. Far below he saw the water whitened by her struggles, and heard one shrill cry for help that seemed to dart upwards along the perpendicular face of the rock, and soar past, straight into the high and impassive heaven. (TU 84)

The mistaken perception of a 'ghost,' the heightened dialogic utterances, the violence and cruel irony in the face of an 'impassive' heaven all contribute towards a consummately Grand-Guignol finale.

For the rest of this chapter, we will turn our attention to two neglected examples of Conrad's shorter fiction: 'Freya of the Seven Isles: A Story of Shallow Waters' and 'The Return'. Both works have traditionally been dismissed as some of Conrad's weakest works, but I believe they can be fruitfully analysed if they are considered in close relation to performance culture. Lawrence Graver, for example, regards 'Freya of the Seven Isles' as a damning example of Conrad's 'deterioration' (163), but if we analyse the novella as an exploration of genre, in particular, classical performance comedy, it is revealed as a much more accomplished work. 'Freya of the Seven Isles' is a romantic love story which imitates the discourse of romantic fiction. Daphna Erdinast-Vulcan argues that the novella 'follows the time-honoured formula of the melodramatic romance' (143). Jocelyn Baines sees the story as an example of 'extreme romanticism' and is annoyed by what he sees as Conrad's deliberate populism in the form of 'occasional lapses into facetiousness or heartiness – presumably a concession to the magazine reader' (392, 376). As Monika Elbert writes, it is a study of the 'power dynamics of possession' (133) with the eponymous heroine the focal desire of masculine possession and/or obsession. However, Elbert also contends that in sections such as the early description of Freya, Conrad resorts to 'the most romantic tropes, even as he tries to resist romantic discourse, in his self-mocking way' (136). It is this self-mocking romance that clearly locates 'Freya of the Seven Isles' as emerging from a tradition of formulaic comedy.

'Freya of the Seven Isles' is in many ways a playfully comic tale with its stock situation of the love and frustrated desires of the eponymous heroine and the malicious intent of her unrequited admirer. Conrad utilizes strategies of comic rhetoric and narrative: the most blatant example being the running joke of 'Nelson (or Nielsen),' a comic device which is significantly abandoned in the final phase of the story. Lawrence Graver intends to dismiss the novella when he describes it as 'flamboyant melodrama' (163). C. B. Cox strives to do the same thing when he argues that 'the characters assume roles suitable for a melodramatic opera' (163), just as Jocelyn Baines argues that 'the style is frankly romantic and the story throbs with movement and passion, becoming at times operatic in form' (376). Despite such attempts to define 'Freya of the Seven Isles' as operatic or wholly melodramatic, a more accurate description, for the most part, would be to see the novella as possessing the unmistakable qualities of the Italian comedy, traceable back to the *commedia dell'arte* of the Italian Renaissance. Lawrence Graver seems infuriated by a novella wherein the 'mood is light' at the beginning (163), but proceeds to allow all of its characters to grow 'to twice the size of life': for Graver, it is 'impossible to take seriously' (164). Graver may be hoping to dismiss 'Freya of the Seven Isles' with his condemnations but inadvertently reinforces the comic aspect of the novella which as a work in the tradition of *commedia dell'arte* needs larger than life characters and an implausible storyline.

Commedia dell'arte is arguably Italian culture's most enduring contribution to world drama and is second only to Shakespeare and the English stage as the Renaissance's most significant dramatic achievement. It is a stylised, highly physical and non-naturalistic form, relying exclusively on the strict formula of its dramatic narrative. It is not a scripted but an improvised form: the plays consist of a collection of two-dimensional characters – frequently archetypal if not stereotypical – who interact in ways that are true to their characters in stock situations. Famous for its use of masks (although it was significantly not an entirely masked theatrical form), *commedia dell'arte* had a major influence on the comedies of Ben Jonson and Molière. Moreover, it continued to flourish as a 'pure' form in its own right and thrived for some two hundred years from the mid-sixteenth century until the mid-eighteenth century when it evolved (or rather dissipated) into more consciously textual and literary plays, most obviously the comedies of Carlo Goldoni, as well as subsequent generations of popular theatre such as pantomime and marionette shows including Punch and Judy (the former character a direct descendant of *commedia dell'arte*'s Pulcinella).

Conrad, of course, expressed his 'love' for the lifeless yet immortal figures in a 'marionette show' (*CL*1 419), and 'Freya of the Seven Isles' is, from a certain perspective, a marionette show: a novella that explores, like classic Italian comedy, a formulaic plot and archetypal characters. This point of contact is made most explicit when Conrad likens Antonia, Freya's Malacca Portuguese maidservant, to 'the faithful cameristra in Italian comedy' (TL 184). In *commedia dell'arte*, the cameristra (chambermaid) figure is Colombina, 'personal maid to the prima donna *innamorata*' (Rudlin 127). The *innamorata* character is the focus of love interest in many *commedia dell'arte* scenarios: the attractive, desirable and fiercely contested object of desire. In such scenarios, the Colombina figure – utterly loyal to her mistress – assists and frustrates the action as necessary. Conrad's description of Antonia being 'in the secret, like a comedy cameristra' (TL 178) reveals a typical Colombina-like privilege and narrative function: in John Rudlin's description, Colombina is the 'still centre of the turning wheel, in on everything that is going on' (130). The fact that Antonia is also to be found making 'funny and expressive grimaces behind Heemskirk's back' (TL 177–8) encapsulates the comedy business of Colombina, a strictly non-masked character – and therefore able to make effective use of facial expression – who has the prerogative to collude with the audience and with the ability, if not obligation, to evoke laughter.

Once we use Conrad's 'comedy cameristra' as our key into 'Freya of the Seven Isles' as Italian comedy, other characters fit comfortably into place. As already indicated, Freya Nelson/Nielsen is the classic Italian *innamorata*. The object of her desire is the charming Jasper Allen, the formulaic *innamorato*. Jasper fulfils the role of the male lover: handsome, noble and whose union with the *innamorata* promises the obligatorily harmonious 'happy ever after' finale. But obstacles and frustrations are essential on this journey. Sometimes this can be in the form of a parent: in Freya's case she has a 'guileless comedy father' who is 'so pathetically comic in his fierce aspect as to touch the most lightsome heart' (TL 177). Nelson/Nielsen is a classic comedy father, ostensibly fierce yet impotent in his struggles to protect or contain a precocious and hotly pursued daughter. In addition, Conrad's line about touching the 'lightsome heart' suggests comic reception; it arguably transforms the reader into a spectator, making us 'see' a comic performer in a comic performance.

Although Jasper may be the romantic male lead, he is nevertheless presented with significant comic exaggeration. When Jasper launches into his romantic daydreams, we are presented with comic innuendo:

> Everything in the world reminded him of her. The beauty of the loved woman exists in the beauties of Nature. The swelling outlines of the hills, the curves of a coast ... (TL 210)

Such gently risqué rhetoric is not dissimilar to many a love poem or letter scene in *commedia dell'arte* where romantic sentiment gradually descends into innuendo. It is not just Jasper's language of love that is comic, his appearance is too:

> Too fine in face, with a literal wave in his chestnut hair, spare, long-limbed, with an eager glint in his steely eyes and quick, brusque movements, he made me think sometimes of a flashing sword-blade perpetually leaping out of the scabbard. (TL 158)

Although even an *innamorato* often provides a wealth of comedy, the fact that Jasper is *too* handsome and enthusiastic in his attitude and physicality makes him not dissimilar to the Capitano of *commedia dell'arte*: the great 'outsider' character who breezes into a staid environment and, inadvertently or otherwise, stirs things up into chaos. The Capitano – and his later development into Scaramuccia (better known in his French manifestation as 'Scaramouche') – was one of 'the most agile players' in *commedia dell'arte* (Rudlin 152). Typically the mock-heroic caricature of a cavalier-like figure, the Capitano bears a flashing sword-blade, wears a lewdly phallic mask and sports a feather in his hat: he has a non-verbal language of movement and gesture remarkably similar to Conrad's description of Jasper. While Scaramuccia's primary plot function is to be a 'stirrer' (Rudlin 153), Capitano is always a fraud who needs to receive his comeuppance and public humiliation. In 'Freya of the Seven Isles,' Jasper may have the manner of a Capitano, but he is not a fraud, and his fate is not a warranted humiliation but unjust in an ending that provocatively abandons the disciplined formula of Italian comedy wherein Jasper would secure a harmonious future with Freya and Heemskirk would have to receive his just deserts. We will return to the ending of the novella in due course, but it is first necessary to explore other aspects of Italian comedy in the work.

Italian comedy requires its villain, and in the Dutch lieutenant Heemskirk we find a perfect example. Some of Heemskirk's lines – such as 'Fooling your father finely, aren't you? You have a taste for that sort of fun – have you? Well, we shall see–' (TL 191–2) – have all the rhetorical and expositional features of a comic aside uttered by a stage villain. Indeed, the alliterative first phrase is a familiar device in the monologues and dialogues of *commedia dell'arte* and is one that would still be utilized by the time of Victorian Melodrama. Heemskirk is a comically unpleasant character who is driven by comically strong passions which makes him a hybrid of the two *Vecchi* ('The Old Men') of *commedia dell'arte*: Pantalone and Il Dottore. Conrad's description of him as possessing 'great flat, brown cheeks, with a thin, hooked nose and a small, pursy mouth squeezed in between' (TL 160) makes him resemble Pantalone, the miserly and vindictive old man of *commedia dell'arte* characterized by his repellent physique and his brown leather mask with its trademark 'long, hooked nose' (Rudlin 93). Some of the characters of *commedia dell'arte* are based on animals. In the case of Pantalone he is a scavenging vulture or wizened turkey, and it is a bird metaphor that springs to Heemskirk's own mind when his passion is humiliated: 'That species of fowl is not to be shooed off as easily as a chicken. Fooled, cheated, deceived, led on, outraged, mocked at – beak and claws! A sinister bird!' (TL 208).

Despite his stinginess and repugnant character, Pantalone is a man of immense influence: 'he controls all the finance available within the world of *commedia dell'arte*' (Rudlin 92). Heemskirk fulfils a similar function, terrifying Freya's father as he embodies the power of the dreaded Dutch authorities: this is why Osborn Andreas argues that the power society has invested in Heemskirk means that 'society itself is the villain of this story' (148). Pantalone is typically an avaricious and emaciated figure, yet Heemskirk is a man given to excess which makes him allusive to Il Dottore. This character – the other *Veccho* in *commedia dell'arte* – is as greedy as Pantalone is miserly. He is rich yet crass and vulgar. He is obese, moving belly-forwards, just as Heemskirk is 'cylindrical' (TL 163). Il Dottore would wear a mask that only covered the forehead and nose: consequently, the 'actor's cheeks are thus revealed and often reddened to show Il Dottore's fondness for the bottle' (Rudlin 100), an attribute shared by Heemskirk whose skin, when drunk, 'quite flamed in the neighbourhood of the flat, sallow cheeks' (TL 193). Heemskirk is a hybrid of Pantalone and Il Dottore: the nose of Pantalone and the cheeks of Il Dottore. The two *Vecchi* are despised figures who serve as obstacles or pests in *commedia dell'arte* scenarios. They are two-dimensional characters driven by base and selfish desires, especially lust and greed. As well as being a nuisance, the *Vecchi* are repulsive to look at with their vices and maliciousness evident in their appearance – in *commedia dell'arte* the good look good and the evil look evil – something we can compare with the assessment of Heemskirk by Freya's servant:

> Antonia was very much afraid of Heemskirk. She was afraid of him because of his personal appearance: because of his eyes and his eyebrows, and his mouth and his nose and his limbs… And she thought him an evil man, because, to her eyes, he looked evil. (TL 202)

We have seen how Italian comedy in the form of *commedia dell'arte* can be seen to define the key players in 'Freya of the Seven Isles,' but it can even be located in some of the minor characters. Consider, for example, the warrant officer who invites Jasper to board the *Neptun*:

> He was a short man, with a rotund stomach and a wheezy voice. His immovable fat face looked lifeless in the moonlight, and he walked with his thick arms hanging away from his body as though he had been stuffed. (TL 212)

This description is like the Zanni in *commedia dell'arte*: the masked and gormless menial servant who bumbles along with his elbows 'bent and the arms half lifted' (Rudlin 69).

Aside from the characters, some other features of *commedia dell'arte* are enlightening in a reading of 'Freya of the Seven Isles'. *Commedia dell'arte* relies heavily on the use of *lazzi*: a repertoire of comic routines. These could be verbal jokes but were more typically examples of physical comedy including slapstick (indeed, the term 'slapstick' derives from the wooden prop invented specifically for Arlecchino – better known as Harlequin – the principal servant character in *commedia dell'arte*). Such routines would be key moments of comic climax in scenes of *commedia dell'arte*. Conrad provides an excellent example of *lazzi* in the episode where Freya slaps Heemskirk's face. The simple spectacle of a woman slapping a would-be suitor is itself a familiar comic situation in its *Schadenfreude*. The 'routine' is further developed – and Heemskirk's indignity further exacerbated – when Freya's father appears on the scene and interprets the Dutchman's agony as being a toothache. But Heemskirk's suffering is presented as inherently comic: 'this cheek nursed with both hands, these wild glances, these stampings, this distracted swaying of the body' (198). Heemskirk's actions would appear to be like the heightened physical actions of *commedia dell'arte*. Conrad's *lazzo* is reminiscent of the 'Lazzo of Fruits and Kisses' described in a performance in Perugia in 1734 in which a romantically-inclined character demands 'the fruits of love' (i.e. a kiss) only to get slapped around the head (Gordon 18). Nelson/Nielsen's bemused comment – 'What is there so amusing in a man being in pain?' (TL 200) – is an absurd question, for, as Samuel Beckett informs us in *Endgame*, 'Nothing is funnier than unhappiness' (101). Of course, Nelson/Nielsen's deadpan bewilderment serves to enhance the comedy of the scene: in other words, a character unmoved by the humour of a scene inevitably makes a scene even funnier.

Jasper's throwaway line – 'Confound his psychology' (TL 170) – takes on greater significance when we regard 'Freya of the Seven Isles' as a tale of two-dimensional comic archetypes and simplistic motivations. However, as much as Conrad enjoys exploring the styles of diverse popular genres he is not content with adhering to one. Conrad has the ability to step in and out of other genres in the sophisticated pastiche of other forms – one thinks of the allusion to melodrama, sensation fiction and journalistic hyperbole in *The Secret Agent*; the parody of pulp romantic prose in 'To-morrow' and so on. In 'Freya of the Seven Isles' Conrad establishes a classical Italian comedy with stock characters and comic routines, but rather than follow this through to a harmonious conclusion, Conrad opts for the anti-comic and ruptures genre with a tragic ending. Indeed, Edward Garnett urged Conrad to consider a happy ending to 'Freya of the Seven Isles,' but Conrad responded that he would sooner see all magazine editors 'drowned in heaps' (*CL*4 464) before he would oblige. By sticking to his principles, Conrad creates a shocking disruption to the well-wrought comedy of the novella, and the work ultimately becomes, in Gail Fraser's words, 'a tragic story of separation and defeat' (Fraser 1996, 35). 'Freya of the Seven Isles' is similar to Henry James's *Daisy Miller* (1879) inasmuch as both are comic love stories in which the eponymous heroines should survive (as Daisy does in James's own 1882 stage dramatization of the novel) but fail to, thus transforming the works into tragedies. Freya was just one of several stock characters in a *commedia dell'arte*-like scenario, but eventually she reaches a highly dramatic, not comic, demise being 'vanquished in her struggle with three men's absurdities' (TL 238).

The conclusion to 'Freya of the Seven Isles' is certainly violent and destructive with its thwarted romance, wrecked ship, degeneration into insanity and premature death: as Elbert writes, Heemskirk's 'rage' fills him with a craving to 'annihilate Freya, the object of his desire' (TL 136), and he succeeds. The bleak conclusion to 'Freya of the Seven Isles' includes an obfuscation of the clarity of comic identity: as Robert Hampson writes, Jasper is 'emasculated by the loss of his ship' (1992, 47) and so, we could argue, he is robbed of the potency of a romantic male lead. The novella concludes, in Elbert's words, with a 'final scene (which) is a crescendo of emotion' (140). The last sentences of the novella, in which the narrator explains to Nelson that his daughter died of a broken heart, read as follows:

> 'Man!' I cried, rising upon him wrathfully, 'don't you see that she died of it?'
> He got up too. 'No! no!' he stammered, as if angry. 'The doctors! Pneumonia. Low state. The inflammation of the... They told me. Pneu–'
> He did not finish the word. It ended in a sob. He flung his arms out in a gesture of despair, giving up his ghastly pretence with a low, heartrending cry:
> 'And I thought she was so sensible!' (TL 238)

The clear diction of comic utterance from earlier in the novella is replaced by hesitancy and incompletion. The medical diagnosis that serves to rationalize Freya's demise is reined back in to romance: a maiden dying of a broken heart.

This shifts the comic narrative of the story into melodramatic tragedy. Indeed, the account of Freya's final days shortly before the above extract is loaded with melodramatic resonance and rhetoric: 'I did not really mean to be a bad daughter to you, papa ... I've been conceited, headstrong, capricious .... Draw the curtain, papa. Shut the sea out. It reproaches me with my folly' (TL 238). It is certainly a very theatrical 'curtain' that Freya wants to see closed in order to end the humiliating spectacle of her comic 'folly'. It is a stark contrast to the death of the female lead in *Victory* wherein Lena embraces and almost relishes her status as Cleopatra-like tragic heroine (Hand 2005, 172–73n). Moreover, if we return to Nelson's moment of revelation at the end of the novella, the reader is made to be the spectator to the heightened practice of melodramatic performance which was characterized with such flinging arms, gestures of despair and heartrending cries. 'Freya of the Seven Isles' marks an attempt by Conrad to use a formulaic comic structure and characters – not dissimilar to *commedia dell'arte* – which he then shifts into melodrama which is itself another form of popular theatre.

'Freya of the Seven Isles' refuses to end harmoniously as classical comedy should. But it also lacks the moral retribution that would be necessary to make it a true melodrama. What we find in the novella is a generic tale which has its genre, structure and formula ruptured and frustrated. Conrad claimed to have adored marionette shows, and it is interesting to consider the writer as puppet master in his work. Arguably, it is the consciously generic works or episodes that reveal this most. One thinks of the twists and violent turns manipulated in order to seal the fate of the unfortunate victims in Conrad's horror story 'The Brute' or the careful manipulation of Winnie Verloc's fate in the melodramatic denouement to *The Secret Agent*. Conrad is dispassionate in the execution of this puppet mastery, and this raises some interesting features to the narration of 'Freya of the Seven Isles'. Monika Elbert contends – partially on the basis of Conrad's own 'Author's Note' where he defines Freya as being 'actively individual' (x) – that Conrad himself is 'possessed with Freya' as she is a construct which 'recall(s) to him his own emotional impotence' (129). Elbert argues that the narrator is one of *four* men in pursuit of Freya (133), and Erdinast-Vulcan believes that the narrator 'tries to become one of the characters' because he is 'not content with being a mere friendly spectator in the drama' (144, 147). The narrator does not want to be one of us, a disengaged reader/spectator, but neither is he able to stand, like Colombina, at the still centre of the comic action. Erdinast-Vulcan celebrates this traditionally much-maligned novella by seeing it as 'an anti-romance, the story of a narrator who will do anything to become a character in his own story' (152). Another way to describe this is to see the narrator as a puppet master who is desperate to be a puppet. But as this is impossible and there is no dramatic role for the narrator as an archetype of comedy, tragedy or melodrama, he mediates us through the dissolution of genre into an ending of bleak nihilism.

In contrast to 'Freya of the Seven Isles' yet no less bleak is 'The Return'. The short story – a long and detailed study of a woman leaving her husband for another man only to return the same evening – was rejected for publication by a number of magazines and eventually only came to print as a part of *Tales of Unrest*. Conrad himself came to have an antipathy towards the short story, while for Albert J. Guerard, 'The Return' is not only one of Conrad's weakest efforts but 'one of the worst (short stories) ever written by a great novelist' (96). For C. B. Cox, 'The Return' is Conrad's 'worst short story' (6) because it demonstrates his inability to write about the 'physical relation' between men and women. This seems at odds with more recent criticism which has come some way in redeeming 'The Return': Gail Fraser, for instance, explains that the sustained study of 'sexual discord' (31) in 'The Return' is what made it an uncomfortable prospect for magazine editors of the time, an argument which suggests that the work is morally difficult rather than incompetent. It is also a tale heavy with Freudian symbolism: Alvan Hervey uncomfortably fumbling with the key in the lock under the gaze of his wife (TU 170), and Mrs Hervey snapping her fan leaving Alvan to 'stoop' and 'grope' for the pieces at her feet (TU 176). Osborn Andreas assesses 'The Return' as an investigation of the problems of conformity: 'to seek the approval of the group may be to find the heavy hand that crushes out the individual life' (35).

'The Return' is undeniably a dramatic work. Indeed, it is interesting to note that even when criticising 'The Return,' some critics turn to drama: Jocelyn Baines sees the short story as 'a psychological drama without any important objective action' (192), and Laurence Graver argues:

> (Instead) of *dramatizing* Hervey's shallowness, Conrad holds it up for immediate disapproval. Thus Hervey is damned by relentless (and tiresome) moral description, alienated from both our interest and our sympathy before he has a chance to *act* (38, emphases added).

'The Return' certainly has a strict and unified focus to its action, time scale and location. In terms of its plot, we can appropriate Osborn Andreas's three 'astounding' moments (35) – the discovery of the letter; the wife's return; and the wife's laughter – and redefine them as key *dramatic* moments. Conrad's avowed 'theatrical imagination' finds some of its most evident expression in this short story's descriptive narrative. At times, this can be in the description of costume appearance: 'His trousers were turned up, and his boots a little muddy, but he looked very much as usual. Only his hair was slightly ruffled…' (TU 136). There are also descriptions which amount to a theatrical choreography such as when we are told that 'Unconsciously he made a step towards her – then another. He saw her arm make an ample, decided movement – and he stopped' (TU 140), 'he clenched his fists and set his teeth hard' (TU 135) or:

> He stamped his foot, tore the letter across, then again and again… He flung down the small bits of paper. They settled, fluttering at his feet and looked very white on the dark carpet, like a scattered handful of snowflakes. (TU 133)

In this simple plot (wife leaves husband; wife returns to husband; husband leaves wife) Conrad explores an eclectic range of performance styles. As in other examples of Conrad's fiction, a textual relationship is established with Shakespeare: Conrad makes an ironic allusion to the world-weary love story of *Antony and Cleopatra* when Mrs Hervey's hair is described as glinting like 'burnished gold' (TU 184), a direct echo of Enobarbus's description of Cleopatra's barge on the Cydnus, like a 'burnish'd throne' with its poop of 'beaten gold' (II, iii, 199–200). In the recent critical attempts to redeem 'The Return,' some arguments have seen the work to be a precursor to more recent drama: Owen Knowles and Gene M. Moore argue that 'The Return' is not dissimilar to the style of Harold Pinter's drama, especially in the achievement of its dialogue which is likened to 'pinterese' (349). There is perhaps an equally convincing argument to see 'The Return' as a precursor to the style (not least in dialogic language) and themes of one of the most significant post-Pinter playwrights, David Mamet. Jocelyn Baines assesses 'The Return' as 'a tragedy of misunderstanding and of failure to connect. There is something strangely compulsive about the story because it seems that these two people are doomed not to make contact' (Baines 193). Such analysis could be effortlessly appropriated as a description of David Mamet's *Oleanna* (1992), another brutal and provocative study of the clash of gender relationships, albeit in a late twentieth-century rather than late nineteenth-century context. Although 'The Return' may suggest Shakespeare, Pinter and Mamet, some lines are emphatically melodramatic. For every elliptical and hesitant proto-Pinter or Mamet line – '... Pain ... Indignation ... Sure to misunderstand' (TU 162) or 'I want ... I want ... to ... to ... know ...' (TU 185) – there is a declamation of high melodrama: 'And, pray, for how long have you been making a fool of me?' (TU 146); '"Pon my soul"' (TU 168); and even '"Pon my word, I loved you – I love you now"' (TU 176).

Most obviously, to the contemporary reader the short story has an Ibsenesque quality. Robert Hampson claims that 'The Return' depicts, like *The Sisters* and 'The Rescuer,' 'the alienated and circumscribed world of the European bourgeoisie' (1992, 85n). This is precisely the same milieu studied and criticized by Ibsen in his Realist plays. Mrs Hervey explains to Alvan that all he required was 'a wife – some woman – any woman that would think, speak, and behave in a certain way – in a way you approved' (TU 177). This social conditioning is also apparent in Alvan's own view of the situation as, according to one of his tortuous (yet naturalistic) utterances, Mrs Hervey has 'failed' in her 'loyalty to – to the larger conditions of our life' (TU 164), a condemnation reminiscent of the appalling bourgeois conclusion that 'One doesn't *do* that kind of thing!' (Ibsen 1961, 364) when the eponymous heroine blows her brains out at the end of *Hedda Gabler* (1890). It is through absurd 'loyalty' to a rotten system and a duplicitous institution – the social conditioning of her class and a betrayed marriage – that Mrs Alving in *Ghosts* (1883) stoically nurses her son, afflicted with congenital syphilis, because of her adulterous husband. In Ibsen's *A Doll's House* (1879), Nora Helmer refuses to descend to Hedda Gabler or Mrs Alving's nadir and escapes from the infernal oppression of bourgeois matrimony as she walks into freedom: '*From below comes the sound of a door slamming*' (1965, 232). In Conrad's short story, Mrs Hervey's bid for freedom fails, and she returns in defeat and humility; and it is Alvan who is permitted to conclude the narrative with the slamming of a door: 'Then below, far below her, as if in the entrails of the earth, a door slammed heavily' (TU 186). Mrs Hervey's return is like the revised finale Ibsen was forced to provide for the 1880 German production of the play (curiously, at the behest of Hedwig Niemann-Raabe, the actress playing Nora [Innes 83]) in which no door slams but rather Nora changes her mind and '*sinks almost to the ground by the door*' (1965, 334).

'The Return' is also reminiscent of August Strindberg, another Scandinavian playwright who strove to denounce the world of the bourgeoisie with a ferocity that outstrips Ibsen. Plays like *The Father*, *The Dance of Death* and *The Pelican* amount to eviscerations of the bourgeois marriage and family. 'The Return' has a barely contained Strindbergian violence to it. Alvan Hervey attempts to pacify his wife by flinging water in her face, 'putting into the action all the secret brutality of his spite' (TU 167) and feeling it would be 'excusable – in any one' (TU 167) to smash the glass tumbler into her face. When Mrs Hervey laughs – a major dramatic scene we will investigate in due course – Alvan considers 'stifling that unbearable noise with his hands' (TU 166). Other moments have a brutality centred, as so frequently in Strindberg, on the gender conflict:

> She panted, showing her teeth, and that hate of strength, the disdain of weakness, the eternal preoccupation of sex came out like a toy demon out of a box.
> 'This is odious,' she screamed. (TU 178)

Strindberg is usually cited as the major precursor to Expressionist drama, and his post-Realist plays shift away from the confines of naturalism even if some of his major themes and preoccupations continue to obsess him. Within 'The Return' itself there are moments that seem to venture into the abstract. At times, the performance dynamic of the short story shifts into the ritualistic:

> His voice rose and fell pompously in a strange chant. His eyes were still, his stare exalted and sullen; his face was set, was hard, was woodenly exulting over the grim inspiration that secretly possessed him, seethed within him, lifted him up into a stealthy frenzy of belief (TU 157)

The Expressionistic quality that is evident in later works such as *The Secret Agent* and *Victory* – and would be detected by dramatic critics of the stage adaptation of the former (Hand 2001b, 7–10) – is utilized in 'The Return'. Expressionist drama characteristically made extensive use of shadows, and in 'The Return,' we are told that 'Behind her the shadow of a colossal woman danced lightly on the wall' (TU 182). In another Expressionistic moment, Alvan beholds his reflection:

> He caught sight of himself in the pier glass, drawn up to his full height, and with a face so white that his eyes, at the distance, resembled the black cavities

in a skull. He saw himself as if about to launch imprecations, with arms uplifted above her bowed head. (TU 158)

Just as some of the drama of *The Return* is variously melodramatic, naturalistic and even expressionistic, it is also proto-absurdist. In 'To-Morrow' (reworked by Conrad for the stage as *One Day More*) Bessie Carvil, in a proto-Beckettian universe, aids her blind father (a figure as monstrous as Hamm in *Endgame*) and her neighbour Captain Hagberd, whose never-ending wait for his son makes him a clown suitable for *Waiting for Godot*. When Bessie's one hope for liberation (for Bessie, the fantasy of freedom takes the form of matrimony and a grand move into the house next door: ironically, into the type of situation that has driven Mrs Hervey to despair) fails her, the door of her father's cottage becomes a Dantean portico which she closes on herself. Like ironic Antigones in a universe of Beckettian nihilism, women such as Mrs Hervey and Bessie Carvil may have aspirations but are both eventually trapped and interred alive. In contrast, other Conradian women, such as Winnie Verloc, the melodramatic heroine of *The Secret Agent*, may find herself the 'free woman' (SA 261), but it is a freedom that is attained through murder and ends in suicide.

It is a man's world for Conrad: Alvan Hervey's bid for freedom is incalculably more successful than his wife's; Andreas argues that Alvan discovers in his 'social outcast status' a feeling of 'euphoria' (39). However, one can be forgiven for expecting his 'freedom' to be as haunted, sullied or guilty as that of other Conrad male characters as diverse as Ossipon (*The Secret Agent*), Axel Heyst (*Victory*) or Captain Davidson ('Because of the Dollars'): men who all find themselves alone when they leave their women or have their women taken away from them. The self-satisfied liberty of Harry Hagberd in 'To-Morrow' is an exception by comparison. The inevitability of a gloomy fate for Alvan especially seems the case given his repeated horror of 'tomorrow'. In this way, Conrad problematises the grand gesture of departure: there is no comfortable comic resolution, no melodramatic finale as Alvan's fate is not clear cut.

The supreme dramatic moment in 'The Return' is the mixture of laughter and sobbing: a 'shrill peal followed by a deep sob and succeeded by another shriek of mirth' (TU 166). The shifting sounds of crying and laughing are unnerving as is the face of Mrs Hervey, 'tear-stained, dolorous' (TU 166) yet laughing: an experience as uncomfortable as hearing the sound of laughter emerging from behind the fixed mask of tragedy. Alvan takes the noise of laughter in the intensely miserable circumstances to be a 'delusion' (TU 166), and yet the reality of the laughter is brutally alienating. He throws water in his wife's face in an attempt to abate 'the horror of those mad shrieks' (TU 167). As Alison E. Wheatley observes in her analysis of Bessie Carvil in the powerful finale to Conrad's *One Day More* (his adaptation of 'To-Morrow'), the image of a woman 'alternating between laughter and weeping, is not unfamiliar in Conrad's novels' (1999, 14). However, in the original short story Conrad does not have Bessie shift from crying into laughter but rather strikes a stark juxtaposition between Bessie and Hagberd: 'She burst into tears [...] He began to chuckle' (T 276). In contrast, the use of this arresting image would seem to have been inherently comic in the Renaissance: at least a similar spectacle is described as an example of *lazzi* – the 'Lazzo of Crying and Laughing' – from a *commedia dell'arte* performance in Rome in 1618 (Gordon 47).

In Conrad's time, the image was used for more tragic impact, and Wheatley acknowledges that this tableau with the crying/laughing woman is 'a commonplace of melodrama' (1999, 14). Although 'The Return' does draw on melodramatic convention, the forcing together of laughter/comedy and crying/tragedy is a device that is precursive to the postmodern plays of Edward Bond. In the two plays that combine to make the two parts of *Jackets* (1989) – one set in feudal Japan and the other in a contemporary European city – there is an equivalent scene in which laughter clashes with despair. In the first part of *Jackets* ('The Village School'), the stage directions show us two of the leading characters transform into '*Two masks:* Chiyo *laughing and* Matsuo *crying*' (Bond 44), roles which gradually reverse until Chiyo '*begins to weep and* Matsuo *to laugh*' (45). In the second part of *Jackets* ('The City'), Mrs Lewis is convulsed with hysterical laughter in a mortuary when she identifies her friend's dead son while the mother of the deceased, Mrs Tebham, is maintained as an image of tragedy. The clash of tragedy and comedy in Edward Bond is an example of what Bond describes as his 'agro effect'. In the case of *Jackets*, the compounding of the explicit extremes of comedy and tragedy creates a moment of alienation for the purposes of social disruption. Conrad may not be striving for social disruption, but it is a technique that is no less alienating. This key moment in *The Return* finds an echo in the overall generic detonation of 'Freya of the Seven Isles'. By throwing laughter into the empty space of tragedy or by creating a formulaic comedy only to wreck it deliberately, Conrad produces works that are disruptive, alienating, confusing and at the same time utterly theatrical.

Chapter 4
From Stage to Screen: 'The Return,' *Victory*, *The Secret Agent* and *Chance*

Robert Hampson

As early as 1897, Conrad confessed to his friend Cunninghame-Graham: 'I greatly desire to write a play myself. It is my dark and secret ambition' (*CL*1 419). This desire was not fulfilled until February 1904, when, with considerable help from Ford Madox Ford, he adapted his short story 'Tomorrow' into a one-act play *One Day More*, which received its first performances in June of the following year (Knowles 53). During the Spring of 1913, while working on *Victory*, he explored the possibility of collaborating on a play with his friend Perceval Gibbon. Later in his career, he was actively involved in the very successful stage-adaptation of *Victory* by Macdonald Hastings (performed from 26 March to 6 June, 1919), and he produced his own stage-adaptations of 'Because of the Dollars' (*Laughing Anne*, 1920, not performed until 2000) and *The Secret Agent* (performed 2–11 November 1922), as well as a film-script based on 'Gaspar Ruiz' (*Gaspar the Strong Man*, not performed).[1] This film-script was first contemplated on 29 March 1915, two days after *Victory* was published in the United States, but not actually written until 1920 (Knowles 1989, 95). In the essay that follows, I want to examine, not Conrad's adaptations of his fiction for the stage or for the screen, but his use of stage and screen conventions in his fiction: the former in 'The Return' and *Victory* and the latter in *The Secret Agent* and *Chance*.

1. A theatrical imagination

In a letter to Edward Garnett, Conrad observed: 'Though I detest the stage I have a theatrical imagination' (17 April 1909; *CL*4 218). Conrad's expression of detestation, however, should not be taken as evidence of ignorance of the theatre or lack of interest. The letter was written in response to receipt of a copy of Garnett's play *The Feud*, which had just been staged at the Gaiety Theatre, Manchester, and Conrad goes on to compare the after-effect of his reading of the play to 'that sort of

---

[1] For a detailed discussion of both the short story and the film script, see Sema Postacioglu-Banon, '"Gaspar Ruiz": A Vitagraph of Desire,' *The Conradian*, 28.2 (Autumn 2003), 29–44.

contentement (sic) the middle plays of Ibsen give' (*CL4* 218). Conrad's familiarity with Ibsen's work is suggested in other letters. For example, Conrad had made a joke about Ibsen's *Ghosts* in a letter to W. H. Chesson: 'The above heading is the address of my burial place and if you are not afraid of Ghosts (nothing Ibsenish) you must come and spend a Sunday in the sepulchre' (7 January 1899; *CL2* 149). Later that year he wrote to Garnett about Garnett's essay on Ibsen in the recent issue of the *Outlook* (26 October 1899; *CL2* 209). 'The Return,' which Conrad wrote two years earlier, also shows familiarity with Ibsen's work, as Peter Keating and Paul Kirschner have pointed out. Indeed, 'The Return' is very obviously a response to, and re-writing of, *The Doll's House*. 'The Return' also shows very clearly Conrad's 'theatrical imagination' and his willingness to draw on dramatic conventions in his fiction.

In the first place, 'The Return' has a clearly-defined three-act structure. In the first act, Alvan Hervey returns home to find a letter from his wife in his dressing-room, announcing that she has left him. The first act ends with a series of off-stage sounds, each decoded by Hervey: a bell ringing somewhere downstairs; then the crash of the front-door closing heavily; then the drawing-room door being opened and flung to; then a voice; then footsteps on the first-floor landing, on the second flight of stairs, coming to a stop outside the door of the dressing-room; and finally the light rattling of the door-handle. A 'theatrical imagination' is evidently engaged in the build-up to this climax.

The second act uses Mrs Hervey's return as the occasion for an extended dialogue between husband and wife. As Conrad's comments on the story reveal, he had a clear conception of the dramatic function of the dialogue. He wrote to Garnett that he was aiming at 'the effect of cold water in every one of my man's speeches': 'I wanted to produce the effect of insincerity, or artificiality.... I wanted the truth to be first dimly seen through the fabulous untruth of that man's convictions – of his idea of life – and then to make its way out with a rush at the end' (29 September 1897; *CL*1, 387). This is evident from the outset, when Hervey's challenging 'Must I go then?' is undermined by the comment 'And he knew he meant nothing of what he implied' (TU 142). As the dialogue develops, Hervey strikes a series of postures. He modulates at one point, for example, from the moral ('I am glad to see that there is some sense of decency left in you') to the sentimental ('After all, I loved you.'), but, in each case, he is merely playing a part. This is clear from the careful description of his actions before this final declaration: 'he appeared to hesitate, as if estimating the possible consequences of what he wished to say, and at last blurted out ....' (TU 151). As 'appeared' and 'as if' intimate, even this apparently spontaneous declaration of love is a performance. The declaration of love also rings untrue because the narrator emphasised at the start of the story that passion was alien to the conventional existence of the Herveys: 'all his acquaintances had said he was very much in love; and he had said so himself, frankly, because it is very well understood that every man falls in love once in his life' (TU 119). At the same time, Hervey's icily civil performance at the start of the dialogue masks a chaos of emotions – including 'flashes of indignation and anxiety' (TU 143) and the desire to make his wife suffer (TU 142). Occasionally, the mask slips and Hervey then gives voice to 'the unconquerable preoccupation with self' that actually underlies his behaviour (TU 146). The scene concludes with Hervey asserting the importance of maintaining appearances for the sake of others, since a scandal would have 'a fatal influence' upon 'the general tone of the class' (TU 164), while also admitting that 'any disclosure would impair my usefulness' in the political career to which he aspires (TU 165). Having, as he judges, gained the upper hand over his wife, he strikes a magnanimous pose ('I forgive you') only to be met by her laughter (TU 166). The glass of water he throws in her face to cure her 'hysterics' violently undercuts the asserted ideals and the magnanimous pose by exposing 'the secret brutality of his spite' (TU 167). Again, the act ends with a strongly theatrical imagining of significant action.

The third act begins with husband and wife in silence at the dining-table together, with Hervey working hard to maintain appearances: 'he remained carefully natural, industriously hungry, laboriously at his ease' (TU 170). Then husband and wife move upstairs to the drawing-room, where a second dialogue takes place between them. This time Mrs Hervey takes the upper hand: she rejects his 'forgiveness' and his declarations of his 'love': 'You wanted a wife – some woman – any woman that would think, speak, and behave in a certain way – in a way you approved' (TU 177). She articulates, disabusedly, the loveless nature of their marriage and her acceptance of it. In the final scene, Hervey announces that he can't accept this way of living and, in an echo of Ibsen's Nora, leaves the house, slamming the front door heavily behind him. Hervey, however, is not fleeing a loveless marriage but rather the replacement of 'tacit complicity' (TU 184) by his wife's 'unfathomable candour' (TU 185).

Secondly, the detailed descriptions of the interior of the Hervey home not only establish the suffocatingly claustrophobic, conventional bourgeois environment that is so important to the story, they also create an elaborate stage-set after the manner of Shavian stage-directions. In particular, the bronze dragon gas-light, the 'marble woman' on the first-floor landing 'holding a cluster of lights' and the 'sketches, watercolours, engravings' on the 'rich, stamped paper of the walls' provide the kind of commentary on the action that stage-furniture supplies in Shavian drama. In 'The Philanderer' (1893), for example, which Shaw wrote in response to the cult of Ibsenism, Act I takes place in the home of a 'New Woman,' Grace Transfield: the walls are 'hung with theatrical engravings and photographs' (all of which are specified) 'but not Eleanora Duse nor anyone connected with Ibsen,' a turret window is filled up with 'a stand of flowers surrounding a statuet of Shakespear [sic]', while 'a yellow-backed French novel' lies open on a table (1977, 99). Act II, in contrast, takes place 'in the library of the Ibsen club,' which is dominated by 'a bust of Ibsen' on the mantelpiece (1977, 124). In 'The Return,' the writhing, bronze dragon with its oxymoronic 'calm convolutions' and 'conventional fury' (TU 124) emphasises the Herveys' subordination of passion to convention. The 'marble woman,' 'decently covered' from her neck to her 'lifeless toes,' suggests both Hervey's reification of his wife and the petrifaction of their passions. The detailed description of the sketches and water-colours performs a similar function to that in Shaw's stage-set: it not only provides a measure of the artistic tastes upon which Hervey prides himself, but it also precisely delineates the sentimental and conventional emotional culture of his class:

> A young lady sprawled with dreamy eyes in a moored boat, in company of a lunch basket, a champagne bottle, and an enamoured man in a blazer. Bare-legged boys flirted sweetly with ragged maidens, slept on stone steps, gambolled with dogs. A pathetically lean girl flattened against a blank wall, turned up expiring eyes and tendered a flower for sale.... (TU 124)

Thirdly, as suggested above, 'The Return' represents a very knowing engagement with *The Doll's House*, and this is part of what might be seen as a more general theatrical self-consciousness. Not only is there an intertextual relationship with Ibsen's play, but Hervey's performances draw on the codes and conventions of popular theatre. By this means, Conrad signals the inauthenticity of Hervey's speeches and actions. As Kirschner notes, Hervey and his wife are presented from the outset as 'products of their class, living in a safe sham world': 'amongst perfectly delightful men and women who feared emotion, enthusiasm, or failure ... who tolerated only the commonest formulas of commonest thoughts' (88; TU 120). Mrs Hervey's attempt to run off with a 'literary man' (TU 121), presumably because she has seen through the loveless performance of their marriage, represents, for Hervey, a 'shameful impulse of passion' (TU 132). This interruption to the safe routines of his existence also has the side-effect of producing, in Hervey himself, a 'loathsome rush of emotion' that breaks through 'all the reserves that guarded his manhood' (TU 130). Conrad observes that 'in the sudden shock of her desertion the sentiments which he knew that in fidelity to his bringing up, to his prejudices and his surroundings, he ought to experience, were so mixed up with the novelty of real feelings, of fundamental feelings that know nothing of creed, class, or education' (TU 131). This conflict between sham sentiments and real feelings is played out in Hervey's internal monologues and in the dialogues with his wife. In his internal monologues, he considers the appropriate 'part to play' in response to this humiliating incident (TU 131). In his encounters with his wife, he goes through a succession of poses, more concerned still with how he appears than with how he actually feels, in which he reproduces, as shown above, various stage cliches. As a result, he has the experience of hearing his own voice 'with the excited and sceptical curiosity with which one listens to actors' voices speaking on the stage in the strain of a poignant situation' (TU 144). If there is an element of popular melodrama in 'The Return,' it is because Hervey introduces it, as he allows himself to be spoken by the resources of his limited culture, and the story's production of meaning requires the reader's recognition of this theatrical performance as the expression of both Hervey's self-alienation and the sham culture to which he belongs. We might compare this aspect of the story's theatrical self-consciousness with Shaw's similar use of citation in 'The

Philanderer' and 'Mrs Warren's Profession'. In 'The Philanderer,' the 'womanly woman,' Julia Craven, has recourse to a 'theatrical method' at moments of crisis, 'throwing herself tragically on her knees at Grace's feet,' for example, to beg Grace not to take her lover from her (Shaw 155). In 'Mrs Warren's Profession,' Mrs Warren's reconciliation with her daughter at the end of Act II produces a tableau in which she 'embraces her daughter protectingly, instinctively looking upward for divine sanction' (Shaw 252). That final gaze upwards, reminiscent of popular sentimental drama, has the result of ironising the tableau, and marking the character's inauthenticity: as in 'The Return,' the citation of theatrical conventions serves to distance us from the theatricalised performance of the character.

2. Scenic method

During February 1914, Conrad had read Ford's recent book *Henry James: A Critical Study*. Ford's study shows a detailed engagement with the New York Collected Edition of James's work and the Prefaces James wrote for it.[2] Ford begins the section entitled 'Methods' by stating that James's Prefaces have already done the critical work of analysing James's 'method,' and he repeatedly cites the Prefaces in his own discussion (1964, 152). (Ford also includes an Appendix on textual variations between the Collected Edition and earlier editions of James's works.) In the Prefaces, James had delineated his 'scenic method'. Blackmur observes that 'the Dramatic Scene was the principal device James used to objectify the Indirect Approach,' and notes that 'his use of the scene resembled that in the stage-play' (xviii). This is most evident in his Preface to *The Awkward Age*. Here James describes his initial sketch for the novel as a central situation surrounded by a circle of lamps: 'Each of my "lamps" would be the light of a single "social occasion" in the history and intercourse of the characters concerned' (1934, 110). The 'Occasion' would be 'really and completely a scenic thing,' and the 'divisions of the form' of the novel would approximate to 'the successive Acts of a Play' (1934, 110). Above all, James registered the importance of 'really constructive dialogue, dialogue organic and dramatic, speaking for itself, representing, and embodying substance and form' (1934, 106). Both Conrad and Ford were very familiar with what James called his 'scenic method'. In a letter to Macdonald Hastings, Conrad refers to the 'scenic drama' of *Under Western Eyes*: 'My artistic aim was to put as much dramatic spirit into the form of a novel as was possible … the dramatisation of the inner feelings – and also of *ideas*, brought out in scene and dialogue' (24 December 1916; *CL5* 696). That scenic method is also much in evidence in *Victory* in its staging of encounters, its dramatic handling of dialogue and in its use of stage directions.

After the narrative prologue, the first two parts of the novel proceed through a series of staged encounters. There is Heyst's dialogue with Morrison in the

---

[2] The Prefaces written for the 1908 New York edition were collected and published, with an Introduction by R. P. Blackmur, as *The Art of the Novel* in 1934.

wineshop in Delli and then on board the brig; there is Davidson's disconcerting exchange with Schomberg in Schomberg's hotel, followed by a surprisingly extended conversation with Mrs Schomberg, who enters the room through 'a door somewhere at his back' (V 38), after her husband has left; there are Heyst's conversations with Lena during the intervals in Schomberg's 'concert-hall' (V 68) and afterwards in the grounds of the hotel; there are Schomberg's unsettling conversations with Jones and Ricardo on board the steam-launch (V 101-3) and later on the hotel verandah (V 111-7); and then there is Schomberg's extended tete-a-tete with Ricardo in the billiard room, which occupies most of three chapters (V 122-9). In each case, there is a precise spatial location and various kinds of dramatic interaction enacted through the dialogue.

The theatrical handling of the novel's various encounters is most obvious in Part III, in the exploration of the developing relationship between Heyst and Lena, where we are given a succession of stage-sets and dialogue supported by what are effectively stage directions. In Chapter 3, the set is the verandah of Heyst's house. The chapter begins: 'Heyst came out on the verandah and spread his elbows on the railing, in an easy attitude of proprietorship' (V 185). Shortly afterwards Lena joins him, and the dialogue between them begins. The dialogue is set up after the manner of a playwright:

> Heyst did not turn round.
> 'Do you know what I was thinking of?' he asked.
> 'No,' she said. Her tone betrayed always a shade of anxiety, as though she were never certain how a conversation with him would end. She leaned on the guard-rail by his side. (V 186)

In both these instances, if the tense used to describe the actions of the participants were to be changed from past to present, the genre of stage directions would be inescapable. As the dialogue develops, Heyst addresses further comments to Lena 'still without looking at the girl,' to which she responds 'after a pause' (V 186). Eventually, he 'turned round and looked at her,' and, instead of oblique comments, he now addresses a direct question to her: 'What is it?' he asked. 'Is it a reproach?' (V 187). Now that they are face to face, indirection gives way to direct questioning. As in drama, the body language and spatial positioning of the characters is as eloquent as the words they exchange.

Subsequently, the action moves to a second set – 'a depression of the sharp slope, like a small platform' (V 190) at the upper limit of vegetation over-looking the sea. Again, the dialogue between them is set up after the manner of a playwright:

> 'It makes my head swim,' the girl murmured, shutting her eyes and putting her hand on his shoulder.
>
> Heyst, gazing fixedly to the southward, exclaimed: 'Sail ho!'
> A moment of silence ensued. (V 190)

The direct and extended conversation that follows marks the greatest moment of intimacy between them. It reveals a potential in their relationship that will never be realised, over-shadowed as it is by that ominous reference to the sail, although it also introduces a further doubt into Lena and gives Heyst the shocking revelation of the calumnious rumours about his relationship with Morrison. The scenic quality is maintained when Chapter 4 closes with what is effectively a curtain: 'The girl glanced round, moved suddenly away, and averted her face. With her hand she signed imperiously to him to leave her alone – a command which Heyst did not obey' (V 215).

For the denouement, Conrad is similarly theatrical. Chapter 11 takes place largely inside the bungalow assigned to Mr Jones. The chapter begins with what reads like stage directions:

> Two candles were burning on the stand-up desk. Mr Jones, tightly enfolded in an old but gorgeous blue silk dressing-gown, kept his hands deeply plunged into the extraordinarily deep pockets of the garment. (V 376)

There is an attention to lighting effects throughout the scene that follows. At a given moment, shortly after Heyst's arrival, Ricardo 'melted' out of the doorframe 'between two flickers of lightening' (V 376) to go to Heyst's bungalow. As the dialogue develops between Jones and Heyst, there are repeated reminders of the 'rolling thunder' (V378) and the flicker of lightening, and, at the end of their dialogue, 'the doorway flickered lividly' (V 389) again, as Jones and Heyst leave to pursue Ricardo. The thunder and lightening is clearly designed to heighten the emotional strain of the scene, but it is a device which is theatrical in its conception rather than novelistic. Chapter 12, a dialogue between Ricardo and Lena in Heyst's bungalow, represents a parallel action. However, since Chapter 11 ends with Jones and Heyst outside this bungalow looking on at events within, there is a sense that the entire action of Chapter 12 is being observed. Jones's 'Behold the simple Acis kissing the sandals of the nymph' (V 393) sets up Ricardo's courtship of Lena as a spectacle for both Heyst and the reader, and the reader's consciousness of the spectators adds a further dimension of menace to the contest between Ricardo and Lena. Again, the conception is theatrical – on-stage spectators observing a private encounter. And the end of the dialogue, with 'the brief report of a shot' and the sudden appearance of Heyst 'towering in the doorway' (V 401), is entirely melodramatic.

At the same time, there is a certain amount of what can only be called 'stage business' throughout the narrative. For example, there is the business with Mrs Schomberg's shawl. Mrs Schomberg helps Lena to escape by wrapping up Lena's 'things' (V 44) in her own shawl and throwing the bundle out of a back window. Subsequently, Davidson returns with the shawl, wrapped in a brown paper parcel, and waits in the billiard-room of Schomberg's hotel, ordering drink after drink, until he has a chance to return it. There is similar business with Ricardo's slipper. During the scuffle between Lena and Ricardo in Part IV Chapter 3, Ricardo loses his straw slipper, but doesn't notice the loss until he has made his hasty escape from Heyst's bungalow through the bathroom window. Lena notices it 'lying near the bath' (V 303) and puts her foot on it to conceal it, when Heyst enters the room. When Heyst lets the curtain fall again, having looked in vain for somewhere to conceal the slipper, Lena finally throws it through the window. A 'faint whistle' (V 304) from outside signals that Ricardo has recovered it. On a smaller scale, in his final dialogue with Heyst, Jones makes repeated use of his handkerchief 'to wipe the perspiration from his forehead, neck and chin' (V 379).

Conrad has clearly allowed his 'theatrical imagination' full play in *Victory*, but his characters are not simply participants in a drama: they are also actors consciously or unconsciously acting out parts. Richard J. Hand, in his recent book, *The Theatre of Joseph Conrad*, has drawn attention to the importance of acting in the novel. Ricardo, for example, displays 'a perfectly acted cheerfulness' (V 335); when under stress, Schomberg, similarly, performs a version of masculinity, putting on his 'Lieutenant-of-the-Reserve' manner, when he feels anxious. At other times, as Hand points out, Schomberg stages a more public performance:

> It became a recognised entertainment to go and hear his abuse of Heyst ... It was, in a manner, a more successful draw than the Zangiacomo concerts had ever been – intervals and all. There was never any difficulty in starting the performer off. (V 95)

In the final section of the novel, ignoring Heyst's instructions, Lena writes a script for herself in which erotic feelings are displaced into idealistic self-sacrifice. She casts herself in a drama of redemption, whose terms and structure of feeling derive from her North London Sunday school lessons and from Victorian constructions of femininity. As in 'The Return,' Conrad brings to the novel an awareness of the theatre that takes the form of attention to the performative and scripted in the construction of individual identity.

3. Successive scenes

As Gene Moore observes, Conrad's earliest documented visits to the cinema occurred in 1920, when he and Pinker went to see Frank Lloyd's 1918 film version of *Les Misérables* at the London Pavilion in Piccadilly Circus on 27 August and Maurice Tourneur's 1919 film version of *Victory* at St George's Theatre in Canterbury in November (40–41). His visit to *Les Misérables* was a research trip for writing a screen-adaptation of his short story 'Gaspar Ruiz,' which he produced, with Pinker's help, in September 1920. However, he must have had earlier experiences of film. Stephen Donovan notes that, in October 1897, Conrad and Stephen Crane ended their lengthy perambulation through Central London in front of 'that monumentally heavy abode of frivolity, the Pavilion' (LE 106) – the very Pavilion to which he would return with Pinker in 1920, which was already 'an exhibition space for cinematic devices' (2005, 44). Donovan also suggests that

Conrad would not have missed 'the cinematic event of 1897, the Diamond Jubilee parade,' a very widely displayed film (2005, 44), and it is also likely he would have seen war-time newsreels. Walter Tittle records a post-1922 conversation with Conrad, where Conrad attacks Charlie Chaplin and 'several so-called educational films that pretended to show a process of manufacture, beginning with the raw material and ending with a finished product' (Ray 161).

Moore records that Conrad had been approached by film-companies as early as September 1913 (32); he and Ford signed a 'moving picture rights' contract for *Romance* in March 1915; and by the end of the same month, Conrad had written to Pinker suggesting 'the eminent fitness of Gaspar Ruiz for pictorial representation' (*CL5* 461). Moore's account of the screenplay notes Conrad's basic filmic vocabulary – a primary division between 'shots of dramatic action,' which Conrad calls 'Pictures,' and the written intertitles of silent cinema, which Conrad calls 'Screen' – and his single explicit direction for camera movement, the marginal suggestion 'that certain "Pictures" should be taken "Close-up"' (38). In a letter to Richard Curle, Conrad described this plan to write a 'cinema scenario' and asserted a preference for the cinema to the stage on the grounds that the stage had 'some sort of inferior poetics of its own' which resulted in compromising 'the very soul of one's work both on the imaginative and on the intellectual side' (18–23 August 1920; *CL7* 163). By implication, film has no such 'poetics'. However, although Conrad describes film as 'merely a silly stunt for silly people,' silent cinema nevertheless had already become well-established and had also developed a 'poetics' which left a trace on his own work.

In America, Thomas Edison had built the first motion-picture machine using celluloid film, the 'Kinetoscope,' in 1889. This and the Mutascope, a hand-cranked flip-book viewer which followed, were essentially peep-show machines.[3] According to Lillian Gish, early American films were often films of vaudeville acts and were often shown as the last act on the programme in vaudeville theatres. In response to the vaudeville actors' strike in 1901, theatre-owners began to show complete programmes of films and, after the strike had ended, this led to the development of 'nickelodeons,' cheap movie houses in small towns and cities across the USA. Whilst the subject matter of early films rapidly broadened, and advanced techniques were swiftly developed, American cinema's origins in the peep-show also had a continuing influence. An early film like *The Kiss* (1896), which was made for the Kinetoscope, has obvious continuities with films such as *The Gay Shoe Clerk* (1903) or *A Search for Evidence* (1903). The former, which revolves fetishistically around the fitting of women's shoes, includes, as Stewart notes, cutting to close-up as the woman raises her skirt, which implicates the spectator as voyeur. The latter, which Stewart describes as a 'Peeping Tom' drama, reverses the expected gender-roles by having a woman searching for her husband

---

[3] Here and elsewhere in this section, I am indebted to Heather Stewart, ed., *Early and Silent Cinema: A Source Book* (London: British Film Institute, 1996); and Lillian Gish (with Ann Pinchot), *The Movies, Mr Griffith and Me* (London: W. H. Allen, 1969).

by peeping through a series of keyholes, each of which reveals a different scene. A film like *Pull Down the Curtain, Susie* (1904) is straightforwardly voyeuristic: its subject, a woman undressing, points to the 'smoking-room' market for some early films. But even films like *The Mill Girl* (1907), an early film of sexual harassment, or Lois Weber's *Suspense*, a woman alone in an isolated house threatened by a burglar, with its emotionally-involving use of split-screen and keyhole shots, draw on the erotics of spectatorship and of close-up. Lillian Gish, who made her name through her work with Griffith, epitomises the erotic spectacle of female suffering in films such as *The Birth of a Nation* (1915), *Intolerance* (1916) and, above all, *Broken Blossoms* (1919).

In Europe, too, the development of cinema coincides with Conrad's writing career. French cinema begins on 22 March 1895, when Auguste and Louis Lumière staged a show of their Cinematographe for the Societé d'Encouragement pour l'Industrie Nationale in Paris. In December, they were giving shows to paying audiences in the Grand Café, Boulevard des Capucines and, by January, they were showing to 2,000 people per day.[4] On 20 February 1896, there was a show of Lumière Brothers' 'Living Photographs' (including *Arrivée d'un Train en Gare*) at Regent Street Polytechnic in London. In the same year, Georges Demeny put together a film programme in a similar vein: it included short films such as *Paris Street-scene* and *Scenes at Marseilles Harbour*. The Lumière brothers were followed by other pioneers who once again developed the range of subject matter and techniques including voyeuristic 'peeping Tom' films as well as fantastic and trick films.

In Britain, cinema developed from two traditions.[5] From the 1830s onwards, there was a technical interest in optical toys such as the praxinoscope, the choreutoscope (a flat strip passing through a lantern with a shutter) and the zoetrope (glass transparencies on a wheel). These all used the rapid succession of still images to produce the effect of continuous movement. They worked with the phenomenon of the persistence of vision and promoted the analysis of motion (and the body in motion) as in the photography of Eadweard Muybridge. In one of the first issues of *Harmsworth Magazine*, a monthly pictorial magazine that began publication in 1898, 140 successive frames from a Lumière Brothers film appeared on the top-right corner of successive pages to produce a flip-book and a hands-on demonstration of how cinematography worked (Chanan 283). In *Lord Jim*, Conrad describes Chester and Robinson dodging into view 'with stride and gestures, as if reproduced in the field of some optical toy' (LJ 174), showing how these new visual technologies increased consciousness of the body, behaviour and movement.[6] In

---

[4] I am indebted to Heather Stewart for this information.

[5] There are also, of course, links between early cinema and theatre. Richard J. Hand reminds me that some of the early films, such as Weber's *Suspense*, owed considerable debts to the popular spectacles of turn-of-the-century melodrama.

[6] Ernest Betts, in *Heraclitus: of the Future of Films* (London: Kegan Paul, Trench & Trubner, 1928), argued that, in the absence of sound, silent audiences attended to 'the other

addition to this technological tradition, there was also, as Michael Chanan points out, the magic-lantern tradition of 'education-cum-entertainment' (272). It is significant that one of the pioneers of British film-making, Cecil Hepworth, was the son of a magic lanternist. The father wrote *The Book of the Lantern* in 1894 and, just three years later, the son published *Animated Photography: The ABC of the Cinematograph* in 1897. This suggests something of the pace of technological development and the speed with which cinema established itself, even if Cecil Hepworth's book tends to see cinematography as a moment in the history of the magic lantern rather than the magic lantern as a precursor to cinema.[7]

Although Louis Le Prince had made moving pictures in Leeds in 1888, Birt Acres and Robert Paul are credited as the originators of British cinema. Acres had shown films at Marlborough House in July 1893 as part of the celebrations of the Duke of York's wedding (with Hepworth as his assistant), and the Acres-Paul film of the Oxford and Cambridge Boat Race in March 1895 seems to have been the first British film for public exhibition.[8] State occasions and sporting events dominate British film in the 1890s. From 1899, Hepworth Films made short (50 foot) documentary 'human interest' films: *Procession of Prize Cattle*; *Comic Costume Race for Cyclists* and many others. One of his principles in selecting subjects is suggested by an observation in *Animated Photography*: he offers advice on photographing 'crowds and street scenes and similar subjects' and notes that they 'always make more or less interesting pictures, having, at all events, the merit of being full of life and movement' (97). From 1900, Hepworth Films moved into news pictures – the departure of the City Imperial Volunteers for the Boer War; Queen Victoria's visit to Dublin; the solar eclipse in Algiers; Queen Victoria's funeral – and illusionist trick films (*The Explosion of a Motor Car* [stop-frame]; *The Egg-Laying Man* [close-up]; *The Eccentric Dancer* [slow-motion photography]). With *Rescued By Rover*, an early doggy film using professional actors and the family pet, Hepworth moved into popular story-telling.

There were other strands of early British film-making. In 1896 Esme Collings, a portrait photographer, made a one-minute film, *A Victorian Lady in Her Boudoir* (or *Woman Undressing*). G. A. Smith, one of the leading members of the Brighton-based school of film-making, made *The Kiss in the Tunnel* (1899). As with early North American cinema, voyeurism was a component of British film-making. Smith was also interested in the use of the close up. In *Grandma's Reading Glass* (1900), the close ups have a narrative motivation: objects looked at by the boy are cut in (as close ups) to represent the boy's point of view, and a circular mask is used to

---

means – gesture, timing, facial expression and grouping – by which an actor's intentions are expressed' (88); cited in Armstrong, 230.

[7] Hepworth notes, for example, how improvements in the development of limelight apparatus as a result of cinematography 'cannot fail to be a lasting benefit to lanternists of all denominations long after cinematography has had its day' (1897, 61).

[8] Here (and elsewhere in this paragraph), I am indebted to Hepworth 1951.

represent the field of vision of the reading glass (Chanan 294).⁹ *As Seen Through A Telescope* (1900) similarly uses motivated close ups as it alternates between long shot and close up to show the spectator with the telescope and the object of his gaze.

As this suggests, Conrad's career as a novelist coincided with the early development of cinema. Thus, as Stephen Donovan notes, *Almayer's Folly* was published 'just two weeks after the Lumière brothers presented their invention to the Sorbonne,' and *An Outcast of the Islands* was published just 'a few days before the Cinematographe-Lumière began its main London engagement at the Empire Theatre of Varieties on Leicester Square' (2005, 42). Conrad, as a resident in or near London and frequent visitor to Paris during the 1890s, was 'ideally placed to follow the emergence of cinema' in Europe (2005, 43). Donovan convincingly demonstrates Conrad's interest in visual technologies, his 'sustained engagement with the visual dynamics of contemporary popular culture,' and 'the importance of visual entertainment for Conrad's conception of literary art' (2005, 20, 24). He shows how, for example, the pre-cinematic technology of the moving panorama (which involved the unwinding of a long, painted canvas in front of a seated audience) is recalled in *An Outcast of the Islands* to present Almayer's dream about his daughter's future: 'Things charming and splendid passing before him in a magic unrolling of resplendent pictures' (OI 320). Similarly, in *The Secret Agent*, Donovan suggests, Conrad again seems to draw on the technology of the moving panorama to describe the thought processes of Winnie Verloc, who 'thought in images' (SA 198), after she has learned of Stevie's death: 'The exigencies of Mrs Verloc's temperament ... forced her to roll a series of thoughts in her motionless head' (SA 182–3) However, the spatiality of this description suggests the technology of the film projector rather than the unwinding canvas of the moving panorama. We might consider Conrad's depiction of Winnie in the light of the work of the American psychologist, Boris Sidis, who, in his book *Multiple Personality* (1905), explicitly uses the technology of cinematic projection to explain hypnoid states: 'The subconscious activity brings out visual perceptions which appear as hallucinations to the upper consciousness. The upper consciousness sees the pictures projected by the subconscious' (cited in Armstrong 215).¹⁰ Subsequent description of Mrs Verloc watching visions of her past life supports this interpretation: she becomes, in effect, a cinematic projector as she gazes at 'the whitewashed wall' with eyes 'whose pupils were extremely dilated' (SA 184). Conrad has repeatedly drawn attention to this wall during this scene and to Verloc seeing 'no writing' on it (SA 181, 182). It is against this blank wall, however, that Winnie effectively projects the 'visions' that constitute her thought processes (SA 183). And the 'visions' themselves are not landscapes (as in the

---

⁹ Chanan describes this use of masking as a technique derived from magic lantern practice.

¹⁰ Freud, in *The Interpretation of Dreams* (1911), also suggested a photographic model for the psyche.

moving panorama) but a cinematic montage of narrative fragments: 'she had the vision of the blows intercepted (often with her own head), of a door held desperately shut against a man's rage (not for very long); of a poker flung once (not very far)' (SA 183). The courtship section of Winnie's visions begins with scenes of domestic drudgery, followed by the brief contrasting image of 'a young man wearing his Sunday best, with a straw hat on his dark head and a wooden pipe in his mouth' (SA 183), and ending with 'the lodger' – 'Mr Verloc, indolent, and keeping late hours, sleepily jocular of a morning from under his bed-clothes' (SA 184). It is easy to imagine the written intertitles that would appear between these sequences – indeed, this last quotation seems already to belong to the genre of intertitle. The married section of her visions is disturbed by the close-up image of Comrade Ossipon, 'the robust anarchist with the shamelessly inviting eyes,' and the 'last scene' is 'the vision of her husband and poor Stevie walking up Brett Street side by side away from the shop' (SA 184) – a long shot that recalls the popularity of street-filming in early cinema. This last vision is described as having 'such plastic relief, such nearness of form, such a fidelity of suggestive detail' (SA 184) – exactly what might be praised in this new medium of film.

Donovan relates this series of visual images to the 'life review' in early films such as *Histoire d'un crime*, but he underplays the impact of cinema on the writing of *The Secret Agent*. Thus, he quotes the later, extended description of Winnie's pictorial remembering of her brother's death, but doesn't comment on the climactic image 'where after a rainlike fall of mangled limbs the decapitated head of Stevie lingered suspended alone, and fading out slowly like the last star of a pyrotechnic display' (SA 196). As Chanan notes, one of the prevalent themes of early cinema (as of more recent cinema) was the acting out of the fragmentation of the body (290). Hepworth's *Explosion of a Motor Car* (1900) ends with the promised explosion, followed by a rain of debris and dismembered limbs. Decapitated (or, more precisely, disembodied) heads were popular in French films. George Meliès 1901 film *L'Homme á la Tête de Caoutchouc* ('The India-Rubber Head') featured a giant, disembodied head, and his 1903 film *Le Melomane* presented a series of disembodied heads perched on telegraph wires. That reference to the image 'fading out slowly' is an effective description of a firework display, but it also suggests the cinematic device of fade out. The intensely visual account of the killing of Verloc is also immensely cinematic:

> He was lying on his back and staring upwards. He saw partly on the ceiling and partly on the wall the moving shadow of an arm with a clenched hand holding a carving knife. It flickered up and down. (SA 197)

This flickering movement is a reader trap: it is not the clenched hand that 'flickered up and down' but the shadow thrown by the gaslight. However, the flickering also suggests the unstable image produced by early projectors.[11] In his attack on cinema in his conversation with Tittle, Conrad complained: 'It merely affords entertainment for people who enjoy sitting with thought utterly suspended and watching a changing pattern flickering before their eyes' (Ray 161). Although he failed to see any writing on the kitchen wall, Verloc has no difficulty understanding the significance of this shadow on the parlour wall. The subsequent paragraph, with its slowing down of time as Verloc contemplates resistance to the impending blow, is the counterpart to the speeding up of time in Winnie's life review, where her whole life is surveyed in a 'few seconds' (SA 184). In both cases, the slowing down of time or the speeding up of time, Conrad can be seen as responding to a new awareness of time and movement resulting from the technicalities of film projection – in particular, hand-cranked cameras and projectors and non-standardised speeds.[12]

Donovan very usefully analyses Conrad's presentation of the murder scene in terms of a 'triptych of artfully arranged *tableaux*,' which he compares to waxwork tableaux of murders such as 'The Last Moments of Mr Maybrick' (staged at McLeod's Waxworks in Glasgow in 1889). However he also notes Conrad's response to W. T. H. Howe who was organising a fund-raising evening of *tableaux-vivants* based on scenes from Conrad's fiction. Conrad claimed to find 'the static quality of a grouping' disconcerting; he noted: 'When writing I visualise the successive scenes as always in motion – a flow of closely linked effects' (16 August 1917; *CL6* 117). This idea of successive scenes 'always in motion' again moves away from the earlier visual culture of *tableaux* towards the new technology of film. Similarly, where he had written to Hastings about 'scenic effects' and 'the *scenic* drama' (*CL5* 656), he wrote to Eric Pinker about his 1923 lecture, 'Author and Cinematograph,' that its '(apparently) extravagant' argument was that 'imaginative literary art' was 'based fundamentally on scenic motion, like a camera'.[13]

4. Visual pleasures

Conrad started *Chance* in 1905, but soon abandoned it and didn't take it up again until May 1911, by which point the film industry was well-established. There are two moments late in *Chance* which suggest the influence of cinema. The first which I want to discuss occurs in Part II, Chapter 6, when young Powell stoops down next to the skylight over the salon to pick up a coil of rope and finds himself looking into the cabin. First he observes Captain Anthony pouring himself a glass of brandy ('or whatever it was') from the decanter and begin reading a book. Then,

---

[11] Hepworth notes 'the inherent faults of cinematography – flickering of the light, and, more especially in the early days, unsteadiness of the picture upon the screen' (1951, 7).

[12] In the conversation with Tittle, Jessie Conrad had championed 'slow-motion pictures as a form providing both amusement and instruction' (Ray 161).

[13] Conrad to Eric Pinker (9 April 1923), in Jean-Aubry 1927, 302.

when Anthony leaves the cabin, Powell shifts his position and finds that his 'angle of view was changed' and the 'field too was smaller': its scope is limited to 'the end of the table, the tray and the swivel chair' (C 414). However, he also now has 'a very oblique downward view of the curtains' (C 415). As he watches, there is a slight 'movement of the curtain,' and then 'tips of fingers ... grasped the edge of the further curtain and hung on there, just fingers and knuckles and nothing else'. Then 'a hand came into view; a short, puffy, old freckled hand projecting into the lamplight, followed by a white wrist, an arm in a grey coat-sleeve, up to the elbow, beyond the elbow, extended tremblingly towards the tray'. Finally, 'this hand, tremulous with senile eagerness, swerved to the glass, rested on its edge for a moment (or so it looked from above) and went back with a jerk'. At the same moment, the 'gripping fingers of the other hand' also vanish (C 417). The passage is striking because of its attention to the mechanics and language of vision. It is also striking because of the staged nature of the event, but the staging is not theatrical. There is an element of the peep-show machine: Powell remains watching because he 'wanted another peep' at Anthony (C 416). However, the main influence on the way in which the poisoning of Anthony's brandy-and-water is represented seems to be cinematic. Not only is there the non-theatrical angle of vision, there is also the fragmenting of the body, the analysis of movement, the interpretation of small details (the tremor of the hand, for example) and the use of close up.

The second, more extended passage which I want to consider is the final chapter of Part I, 'On the Pavement'. It begins as another scene of spying: Marlow decides to wait outside the Eastern Hotel to 'see what would come of' Fyne's visit to Captain Anthony (C 198). He intercepts Flora, and the dialogue between them is interspersed with alternating close-ups and long shots. Thus, Marlow observes early on: 'The mouth looked very red in the white face peeping from under the veil, the little pointed chin had in its form something aggressive' (C 201). Later we are given a long shot of the East India Dock Road: 'the great perspective of drab brick walls, of grey pavement, of muddy roadway rumbling dismally with loaded carts and vans lost itself in the distance' (C 204). Then there is a close-up of Flora's dress ('Close fitting and black, with heliotrope silk facings under a figured net') followed by another street scene ('Every moment people were passing close by us singly, in twos and threes ... they passed us in their shabby garments, with sallow faces, haggard, anxious or weary, or simply without expression, in an unsmiling sombre stream'). The use of colour (the red lips, the heliotrope silk facings) perhaps argues against a consciously cinematic conception of this chapter, as do the references to sound.[14] For example, a later description of the street begins with 'the odious uproar of that wide roadway thronged with heavy carts,' whereas, in setting up the poisoning episode discussed above, Conrad emphasises the lack of sound: Marlow records that 'Powell explained to me that no sound did or perhaps could reach him from the saloon' (C 416). However, Donovan has demonstrated

---

[14] However, as Katherine Baxter has pointed out to me, colour-tinting of film was in use from around 1910.

Conrad's engagement with the visual dynamics of contemporary culture, and has also noted Conrad's 1923 claim to have seen '"certain experiments" in sound and colour film' (2005, 45; citing Ray 186). It is possible (indeed, likely) that, in narrating this chapter, Conrad has drawn on and incorporated the visual language of film.

Finally, I want to consider Flora and the erotic spectacle of female suffering. As Armstrong notes, cinema's 'mechanisms of desire' have always been 'a subject of anxiety' (239).[15] In *Chance*, Conrad engages with both the ethics and the erotics of looking. Marlow, typically, raises the ethical implications of Powell's spying on Anthony by ostentatiously refusing to consider them: 'As to the delicacy of Mr Powell's proceedings I'll say nothing' (C 416). However, he then immediately adds that Powell found 'a sort of depraved excitement in watching an unconscious man – and such an attractive and mysterious a man' (C 416). Powell himself expresses his unease at the 'low' trick he had literally stooped to: 'For, after I had stooped, there I remained prying, spying, anyway looking, where I had no business to look' (C 412). He tries to excuse his behaviour as natural and unavoidable: 'He who has eyes, you know, nothing can stop him from seeing things'; he tries to affirm the benign motive for his spying: 'there could have been nothing inimical in this low behaviour of mine'; and he also tries to blame Franklin 'always talking of the man' so that 'really he seemed to have become our property' (C 412). However, the more he tries to excuse himself the more issues he raises: the benign or malicious intention behind observing; the objectification and appropriation of the person observed. To these Marlow adds the erotics of the gaze.

These questions are particularly important in a novel which focuses, in part, on the victimised Flora de Barral and, in part, on the concept of masculinity of her rescuer, Captain Anthony.[16] If we return to the visual economy of 'On the Pavement,' the first close-up of Flora ends with Marlow's judgement that she was 'a desirable little figure' (C 201). The second close-up on her dress leads to a similar erotic evaluation: 'it accentuated the slightness of her figure, it went well in its suggestion of half-mourning with the white face in which the unsmiling red lips alone seemed warm with the rich blood of life and passion' (C 205). A later close-up produces a similar response: when she lowers her glance so that 'her dark eyelashes seemed to rest against her white cheeks,' Marlow records that it 'was so attractive that I could not help a faint smile' (C 214). Throughout this encounter, close-ups of Flora lead immediately to an erotic response. The scopophilic instinct leads to pleasure being taken in regarding another person as an erotic object.

---

[15] Armstrong cites Miriam Hansen, *Babel and Babylon: Spectatorship in American Silent Film*, Cambridge MA: Harvard University Press, 1991, and Richard Maltby, 'The Social Evil, the Moral Order, and the melodramatic Imagination, 1890–1915' in Bratton et al. 214–30.

[16] As Andrew Michael Roberts has shown, it also involves a series of male figures competing to demonstrate their superior knowledge of 'woman,' but actually betraying 'a secret sharing of male ignorance'. See Roberts 1993, 7–23, and 2000, 154–62, 159.

However, that pleasure has to be explored further. Toril Moi has written of 'the voyeur's desire for sadistic power, in which the object of the gaze is cast as its passive, masochistic, feminine victim' (180). As Marlow knows, Flora is already a victim, and, in the analysis of the beginning of Flora's relationship with Anthony that he now offers, Flora's victim-status has an important part. First of all, he speculates about what attracted Anthony to Flora:

> It might have been her pallor ... that white face with eyes like blue gleams of fire and lips like red coals. In certain lights, in certain poises of head it suggested tragic sorrow. Or it might have been her wavy hair. Or even just that pointed chin stuck out a little, resentful and not particularly distinguished, doing away with the mysterious aloofness of her fragile presence. (C 217)

In this close reading of her physiognomy, Marlow clearly identifies with Anthony and his viewing of Flora. Later, presumably drawing on Flora's account, Marlow suggests that 'her misery was his opportunity': 'he rejoiced while the tenderest pity seemed to flood his whole being' (C 223–4). Laura Mulvey has discussed how women are 'simultaneously looked at and displayed, with their appearance coded for strong visual and erotic impact' (19). This certainly applies to Marlow's presentation of Flora here. Again, as Mulvey suggests, these passages break the diegesis 'to freeze the flow of action in moments of erotic contemplation' (19), as the face of Lillian Gish would in the cinema. Anthony's look, Marlow's look and the reader's converge on the exhibited face and figure of Flora, and Flora is forced to perform under this cinematic gaze. At the same time, Marlow's emphasis on the marks of her ill-treatment being part of her attraction, and his suggestion that her powerlessness confirms and augments this, renders this identification and convergence of gazes uneasy for the reader by exposing the sadistic basis of this visual pleasure.

5. Conclusion

Although *Close Up*, the journal set up by Kenneth Macpherson, Bryher and H.D. to explore the aesthetic possibilities opened up by cinema, didn't start publication until 1927, coinciding with the beginning of sound, cinema was well-established by the early years of the twentieth century, and Conrad's work shows how some of those aesthetic possibilities are already being explored in fiction of the first two decades (see Donald, Freidberg and Marcus). In his 1936 essay, 'The Work of Art in an Age of Mechanical Reproduction,' Walter Benjamin writes of the effects of film with its changes of place and focus, its fracturing of action into 'a series of mountable episodes,' and, more specifically, of the effects produced by the camera: 'its interruptions and isolations, its extensions and accelerations, its enlargements and reductions' (223, 239). For example: 'With the close-up, space expands; with slow motion, movement is extended' (230). The new technology of cinema had an inescapable impact on the sensory apparatus, and it reconfigured the understanding of time, space and movement. As Benjamin puts it, the camera introduces an 'unconscious optics,' enriching the field of perception and promoting the unconscious negotiation of a changed environment through apperception (230, 233).

In *The Senses of Modernism*, Sara Danius argues that these new technologies of perception were not opposed to, but were constitutive of, high modernist aesthetics (3). She shows how, through developments in perceptual technologies between 1880 and 1930, 'categories of perceiving and knowing are reconfigured' (3). Benjamin suggested that 'a different nature opens itself to the camera than opens to the naked eye' (238): Danius argues that the notion of the 'naked eye' was an invention – and 'the terms through which it was articulated' were re-shaped through the introduction of the new technology. She cites a passage from *The Guermantes Way*, where Proust summons up the image of 'the dignified emergence of an Academician who is trying to hail a cab,' and then imagines how that image would be recorded by a photographic plate, where the focus shifts to 'his tottering steps, his precautions to avoid falling on his back, the parabola of his fall' (Proust 142). Although Proust refers to a photographic plate (*plaque photographique*), the description draws rather on cinematography: the breaking down of movement and the observer's attention to corporeal signs. Indeed, the description shows very precisely how the 'unconscious optics' of cinema re-shape ordinary vision and enter into fiction. In Danius's words, 'specific technoscientific configurations and their conceptual environments enter into and become part of' aesthetic strategies (11): technological change 'makes available new sensory domains that open themselves to artistic exploration' (12), and technological transformation 'helps articulate new perceptual domains' (17). Accordingly, Danius concludes that a 'sustained reconsideration of aesthetic modernism' has to include 'a historically reflexive and multi-levelled attempt at incorporating the operations of the perceptual technologies of the second machine age into the modernist enterprise' (196).

In this essay, I have shown Conrad's self-conscious engagement with dramatic form and conventions. I have also tried to demonstrate a similar, though perhaps unconscious, engagement with early cinema. Danius argues that new perceptual technologies impact on the sensory apparatus and reveals how those re-configurations of the senses shaped modernist aesthetic practices in a 'nexus of perception, technological change, and literary form' (1). Conrad's work demonstrates this in practice.

Chapter 5
'Post-impressionism' and the Cinema: How We Are 'Made to See' in Conrad's *Victory*

Suzanne Speidel

Joseph Conrad and Early Cinema

The words and works of Joseph Conrad have frequently been cited by those seeking to demonstrate the influence of the novel on the medium of film. Since George Bluestone's groundbreaking study of film adaptation in 1957, it has been common-place for adaptation critics to include a discussion of Conrad's 'Preface to *The Nigger of the "Narcissus,"'* and to quote the author's bold declaration of intent: 'My task, which I am trying to achieve is, by the power of the written word to make you hear, to make to you feel, – it is, before all, to make you *see*' (NN 5).

More recently, however, such allusions have contained some circumspection: Brian McFarlane, for example, points out that we should not take Conrad to represent the aims and practices of novelists en masse, since he was writing at a time of 'crucial changes in the (mainly English) novel ... changes which led to a stress on showing rather than telling and which, as a result, reduced the element of authorial intervention in its more overt manifestations' (4). Here Conrad's desire to 'make us see' is placed within the contextual framework of modernism, in which 'seeing' is frequently given special focus. The act of seeing, often ceded in modernist novels to the realm of characters rather than extradiegetic narrators, becomes at once an event within the story and a rich area of narrational innovation and instability. Thus in *Heart of Darkness*, we find what Ian Watt has termed 'delayed decoding': when Marlow's Congo steamer is under attack it is not the firing of arrows which is the subject of the story, but Marlow's dawning realisation that this is what is occurring. The narrative rendering of this is striking in its, at first, puzzling specifity, 'little sticks' (Y 109) as opposed to arrows, and so highlights for us how language might seek to capture such perceptual processes (Marlow's progress from observation to understanding).

It is, of course, precisely this investigation of perception itself which critics of Conrad and Ford Madox Ford, following the example of Ford himself, have dubbed literary impressionism (see Ford 1924). For those wishing to argue for the influence of the film on the novel, Fordian impressionism, with its stress on 'seeing,' offers an inviting starting point, and undoubtedly Conradians remarking on relationships between Conrad's narratives and film have frequently done so whilst examining the impressionist credentials of Conrad's novels. For Todd K. Bender, for example, it is perception rendered as 'fragmented broken sequences of images' and 'fluidity of time' which most clearly mark the narratives of both Conrad and Ford as 'cinematic' (51, 56).

An alternative to the impressionist approach has been put forward by Stephen Donovan in his impressive study 'Sunshine and Shadows: Conrad and Early Cinema'. Adopting a historically specific, rather than a metaphoric, stance towards cinema Donovan sets out his aim of tracing the influence of early, pre-narrative cinema on Conrad's writing. Whilst initially allowing that Conrad appears an 'unpromising object of enquiry' for this type of investigation, Donovan is able to open up a wealth of possibilities for the impact of film on literature by proposing that we 'include negative reactions to cinema' within the field inquiry (2003, 238). Under this rubric, Conrad's work is transformed into a potentially rich set of responses to the advent of cinema, manifesting a tacit, yet significant, distrust for the new phenomenon of the moving photographic image.

Conrad's dislike of both photography and cinema is well documented. Donovan points out that Conrad 'once described the aim of the "artistic!" photographer … as "being always to obliterate every trace of individuality in his subject"' (*CL2* 105; cited in Donovan 2003, 249). As late as 1920, Conrad declared that 'The Movie is just a silly stunt for silly people' (1928, 114).

Conrad's objections to photography and cinematography seem to stem chiefly from the supposition that such technologies achieve a high degree of authenticity in their representations. He protests against this claim in even the most casual observations on the subject – in his Preface to Thomas Beer's biography of Stephen Crane, Conrad recalls a visit to Crane's home, during which a photograph was taken. Conrad describes the photograph as follows: 'Though the likenesses are not bad it is a very awful thing. Nobody looks like him or herself in it. The best yet are the Cranes' dogs …' (LE 155). In this instance Conrad's irreverence towards photography is nicely captured in the remark that it is the dogs who fair best in the process. Curiously Conrad also asserts that whilst the 'likenesses' are 'not bad,' nobody looks 'like' themselves. Presumably the word 'likeness' is used here chiefly to mean 'graphic image' rather than 'similarity' or 'semblance,' yet there remains something equivocal in the comment. The repetition of 'like' in 'likeness' and 'looks like' invites us to consider that what is asserted here is that even when photography captures a visual resemblance, what is shown is still far removed from the experiences of 'seeing' – and the experiences of 'being'. The mechanics of the camera and of photographic development have 'obliterated … individuality.'

In his discussion of *The Nigger of the 'Narcissus'* (1897) in relation to early cinema Donovan throws new light on Conrad's famous 'Preface'. Rather than aligning Conrad's manifesto, as adaptation critics have done, alongside the aims of cinema, Donovan sees it as a reaction against the new ways of seeing being offered by the cinema in the closing years of the nineteenth century. It is only with the *novel*, Conrad seems to be saying, that the artist can *really* 'make you see'. The ways of seeing open to the novel which cannot, in Conrad's view, be offered by the cinema are perhaps most clearly suggested by a play on words, which Conrad makes more than once, on possible meanings of the phrase 'moving pictures'. In an interview given during a visit to the United States (Conrad's only visit there, made in 1923), Conrad comments: 'Before the cinematograph was invented ... fiction-writers tried to make moving-pictures. This was the first essential of a good story – that it move. The trouble with moving-pictures is that they don't show, except in a superficial way, what the characters are thinking' (Smith 186). Similarly, in a lecture entitled 'Author and Cinematograph,' delivered during the same American trip, Conrad observed: '...fundamentally the creator in letters aims at a moving picture – moving from the eye, to the mind, and to our complex emotions which I will express in one word – heart' (Schwab 346). In both these instances the notion of a '*moving* picture' is given a double meaning: 'to move' refers both to physical movement in space across time, and to a capacity to evoke an emotional response (stories must *move us*). These two meanings are connected by the type of narrative movement – the type of showing – that Conrad posits as specific to the novel: that is, the movement of the narrative voice into the mind of characters, the revelation of what characters see, think and feel.

This then takes us back to the notion of impressionism, except, of course, that in Conrad's accounts the novel's ability to occupy the realm of a character's consciousness, and to show the outside world as seen from within, is not posited as evocative of cinema's manipulation and fragmentation of time and space. For Conrad, it is precisely here that cinema falls short. This reinforces Donovan's interpretation of 'Preface to *The Nigger...*' – namely, that we might read impressionist traits and aims as reactions against cinema, as efforts to find territory, and ways of seeing, which the cinema cannot offer, and could not usurp.

Perhaps Conrad's pointed dislike of the Stephen Crane photograph is telling, given that this picture also features Conrad himself. One particular challenge cinema offered the novel was a new encounter with the notion of self-image. As we shall see, the development of the cinematograph in its early years was to give special prominence to self-image, and the invitation not just to view, but to view *oneself*, was an important ingredient of what Tom Gunning has termed 'cinema of attractions'.[1] In the music halls and fairgrounds where such exhibitions took place, moving images of the viewers themselves were frequently offered as prize exhibits. In other words, cinema provided viewers with a new opportunity to see themselves from the 'outside,' so to speak – potentially, to see themselves as others see them.

---

[1] Borrowing from Sergei Eisenstein's theatrical theories and experiments, Gunning uses this term to describe the dominant modes of cinema in its earliest years (from 1895 to around 1906). 'Cinema of attractions' refers to 'a conception that sees cinema less as a way of telling stories than as a way of presenting a series of views to an audience, fascinating because of their illusory power ... and exoticism' (57). 'Cinema of attractions' was thus primarily exhibitionist, celebrating its own capacity to show.

Thus whilst modernist literature (particularly those works we might consider impressionist) executed a narrative movement inwards, depicting, as Bender puts it, 'the fleeting moment of intersection when the exterior world impinges on a sensitive consciousness,' cinema offered a new construction of self as seen as a constituent in the observed exterior landscape (6). With the verisimilitude offered by the cinematic attraction of movement, the 'sensitive consciousness' faced a new complication in perception and understanding: self-knowledge was bound up more than ever before with the processing (both cognitive and chemical) of an external self-image. This suggests that even as impressionist writers responded to the properties of film by employing the novel to 'make us see,' cinema necessitated further developments in the novelistic form, since the way we saw, and what we saw, was rapidly evolving, subject to the powerful influence of the moving image.

When considering the possible influences of the cinema on the work of Joseph Conrad, it is perhaps useful to tread a line somewhere between the approaches outlined thus far. Clearly, a simple aligning of his writing with the properties of cinema, such as Bluestone posits, cannot account for the way Conrad's novels, and other modernist works, manifest an anxiety about the influence and effects of the cinematic age. Indeed we might see cinema as having fuelled a certain cynicism (detectable in the works of Conrad, Ford, Joyce and others) whereby 'to see' is increasingly synonymous with self-delusion.[2] Having said this, it is equally clear that Conrad's novels display other cinematic influences besides hostility, and Conrad's analogy that writers seek to create 'moving pictures' is echoed in studies of impressionism such as Bender's, which explore how Conrad's narratives display metaphoric reflections of filmic techniques. It is particularly the techniques of narrative cinema that provide material for such comparisons, and in studying the relationship between Conrad's writing and early cinema, it becomes clear that at times his work adopts strategies of imitation as opposed to, or indeed alongside, strategies of critique.

Certainly in Conrad's later life it is possible to detect some thawing in his outlook towards cinema, particularly when – characteristically mindful of his income – he began to recognise the potential financial benefits of cinema's investment in literary sources. Gene M. Moore, pointing out that the sale of the film rights to *Victory, Chance, Romance* and *Lord Jim* to the New York agent Alice Krauser brought Conrad $20,000, comments that this windfall 'affected the nature of his involvement with the new medium' (35).[3] Evidence of this change can be

---

[2] This idea emerges as a powerful theme in novels as diverse as Conrad's *Lord Jim* (1900), Ford's *The Good Soldier* (1915), and Joyce's *A Portrait of the Artist as a Young Man* (1916).

[3] Moore calculates that this sum was in fact 'roughly one sixth of Conrad's entire fortune'. Moore also notes that Conrad's lifestyle changed significantly as a result of the deal: he purchased 'a 30-horse-power, four-cylinder Cadillac, and ... moved to his last and largest residence, Oswalds, in Bishopsbourne near Canterbury' (34).

seen in Conrad's willingness to compose his American lecture on the similarities between the novel and the film. Even more persuasively, in 1920 Conrad, assisted by his agent, J. B. Pinker, actually wrote a screenplay – *Gaspar the Strong Man* – adapted from his 1906 short story 'Gaspar Ruiz' (the screenplay was rejected by Famous Players-Lasky in 1921). Furthermore, in the same interview that Conrad commented on the difficulties cinema has in showing 'what characters are thinking,' he apparently also remarked to interviewer James Walter Smith that he considered cinema 'miraculous'.

It is clear, then, that in his later life Conrad's attitude towards cinema might at least be characterised as 'mixed'. Something of this ambivalence can be seen in the way that Conrad wrote about his American 'Author and Cinematograph' lecture, which he in fact delivered twice, once at the City Garden offices of Doubleday, his American publisher, and once at the New York home of Arthur Curtiss James. In a letter to Eric Pinker, Conrad comments:

> I ... have sketched out the outlines of a lecture, or rather of a familiar talk, on the (apparently) extravagant lines of the imaginative literary art being based fundamentally on scenic motion, like a camera: with this addition that for certain purposes the artist is a much more subtle and complicated machine than a camera, and with a wider range, if in the visual effects less precise – and so on and so on, for an hour; with a mixture of jocularity and intense seriousness ...
> (Jean-Aubry 1927, 302–3)

Several sentences later, Conrad adds in parenthesis – and out of the blue – 'Don't imagine that I am going to be impertinent to the cinema; on the contrary I shall butter them up.' In this letter it is possible to detect a combination of attitudes: the tone is undoubtedly facetious, but perhaps also defensive (he anticipates accusations of impertinence). There is a suggestion of self-consciousness, an awareness on Conrad's part that he is 'buttering up' – giving a desired performance for commercial ends. Yet the fact that Conrad recounted to Eric Pinker the completion of his lecture suggests some satisfaction in the topic (as well as some anxiety about his audience's response).

In considering the influence of cinema on the work of Joseph Conrad it is important to find ways of reflecting the ambivalence and contradictions which the question encompasses. Indeed we might think of cinematic influences as emerging in a number of different ways. Conrad's novels were written during the birth and first growth of the cinematic – the visual – age, and they reflect the experiences of this age. These are reflected in the novels' focus on 'seeing,' but might also be detectable in an evolution in the ways that 'seeing' is itself seen across Conrad's career. Certainly the visual properties of cinema – which themselves evolved over time – put the project of 'making us see' under pressure, and Conrad's works may be understood in terms of their varied, changing responses to the cinematic zeitgeist.

Victory and Narrative Cinema

Conrad's *Victory* seems a particularly appropriate novel to examine for evidence of cinematic traces. Published in 1915, and written between April 1912 and May/June 1914, the novel was produced during an era when cinema was making dramatic leaps in its evolution towards narrative.

There are a number of landmark dates in this transition, one of which is the Nickelodeon boom in the United States, which began in 1906, and prompted a world-wide increase in film production, giving new impetus for the medium to develop.[4] The move towards narrative can thus be seen as primarily commercial, with attempts to stabilise the chaotic distribution and exhibition of films resulting in the building of movie theatres (whose name originated from the entrance charge of a nickel), which required mass production to fill their schedules and cover their costs. The formal transition towards narrative was consolidated by a number of important developments between 1907 and 1913, such as the increase in multi-reel films, the sophisticated use of cross-cutting to show parallel actions (as pioneered – though not invented – by D. W. Griffith), and a gradual tendency towards closer shot-scales.[5] The years from circa 1913 to 1919 are generally recognised as the period when what is now the dominant mode of film grammar, often referred to as 'continuity cinema,' was elaborated. Continuity cinema refers to a system of film editing which depicts a continuous, clear narrative action so that cuts between shots are not elliptical, disruptive or confusing. The techniques associated with continuity editing – such as matches on action and eyeline, as well as correct handling of screen direction – serve to explain, and smooth over, cuts within a scene.[6] It was the American studio Vitagraph, and especially director Ralph Ince, who led the way, and others, in the context of international film distribution, soon followed.

Conrad's *Victory*, therefore, emerged at a particularly vibrant point in cinema's evolution – especially in its narrative innovation. It was a point when cinema's influence was well-established, but when its narrative techniques were fresh and innovative, and when it was also gradually becoming clear what type of stories

---

[4] See Barry Salt 1990.

[5] See Barry Salt 1992.

[6] 'Screen direction' refers to 'the 'right-left relationships in a scene ... determined by the position of characters and objects in the frame, the directions of movement, and the characters' eyelines. Continuity editing attempts to keep screen direction consistent between shots.' (Bordwell and Thompson 822). A 'match on action' is 'a cut which joins two shots of the same gesture, making it appear to continue uninterrupted' (Bordwell and Thompson 822). An 'eyeline match' is 'a cut obeying the axis of action principle, in which the first shot shows a person looking off in one direction and the second shows a nearby space containing what he or she sees' (Bordwell and Thompson 820). (It should be noted that some dispute exists about the development – and importance – of the 'axis of action' in continuity cinema; see Salt 1992, 172.)

cinema seemed best suited to tell. Indeed the period from 1912 to 1914 surely constituted a fitting moment to begin to understand the impact of cinema on the modern world, as is reflected in the first, tentative burgeoning of both avant-garde cinema, and writings about cinema, at this time.[7]

In his second 1923 lecture on 'Author and Cinematograph' Conrad chose to support his thesis with readings from *Victory*. It is easy to see why he felt that this novel would go down well with his American listeners, given that it was *Victory* which constituted Conrad's greatest popular – and commercial – success. Robert Hampson, in his introduction to the novel, specifically discusses *Victory*'s status within Conrad's career in terms of its contrast to earlier novels which 'had not achieved the popular success he sought' (1989, 11). As Hampson makes clear, a change in fortune was to occur with the success of *Chance* (1914) in the United States, and this paved the way for the popularity of *Victory*, whose proceeds relieved Conrad of 'the pressure of having to write in order to live' (1989, 14).

Writing in *Conradiana*, Peter Mallios takes up Hampson's point: citing Conrad's earlier pecuniary difficulties, and the new-found prosperity afforded by *Chance*, Mallios comments wryly that 'One may readily imagine ... what was on Conrad's mind when he began *Victory*, which was originally envisioned as a novella, under the working title "Dollars"' (148).[8] This suggests that *Victory* was written with the same commercial imperatives in mind which shaped the development of film narratives, and it offers the intriguing possibility that Conrad's thawing towards cinema, often attributed to the sale of *Victory*'s screen rights, was perhaps already in process before the novel was begun. Certainly, if we examine some of the critical debates which *Victory* has engendered, the notion of some change of heart towards cinema narratives is persuasive.

That *Victory* has provoked criticism as well as admiration is well known, and for its detractors it is the novel's apparent popular elements which are at fault. Mallios provides us with a very useful account of both sides of the argument, citing, amongst others, Albert Guerard's particularly apropos condemnation of the novel:

> The gross over-evaluation of *Victory* is of such long standing that it will not be easily corrected. *Victory* is Conrad for the high schools *and the motion pictures,*

---

[7] Between 1912 and 1914 painter Leopold Survage planned out, though did not produce, an abstract animation, a project examined by Guillarme Apollinaire in his journal *Les Soirées de Paris*. Survage's work was preceded by experiments in hand-printing raw film by futurists Ginna and Corra as early as 1910. See Rees, 'Cinema and the Avant-Garde'.

[8] Both Mallios and Hampson draw attention to the fact that Conrad wrote the short story 'Because of the Dollars,' which features *Victory*'s Captain Davidson, whilst composing *Victory*. The title, as Mallios implies, is still more suggestive of Conrad's priorities during this period. See Mallios, footnote 10 (177), and Hampson 1989, 12.

the easiest and generically the most popular of the novels. (255, emphasis added; cited in Mallios, 151)

Conrad's *Victory* has been a prime target for that school of thought amongst Conrad scholarship which holds that the author's rise in popularity also signalled his decline in artistic achievement. Mallios's account makes clear that it is the novel's tendency towards melodrama – its reliance on (exaggerated) character types, conventional story situations, and 'sentimental' themes – which is often deemed one of its chief failings. That *Victory* is defined by, and censored for, the readiness with which it can be 'generically' placed is particularly significant for the novel's affinities with cinema, since no other narrative form has so thoroughly embraced genre as a means of telling and, of course, marketing stories. Guerard makes this connection abundantly clear: for him to write generically (which is inherently to write *badly*) is to write 'for the motion pictures.'

Obviously attacks on the novel have been vigorously repudiated, and some of the grounds upon which the defence is mounted have further implications for the purpose of this study. A number of Conrad scholars have sought to scrutinize what Robert Hampson calls the novel's 'synthetic, composite nature' (1989, 15). This line of enquiry sees *Victory* as incorporating a mosaic of allusions and narrative antecedents, along the lines of James Joyce's 'mythic method,' so that, for example, Heyst and Lena serve as allusions to Prospero and Miranda, whilst Pedro corresponds to Caliban, Wang to Ariel, and so on (Hampson 1989, 18–19). Other such connections include parallels with Villiers de l'Isle Adam's play *Axël* (1828) (Hampson 1989, 17), with Stefan Zeromshki's *Dzieje grechu* (*The History of Sin*, 1908) (Busza),[9] and with Robert Louis Stevenson's *The Ebb-Tide*.[10] Such a conception of the novel as a work which reproduces aspects of other texts posits it as fertile ground for this study, since it suggests that the novel's meaning is located precisely in its instances of allusion.

Indeed, Peter Mallios takes the 'mythic method' argument a stage further, drawing on the work of Brian McHale to suggest that *Victory* articulates a 'postmodern' ontological crisis, where the 'blurring of the boundary between "text" and "reality"' becomes 'an expression of the plasticity of the "postmodern" world.' Mallios elaborates as follows:

> ... anticipating a contemporary moment in which textualized agencies like the media have such great power to *make* reality through their words, Conrad presents a world in which the most visceral realities are fictions, where what is most 'literary' determines what is most 'real'. (159)

---

[9] Cited in Mallios 158. For an extensive list of studies tracing further allusions see Mallios and Hampson 1989; see also Watts 1994.

[10] Watts describes *Victory* as 'an amalgam of literary materials borrowed from many locations and fused in unstable combination' (1996, 133).

This interpretation of the novel offers further possibilities for the way in which *Victory* might reflect the early experiences of the cinematic age. More than any other representational form, cinema was surely the medium which launched the twentieth century into the postmodern condition to which Mallios refers, and many of Conrad's initial objections to photographic media – that photographs 'obliterate individuality,' for example – acquire a new force and meaning in the light of a postmodern concern for how representation may (re)produce 'reality'. For Mallios, McHale's distinction between 'modernist' and 'postmodernist' distinguishes *Victory* from preceding Conrad novels, since the latter are modernist in their focus on 'questions and crises of epistemology (how we know what we know)' whilst the former is postmodern in its pre-occupation with 'questions and crises of ontology (the stability of Being itself)'. Mallios argues that one reason why *Victory* has been critically maligned is that it has been 'misidentified as a "modernist" novel' (Mallios 179n).

Perhaps another way of putting this is to characterise *Victory* as a novel where, more than ever before, Conrad explores the implications of being '*made to see*.' Thus *Victory* marks a move away from Conrad's earlier, impressionist manifesto towards what we might term 'post-impressionism' – that is, towards an acknowledgement that 'making us see' involves a problematic process of 'fabrication' (in which language produces sight and 'the seen,' rather than simply capturing or representing them). The novel achieves this through its strategies of replication, where stories and narration take us to the models which are imitated – to Shakespeare, to melodrama, and to film.

Victory and Cinematic Narration

Part I of *Victory* offers plenty of material for Conrad's theory on the 'camera-like' properties of 'literary art'. The opening chapters repeatedly make reference to vision and visibility, and set up a notion of spectatorship as key to the narrative organisation of the story. Thus, the events of Heyst's life leading up to his meeting with Lena are presented to us in the form of a series of 'sightings': Heyst 'had been seen' in Manila, and 'he was likewise seen' in Saigon (V 7); he 'vanished … in the direction of New Guinea,' then 'swam into view … in a native proa full of Goram vagabonds' (V 8); following Morrison's death, he 'disappeared for a time,' 'became visible again rather suddenly' (V 22), then 'faded completely away' (V 25); until at last he 'suddenly reappeared in the world, broad chested, bald forehead, long moustaches, polite manner, and all.' (V 31)

Much of this emphasis on observation has nautical connotations, as is made clear by the presence of Captain Davidson, the story's principal eyewitness ('Davidson's attitude was that of a spectator,' we are told [V 49]), who literally watches from his ship for 'signs' from (or of) Heyst. The metaphor of Heyst 'swimming into view' provides an obvious link to telescopic sightings, though it is also reminiscent of the focal adjustments of a camera lens. The notion of Heyst 'fading away completely,' meanwhile, offers a more obvious cinematic evocation in that it is reminiscent of the dissolve, or the trick film.

Furthermore, narrative presentation in the form of a series of views through a telescope has itself cinematic associations: the earliest point of view shots, known as 'vignette' shots, presented characters' views through telescopes, magnifying glasses, and key holes, usually suggested by an appropriately shaped, black mask around the image.[11] The vignetted POV shot remained the method of presenting point of view until 1908 – after which the earliest attempts at unvignetted POV frequently mimicked those narrative situations where previously vignettes were used (the view from the ship[12] being an obvious, pertinent, example).[13]

What is stressed in the novel's opening is the distance from which Heyst is viewed. Indeed he is frequently presented to us second- or third-hand, with an anonymous first person narrator reporting the accounts of others, on their dealings with, or remote sightings of, Heyst. The casual, hearsay style with which the narrator dips in and out of such anecdotes makes the strategy appear less significant than the narrative structure it imitates, namely the double-framework structure of *Heart of Darkness*.

What is conveyed is the sense of a universal view, and it is the pronoun 'we,' rather than 'I' which dominates ('we' being, presumably, the loose community of sailing men who travel, and inhabit, the Malay Archipelago). The narration evokes an array of background spectators, nonchalantly, intermittently taking in the life of Heyst: '… we all concluded that Heyst was boarding with the good-natured – some said: sponging on the imbecile – Morrison…' (V 19): 'A few of us who were sufficiently interested went to Davidson for details' (V 28). This technique differs from what is practiced in *Heart of Darkness* in that here the processes of 'seeing' are not explicitly investigated: the spectatorship is collective, and unlike Marlow, it takes its views for granted. This unconcerned outlook evokes the notion of being 'made to see' – of accepting a preconception, a mass view, and the surreptitious ease with which such illusions are established is reflected in the narration's deceptive simplicity.

---

[11] Examples of this are found in *Grandma's Reading Glasses* (G. A. Smith, 1900), *As Seen Through a Telescope* (G. A. Smith, 1901), and *Peeping Tom* (Pathé, 1902). These very early experiments with point of view did not feature literal shots from a performer's line of vision. Instead they constituted the first examples of scene dissection through cuts to close-up. (See Salt 1992, for an account of the development of point of view shots.) From hereon I will adopt what has become standard Film Studies practice in referring to point of view constructions, the abbreviation POV.

[12] Examples of this are found in *Saved by the Wireless* (Vitagraph, 1909) and *Back to Nature* (Vitagraph, 1910).

[13] Salt notes that the development of unvignetted POV was surprisingly slow and awkward in that 'most early filmmakers had some conceptual or aesthetic difficulty' matching the angle correctly between the shots of a POV construction, a problem which had not arisen with the earlier introduction of vignetted POV (1992, 51, 96).

Thus one way we might consider *Victory* as 'Conrad for the motion pictures' is in its evocation of mass perception, and mass perception which mimics Conrad's own reservations about cinematic presentation. The view of Heyst is constructed entirely from the outside, a 'superficial' image in which his individuality cannot be detailed, yet which is widely, seductively assumed to be accurate.

The reader is left in no doubt that such views are inaccurate, and waits for a close-hand introduction to Heyst. Indeed the move in Parts II and III away from a first person, outsider narrator to a third person narration in which Heyst himself is our principal focalizer tempts us to assume that the novel plots a course from false versions of Heyst to a 'true' one. Yet this would be to presuppose that Heyst's own view of himself is accurate, and indeed that 'true' views are even achievable, and *Victory* implies that we cannot rely on either assumption. Heyst, like Davidson, views himself as an observer – crucially he classes himself as an '"*independent spectator*"' (V 196, emphasis added) – and this results in a struggle to reconcile two sets of contradictions: he sees himself as a bystander, an audience member, when he has already been cast (by the narrative, by others, by himself) as the lead performer; and he believes his vision is separate, above the mass view, when he is just as susceptible to the effects of collective delusions as anyone else.

Victory and Cinematic Self-Image

In common with a number of other Conrad novels, *Victory* deals with the self-image of its lead characters. Where *Victory* differs – where it marks itself as a 'post-impressionist' rather than an impressionist novel – is in the particular stress it places on the self as a 'textualized' concept. This notion is at once a product of the cinematic age, and is explored through the novel's resemblances to cinematic narratives.

The phenomenon of 'self as text' is detectable in cinema's earliest, pre-narrative forms. In 1895 the Lumière brothers promoted their new product by filming interested parties and inviting them to view the results (one surviving example being *Congress of Photographic Societies at Neuville-sur-Saône*).[14] That this experience was soon to be widely on offer is demonstrated by the work of Sagar Kenyon and James Mitchell, whose recently unearthed collection[15] contains many films of ordinary British people (one showing the distribution of flyers advertising the fair where the film would be screened).[16] The importance of this phenomenon is suggested by R. W. Paul's 'comic episode' film, *The Countryman and the Cinematograph* (1901). Here a 'village idiot' encounters cinema for the first time,

---

[14]   See *The Movies Begin, Volume Two: The European Pioneers* (A Kino on Video DVD; Copyright Kino International Corp, 1994).

[15]   800 rolls of nitrate film, shot between 1897 and 1913, discovered in the basement of their former premises in Blackburn in 1994, have since been restored by the British Film Institute.

[16]   See *The Lost World of Mitchell and Kenyon* (A BFI DVD; Copyright BBC 2004).

and runs away in terror at the sight of a moving train, but is lured back when he sees himself onscreen (whereupon he points, excitedly, at his own image).[17]

Studies of the influence of early cinema have tended to focus on the presence of movement and its effects in those films where movement itself constitutes the main 'attraction' (as in the Lumières's *Arrival of a Train*, 1895). Perhaps because the photograph preceded the moving image by seventy years, less attention has been paid to effects of the recording and reproduction of the human image. Yet the verisimilitude afforded this image by the addition of movement clearly was striking to early audiences, as the exhibition of films of the audience itself demonstrates, and the cinematograph brought the reproduction of self-image to the masses in ways that had never been achieved before.

What early, pre-narrative films also suggest is the response of the filmed subject to the phenomenon of self as recording, and self on display. A recurring reaction of those filmed is a tendency to perform. Thus in *Congress of Photographic Societies...*, congress members look to camera, doffing their hats; similarly in Mitchell's and Kenyon's films the waving (and throwing) of caps is a frequent reaction to the camera's presence. The temptation to perform is detectable in the simplest of early films: even *Workers Leaving the Factory* (1895), the very first Lumière film, contains examples – such as the exaggerated dips and swerves of a bicycle (executed, not by the rider, but by a man behind the bicycle, who is pushing it, and holding it up). Another instance occurs in a Mitchell and Kenyon film reminiscent of the Lumières's first movie: here the mill workers in question move too slowly and self-consciously for the filmmakers' liking. The film shows James Mitchell himself directing the crowds, and gesticulating so elaborately that his are the most conspicuous actions featured. (This example is useful as it suggests that the performance signs displayed are not purely a matter of response to filmmakers' instructions.)

The age of cinema, it seems, encouraged an age of performance. The dominance of narrative cinema after 1906 meant that opportunities for viewers to view themselves gradually declined after 1906, but narrative brought new types of performance to the forefront. A number of film historians, in accordance with D. W. Griffith, have viewed advances in narrative sophistication and film technique as producing greater restraint, or 'verisimilitude,' in performance gestures, seeing the increased use of close-ups and editing as reducing the need for emphatic gesture (cinema is therefore seen as heralding less 'theatrical' acting styles).[18] More recently, however, research into the relationships between early cinema and theatre suggest that the transition towards understatement was more complex than this. Ben Brewster and Lea Jacobs, for example, argue that until the late 1910s acting in cinema was more emphatic and more pictorial (more

---

[17] See *The Movies Begin, Volume Two*.

[18] See 'D. W. Griffith Speaks'. Roberta Pearson distinguishes between 'verisimilitude' and a 'histrionic' acting code, associating the latter with theatricality (*Eloquent Gestures*); see also James Naremore, and Janet Staiger.

reliant on posed 'attitudes'), than was late nineteenth century theatre, due to a need to compensate for the absence of dialogue, the size of performers when in long shot, and the short duration of one- and two-reelers. According to Brewster and Jacobs, close and medium shots frequently served to emphasize, rather than replace, performance poses. The influence of classical painting and statuary on the 'attitudes' of pictorial acting suggests some of the paradoxes which performance caused for early cinema: the apparently realist medium of film evoked artificiality through acting styles reliant on stock gestures, which themselves imply an address towards spectatorship.

Thus textual analysis of early films offers some intriguing possibilities about how the influence and effects of the cinematic age might have been felt by an impressionist writer like Conrad. Cinema created collective spectatorship, and also suggested that the response to this was the performance of collective, recognizable 'signs'. Cinema therefore highlights a theme already dear to Conrad, and explored in a novel like *Lord Jim* (1900), namely how human behaviour is shaped by mass perception and expectation. Of course, what cinema as a narrative medium also produced were popular narratives, themselves promoters of behavioural codes. *Victory* is a novel which responds to such paradoxes – to an age where performance seemed to be at once exposed and promoted, and where the new, miraculous medium of cinema was haled for its authenticity, and enjoyed for its artifice and play-acting. Seen in this light the new cinematic age does indeed emerge as the dawning of a new postmodern era, in that the behaviour and experiences which seemed most 'true' were also those which were most conspicuously rehearsed, reproduced and exhibited ('exhibition,' of course, in the sense of both physical performance and cinematic projection).

It is noticeable that the terms in which characters are described in *Victory* at times evoke elements of cinematic performance. Lena, whose 'statuesque' quality gives her 'the charm of art tense with life,' is able to produce a smile when Heyst demands it: '… the effect of the mechanical, ordered smile was joyous, radiant. It astonished Heyst. No wonder, it flashed through his mind, women can deceive men so completely' (V 81). Captain Davidson's encounter with Mrs. Schomberg, meanwhile, produces this account of the innkeeper's wife:

> Nobody had ever suspected her as having a mind … One was inclined to think of her as an It – an automaton, a very plain dummy, with an arrangement for bowing the head at times and smiling stupidly now and then. (V 40)

At such moments characters produce 'on cue' behaviour, which conforms to recognizable performance signs. The gestures are 'automated,' connotatively divorced from the human feeling beneath (furthering their association with mechanical cinematic presentation). They are delivered by characters who are, literally and figuratively, 'going through the motions,' so that here performance seems to be condemned as a source of human misery, in which those who are misunderstood or neglected seem to collude in their own mistreatment by producing the behaviour most expected of them. Specifically, these performances are ascribed to the novel's women characters, demonstrating on the one hand, learned feminine conduct towards men, and on the other, learned masculine perception of women.

Indeed, in *Victory* the notion of performance is frequently evoked in connection with gendered behaviour. Schomberg's regret and wounded pride, for example, brings to mind certain masculine gender roles: 'Ah, if he had only had that girl with him he would have been masterful and resolute and fearless – fight twenty desperadoes – care for nobody on earth!' (V 109). Schomberg's delusional attempts to cast himself as a fearless, courageous hero are incongruously reminiscent of the youthful protagonist of Conrad's *Lord Jim*, who 'saw himself saving people from sinking ships, cutting away masts in a hurricane, swimming through a surf with a line' (LJ 6). In both instances, the hyperbolic catalogue of action makes clear that the envisaged role is drawn from fictional narratives (indeed Jim 'live[s] in his mind the sea-life of light literature' [LJ 6]), and early cinema also played a part promoting images of 'manly' courage and physical prowess. Whilst the star system (promoting individual heroic personae) was in its infancy in the 1910s, male physique and strength were celebrated in such pre-narrative genres as the boxing movie.[19] The propensity of commercial narrative cinema to promote aggressive, romantized masculinity, meanwhile, is aptly illustrated by the 1919 film of *Victory* which was the product of Conrad's screen rights deal.[20] Here Heyst (Jack Holt) shoots Ricardo (Lon Chaney), and the subsequent intertitle reads: 'Something has indeed happened to Heyst. He was no longer the slave of an idea, but a man, free to slay and die for his woman.'

Of course, Conrad's Heyst never experiences this dubious liberation. Yet Heyst's life (and death) are undoubtedly shaped by his complex, ambivalent relationship to such images of masculinity, and the tragedy which befalls both him and Lena demonstrates the novel's curious stance of at once condemning and condoning the playing out of roles. The role which Heyst adopts – his detached spectator stance – seems specifically designed to avoid the construction of masculinity favoured by Schomberg and Jim (as is demonstrated by his acute embarrassment when he rescues Morrison). Apparently Heyst neither wishes to form emotional bonds, nor to play to the crowd; and yet his performance still emerges as a response to public opinion, his polite remoteness an act of self-preservation in the face of the malicious misconceptions of others. Interestingly, Heyst too has an 'on cue' smile, 'the Heyst smile' (V 375), making his reflection on potential female duplicity particularly ironic.

The most thorough analysis of Heyst's performed self-image is provided in Robert Hampson's *Betrayal and Identity*. Hampson argues that Heyst's chosen role is founded on a contradiction, since he has based his detached stance on advice given to him by his father – itself powerful evidence of filial attachment.

---

[19] Miriam Hansen has demonstrated that, surprisingly, women flocked to boxing films, 1ff.

[20] Maurice Tourneur dir., *Victory*, Famous Players-Lasky (1919).

For Hampson, Heyst's sceptical, detached persona is at odds with his 'repressed emotions' – for Lena, for his father, and even for the unfortunate Morrison – and it is the '"real truth"' about these relationships that *Victory* gradually reveals (1992, 232; 1989, 62). Of course, what this means is that the 'truth' that Heyst suppresses is itself the stuff of fiction, for what the cynical, diffident Heyst really longs to do is to rescue the pretty girl from the clutches of the lecherous hotel keeper. This irony is in itself an indicator of the power of prescribed roles, since it suggests that even repressed, subconscious desires are the product of external conditioning.

Mallios identifies this paradox in the novel's treatment of romantic relationships:

> Conrad's point is that we never speak about love in our 'own' voices: that 'love,' that experience which seems to demand that and feel like we are speaking our truest most individual selves, is actually the most overwritten, oversung, and hypertextualized experience known to humanity. (159)

Thus it is not the case that the novel denounces Heyst's foray into the realm of melodrama, or suggests that his emotions are insincere. Indeed, if anything, it is Heyst's reticence in his new role of romantic hero which appears to be at fault, because he is unable to play the part in such a way that Lena recognises his commitment to it (and to her). Lena expects 'signs' of love from Heyst, and when these are not forthcoming she seeks to earn them through an 'act' of feminine self-sacrifice.

Lena's 'victory' is recounted as follows:

> Exulting, she saw herself extended on the bed, in a black dress, and profoundly at peace; while, stooping over her with a kindly, playful smile, he was ready to lift her in his arms and take her into the sanctuary of his innermost heart – forever. (V 407)

The fictional origins of Lena's heroine role are made clear with the linguistic flourish ' – forever.' Like Jim, Lena 'sees herself,' and the novel painfully conveys how what we are 'made to see' shapes what we are made to be. Dying in her lover's arms, Lena seems to miss the significance of her life's last moments, because she is pre-occupied with an image of herself in her lover's arms. Poignantly in death, Lena seems to resemble a cinema viewer, watching a big, romantic scene (her own) playing out before her. Ultimately the novel's depiction of Lena's death sets up a contraction, in that it both censures the performance of a prescribed role (Lena's), whilst also prompting us to wish that Heyst could have played the romantic lead better. This ambivalence is reinforced by the intricacies of the novel's employment of the rescue motif, which the novel seems both to parody and embrace.

Victory and Cinematic Stories

Victory's artificial, imitative qualities are normally seen in the light of its allusions to literary genres and works, but they are also produced by the novel's resemblance to cinema. Both in its story and its plot *Victory* borrows from commercial, narrative films, particularly in its employment of the rescue motif. Tales of daring rescue, inherited from nineteenth-century melodrama, were staples of narrative cinema before the famous climax of Griffith's *The Birth of a Nation* (1915), having been exploited to full effect by Griffith in such earlier films as *The Fatal Hour* (1908), *The Lonedale Operator* (1911) and *The Girl and her Trust* (1912). The popularity of the rescue scenario is illustrated by that fact that it was parodied in *The Bangville Police* (1913), the first Keystone Kops comedy.

Conrad's *Victory* also mimics a related Griffith technique, namely parallel editing to create suspense (usually by cutting back and forth between victims and rescuers). In *Victory* the narrative 'cuts' between Heyst and Lena, on the one hand, and Mr. Jones and Ricardo on the other, so that we anxiously anticipate the actions of the latter whilst witnessing the blossoming relationship between the former. Thus Chapters Four to Eight, Part II, recount the time that Ricardo, Jones and Pedro spend at Schomberg's hotel (alerting us to their intention of robbing Heyst), whilst Chapters One to Five, Part III, detail Heyst's and Lena's life on Samburan (as we await the arrival of the 'desperadoes'). The second half of Part III, and Part IV continue this pattern, switching between the bungalows of the two parties. The close of Chapter Nine, Part II even contains a highly cinematic transition between the two parallel storylines, with a point of view link between the two – as Heyst smokes at night outside his bungalow, his lighted cigar is seen by Ricardo outside his:

> It was noted as a symptom of importance by an observer with his faculties greedy for signs, and in a state of alertness tense enough almost to hear the grass grow.
> Chapter 10
> The Observer was Martin Ricardo. (V 259–60)

This moment resembles an unvignetted POV construction ('a shot taken with the lens pointing along the direction of the view of a character shown in a previous or subsequent shot' [Salt 1992, 327]),[21] with Ricardo revealed as the subsequent viewer of a previously 'shown' spectacle. Thus *Victory* offers a highly cinematic

---

[21] The unvignetted POV shot was established, though in its infancy, by 1914, occurring most frequently in films made by Vitagraph (e.g. Rollin S. Sturges's *The Craven* [1912], William V. Ranous *Poet and Peasant* [1912] and Ralph Ince's *His Last Fight* [1913]); see Salt 1992, 94–6. Admittedly it is debatable the degree to which Conrad was consciously aware of this development: Moore, for example, points out that Conrad appears to have struggled writing his screenplay, and that he wrote to Pinker of 'not knowing how a moving pictures story is composed' (40).

presentation of the anticipated stand-off, with confrontation staged across opposing spaces on Samburan. The conventions of cinema reinforce the 'textualized' nature of Heyst's and Lena's story, since *Victory*'s narrative mirrors the practices of continuity cinema that the medium's commercial imperatives helped to shape.

Yet ultimately, what is suggested about the cinematic age remains highly ambivalent, in that the novel does not straightforwardly critique the 'post-impressionist' world it depicts, in which consciousness is shaped by what we are 'made to see'. This ambiguity is underlined by the novel's ending, where we encounter yet another thwarted rescuer, in the form of Captain Davidson. Davidson, our observer figure in Book I, materialises again with ludicrous abruptness after Lena's shooting (indeed he almost seems to literally materialise, in the manner of a trick film). Earlier, when Lena and Heyst go in search of Wang, Heyst speculates (as the reader is tempted to do) on the possibility of a rescue by sea, but dismisses this with the observation that 'Davidson passed westward ten days ago" (V 352). However, in the final chapter we learn that Davidson, alerted by Mrs. Schomberg that Heyst is in danger, has turned back mid-voyage.

According to the conventions of the rescue-genre, this ought to signal the suspenseful salvation of the lovers, with Davidson's journey paralleling the drama unfolding on the island. Indeed, Davidson does arrive in the dead of night on the night that the crisis occurs (fittingly negotiating thunderstorms to do so). However, he does not perform a heroic rescue, because the fastidious Davidson is as restrained as Heyst himself, and – farcically in keeping with his spectator's stance – decides to wait until morning before intruding. Alerted to his mistake by the sight of Pedro's body, he arrives at Heyst's bungalow just too late, instead of just in time.

The narrative's awkward articulation of Davidson's entrance emphasises the absurdity of this failure. Davidson's reticence serves as a parallel to Heyst's failure in the role of heroic saviour, and the behaviour of both characters demonstrates that there is folly in *refusing* to be 'made to see,' in declining allocated, expected roles. Whilst both men are partially vindicated by the presence of Ricardo as a dubious representative of masculine assertiveness, their passivity is also mocked through the futile, near-miss nature of Lena's death. Thus we are left with an impossible dilemma, in that attempts to evade popular expectations are seen to be as destructive as oblivious collusion with them. Indeed the novel suggests that we ignore collective conceptions of our own image at our peril. The paradox remains insoluble, and as such it captures the challenges to self-knowledge and perception which the new cinematic age heralded.

Cinematic Development and Conrad's Victory

Scholars of early cinema history have tended to view the development of narrative cinema, as well as the growth of movie theatres, as a step in the cinematograph's gradual social metamorphosis – the move out of the fairground, coupled with the adoption of forms and narratives recognisable from the novel and the theatre, began to attract the middle classes to the cinema. Film was no longer considered a 'mere' spectacle for the entertainment of the masses, but a medium capable of conveying complex stories and messages – indeed of sustaining an adaptation of a novel by a writer like Joseph Conrad. It is possible that these transformations in form and attitude also influenced Conrad in his apparent thawing towards the cinema.

Yet the project of exploring early cinema's influences on a contemporaneous novelist, such as Conrad, suggests a far more complex process of cross-fertilisation between media than this type of assumption implies. Cinema obviously drew on popular, as well as high culture sources, and even as the medium gained respectability through the adaptation of a novel like Conrad's *Victory*, it was itself influencing the very forms and themes of such literature through its reworking and promotion of genres like the melodrama (thus the existence and practices of the film industry had already played a part in shaping the material of Conrad's novel that Famous Players-Lasky purchased, and transformed for the screen, in 1919). Similarly, the cinema responded to the challenge that films 'don't show ... what people are thinking' with the development of a sophisticated film grammar which included POV constructions, and these in turn influenced the handling of character point of view in novels, creating new frames of reference, and narrative approaches, in the project of 'making us see.'[22]

The cinema has also been highly influential in evoking a postmodern sensibility in which human experience is understood in terms of how we are 'made to see' – since cinema, quite literally, shows us the world through someone else's lens. Conrad's *Victory* portrays a world where characters are inescapably shaped by how they are 'made to see' *themselves*, yet Heyst and Lena are both in effect blind to how they are seen (and valued) by each other. At once melodrama and critique of melodrama, the novel warns of the dangers of rejecting, as well as fulfilling, certain roles in the eyes and lives of other people. Indeed *Victory* serves as an effective metaphor for commercial cinema (and also embodies Conrad's own experiences of the cinematograph), since it shows us the benefits, temptations and difficulties which come with giving the performance an audience expects and desires. With the writing of the commercially successful *Victory*, the sale of his novels' film rights, and the writing, and rejection, of the screenplay *Gaspar the Strong Man*, Conrad was to discover the possible profits and price of such performances.

By the end of the First World War a clear cinematic victory had been won by the film industry of North America (and the American film industry of the west coast), and it was, of course, in Hollywood that Famous Players-Lasky (later to become Paramount) produced *Victory*, the first film adaptation of Conrad's work. The war had weakened European industries to the point where even the previously-

---

[22] These reached a high point in the decade following the publication of *Victory* in the works of Virginia Woolf, where the novels' fluid, multiple focalisation mirrors very precisely the continual realignment of the camera necessitated by the eye-line matching of continuity cinema.

thriving French film industry could no longer pose a serious economic threat to Hollywood, and from this point onwards a gulf opened up in international film-making practices, as well as in our cultural perceptions of them. Exacerbated by economic necessities and national ideologies (and, importantly, also *exaggerated* within critical discourses) America was to become the home of mainstream narrative cinema, driven by commercial imperatives, whilst Europe became the home of 'artistic,' socially 'worthy' film-making, driven by individual creativity (and, frequently also, government subsidies). Indeed the film industry today remains in the grip of precisely that quandary which Conrad's *Victory* explores – namely the difficulties and benefits, the risks and rewards, of projecting the image that the viewing public expects. Whilst on a thematic level the novel leaves this matter unsolved, Conrad's allusive style – which mixes with ease its wide array of sources – suggests that it is *Victory* itself which offers an ingenious negotiation of this dilemma of the cinematic age.

Chapter 6
Gorgeous Eloquence: Conrad and Shadowgraphy

Stephen Donovan

> I call these sketches Shadowgraphs, partly by the designation to remind you at once that they derive from the darker side of life, partly because, like other shadowgraphs, they are not directly visible. When I take a shadowgraph in my hand, it makes no impression upon me, and gives me no clear conception of it. Only when I hold it up opposite the wall, and now look not directly at it, but at that which appears on the wall, am I able to see it. So also with the picture I wish to show here, an inward picture that does not become perceptible until I see it through the external.
>
> – Søren Kierkegaard, *Either/Or* (171)

> He lived then before me; he lived as much as he had ever lived – a shadow insatiable of splendid appearances, of frightful realities; a shadow darker than the shadow of the night, and draped nobly in the folds of a gorgeous eloquence.
>
> – Joseph Conrad, *Heart of Darkness* (1899) (Y 155)

I.

Few readers of Conrad can have failed to notice the peculiarly intense depiction of light and dark in his work. Indeed, the phenomenon has prompted one critic to declare: 'I doubt whether there is any writer in the English language employing so often words like *sombre…, gloomy, dark, ghosts and shades, shadows*' (Morf 195, his emphases). In places, it is true, Conrad's fondness for this trope degenerates into those stylistic excesses of circumlocution and pastiche that the *Daily Chronicle* once condemned as 'surplusage' (Sherry 64): 'tenebrous immensity' in *Lord Jim* (102); 'Cimmerian gloom' in *The Inheritors* (154); 'opaque, lightless patches' in 'The Secret Sharer' (*'Twixt Land and Sea* 133); and 'darkling shade' in *Victory* (301). For the most part, however, Conrad's evocations of light and shadow are pleasingly effective, as when the narrator of 'The End of the Tether' relates how 'the smoke pouring backwards from the funnel eddied down behind the ship, spread a thin dusky veil over the sombre water' (Y 257). At their best, they have an evocative force that has rarely been equalled in the language. Thus Marlow recalls the leave-taking of Kurtz's mistress in *Heart of Darkness*: 'Suddenly she opened her bared arms and threw them up rigid above her head, as though in an uncontrollable desire to touch the sky, and at the same time the swift shadows darted out on the earth, swept around on the river, gathering the steamer into a shadowy embrace' (Y 136).

Friends and contemporaries were also sensible of an authorial preoccupation that found expression in the titles of such well-known works as *Heart of Darkness* and *The Shadow-Line*. In an important early appraisal of Conrad's writing Edward Garnett paid tribute to 'this artist's living world of men and shadows,' and the motif was to become a favourite among reviewers (Sherry 106). 'You see Verloc seeing the shadow of the arm with the clenched hand holding the carving-knife,' explained the London *Star* approvingly in its otherwise hostile review of *The Secret Agent* (Sherry 198). The *New Statesman* declared that the protagonists of *The Rover* 'seem to fall together through the crust of ordinary experience into a shadowy grander world' (Sherry 361). And Conrad's good friend Arthur Marwood even went so far as to characterize *Victory* as a study of 'dancing shadows' (*CL5* 465). In turn, Conrad's detailed renderings of the play of shadows inspired some of the most effective graphic interpretations of his work, including Maurice Greiffenhagen's pointillist treatment of 'Typhoon' in *Pall Mall Magazine* and Thornton Oakley's Munch-like illustration of 'An Anarchist' in *Harper's Monthly*.[1] By the time Max Beerbohm published his witty parody of 'The Lagoon' in 1912, descriptions of shadow had become instantly recognizable elements of the Conradian style: 'The roofs of the congested trees, writhing in some kind of agony private and eternal, made tenebrous and shifty silhouettes against the sky, like shapes cut out of black paper by a maniac who pushes them with his thumb this way and that, irritably, on a concave surface of blue steel' (Beerbohm 129).[2]

In the late 1940s F. R. Leavis argued that passages such as the grove of death in *Heart of Darkness* – a 'gloomy circle of some Inferno' whose moribund 'black shadows' lie motionless in a 'greenish gloom' (Y 66) – evinced Conrad's commitment to an 'art of vivid essential record' that, when successful, attained a numinous quality (204). Since then, Conrad's shadows have continued to fascinate students of his work, standing as a kind of visual corollary to the ideological ambiguities that characterize his representation of colonialism, feminism and revolution. In his influential survey *Joseph Conrad: Achievement and Decline* (1957), Thomas Moser proposed that the interplay between light and dark in *The Nigger of the 'Narcissus'* and *Heart of Darkness* be understood as a dialectical allegory of truth and falsehood (47). This line of argument was developed further by Albert J. Guerard in *Conrad the Novelist* (1958), whose analysis of the novella's 'night journey into the unconscious' interpreted darkness and shadow as giving symbolic expression to primal psychological fears, above all, 'a radical fear of

---

[1] See *Pall Mall Magazine* 26.105 (January 1902), 95, and *Harper's Monthly Magazine* (European edition) 113.675 (August 1906), 406.

[2] Compare Conrad's original: 'In that fleeting and powerful disturbance of his being the earth enfolded in the starlight peace became a shadowy country of inhuman strife, a battle-field of phantoms terrible and charming, august or ignoble, struggling ardently for the possession of our helpless hearts.' (TU 193–4).

death, that other darkness' (39, 47). Subsequent commentators would present *Heart of Darkness* as a reworking of classical or Judeo-Christian myths in which the lightless world of the Congo Free State constitutes a modern equivalent to the chthonian realms of antiquity and the Valley of the Shadow of Death in Psalm 23.[3]

More recently, Conrad's lexicon of shadows has figured in scholarly discussions of topics as varied as the Victorian discourse on race, metropolitan topography, scientific theories of entropy, and painterly techniques of Impressionism and *chiaroscuro*.[4] Richard J. Hand has identified Conrad's debt to the spectacular effects of Grand-Guignol theatre in *Laughing Anne*, the stage version of a tale whose hero is introduced as languishing under a 'spiritual shadow' (WT 171).[5] The abrupt stage direction '*Dusk falls,*' notes Hand, 'was indeed a stylized moment, but like Conrad's startling descriptions of shadow and light ... seemed to acquire an Expressionistic quality in performance' (Hand 2001a, 111). The writer's fascination with the special properties of light has also been discussed in relation to contemporary developments in visual technology, notably X-rays and projected motion photography.[6] Even so, and despite a resurgence of interest in the performative aspects of his writing, Conrad's obsession with shadows has not yet been considered in terms of the possible influence of the performing arts and, above all, the popular practice known variously as shadowgraphy, shadow theatre, shadow-play, *ombres chinoises*, or Chinese shadows.

---

[3] See, for example: Ian Watt, 'Impressionism and Symbolism in *Heart of Darkness,*' in *Joseph Conrad: A Commemoration*, ed. Norman Sherry (London: Macmillan, 1976), 37–53 especially 45–6; and the essays by Jerome Thale, Lillian Feder, and Robert O. Evans in *The Art of Joseph Conrad: A Critical Symposium*, ed. R. W. Stallman (Athens: Ohio University Press, 1982).

[4] See Patrick Brantlinger, *Rule of Darkness: British Literature and Imperialism, 1830–1914* (Ithaca: Cornell University Press, 1988), 262–3; Hugh Epstein, 'A Pier-Glass in the Cavern: The Construction of London in *The Secret Agent,*' in *Conrad's Cities: Essays for Hans van Marle*, ed. Gene M. Moore (Amsterdam: Rodopi, 1992), 175–96; Cedric Watts, *Preface to Conrad*, 83–5; John G. Peters, *Conrad and Impressionism* (Cambridge: Cambridge University Press, 2001), 30–31.

[5] See Hand 2002, especially 50–52. On the lighting effects used in Grand-Guignol, see Hand and Michael Wilson, 60–64.

[6] See Jeremy Hawthorn, 'Optical Toys and X-ray Machines: Seeing and Believing in *Lord Jim,*' in *Lord Jim de Joseph Conrad,* ed. Nathalie Martinière (Nantes: Editions du Temps, 2003), 74–94; Martine Hennard Dutheil de la Rochère, 'Conrad's Anatomy of Empire in *Heart of Darkness:* Body Politics and The Hollow Men of Empire,' *Conradiana* 36.3 (2004): 185–205. See also Sema Postacioglu-Banon, 29–44, and Gene M. Moore, ed. *Conrad on Film* (Cambridge: Cambridge University Press, 1997).

II.

The art of manipulating shadows by hand dates back thousands of years. Widely recognized as an integral part of the cultural heritage of many societies, its most important examples include the *Wayang* shadow theatre of Java, the *Utsushi-e* theatre of Japan, and the *Karagöz* and *Karaghiozis* puppet theatres of Turkey and Greece. It says much for the importance of this ancient mode of entertainment that shadowgraphy supplies the structuring conceit of one of the most influential descriptions of human consciousness in Western philosophy: the allegory of the cave in Book VII of Plato's *Republic*.

Although we have no way of knowing where Conrad saw shadowgraphs for the first time, he would have had plenty of opportunities to attend shadow shows during the twenty-five years he spent travelling the world. Even after his retirement from the sea, the shadow theatre was never far away. On any of his several visits to Paris, for example, he could have spent an evening among the avant-garde artists who flocked to Henri Rivière's Théâtre des Ombres in the Chat Noir cabaret in Montmartre. Opened in 1881, this highly sophisticated shadow theatre staged numerous shorter and longer plays using teams of puppeteers, powerfully lit screens, lavishly painted backdrops, colour lighting, and a battery of special effects. When the Théâtre des Ombres closed in 1897, a host of imitators rushed to capitalize upon the medium's renewed popularity. Thus Olive Cook evokes the richness of Parisian shadow theatre at the turn of the twentieth century:

> Among these were the Boîte à Musique; the Conservatoire Montmartre, where Alfred de Musset's *Ballade à la Lune* was made into a shadow play; Le Théâtre Antoine, where Rivière's *Wandering Jew* was performed; Le Théâtre des Mathurins, where Lucine Metivet wrote the poems and cut the shadows for two entertaining pieces, *La Belle au Bois Dormant* and *Aladin*; and Les Quatz'arts, which most nearly resembled Le Chat Noir in character, reviving the most successful of Henri Rivière's shadow shows, including *La Marche à L'Étoile* and *L'Enfant Prodigue*, and enlarging the repertoire after the turn of the century with several new pieces, among them Steinlein's *Une Page d'Amour*, *La Marche des Députés* by Dominique Bonnaud and Numa Blès, and an aquatic fantasy by Edmond Lempereur called *Le Serpent du Mer* and *La Chevauchée des Satyres* with verse by Gaston Pollonais and shades by Brunner. In 1904 Dominique Bonnaud and Numa Blès opened a new shadow theatre known as La Lune Rousse, which survived until the outbreak of the First World War in 1914 (77).

We are, perhaps, hearing an echo of the exquisite articulated metal and paper silhouettes of shadow shows such as these when, in the opening scene of *The Nigger of the 'Narcissus,'* Conrad describes how 'in the illuminated doorways, silhouettes of moving men appeared for a moment, very black, without relief, like figures cut out of sheet tin' (3).[7]

In our own era the shadow show has survived as a domestic entertainment for children in which the performer uses either his hands or paper cutouts to create profiles of animals or human heads that emulate, usually in a comically distorted fashion, the natural shadows cast by these subjects ('Whether it was the droop of his head, play of light, or some other subtle cause his nose seemed to have grown perceptibly longer,' observes Conrad's narrator in *The Arrow of Gold* [260]). Despite its relative simplicity, this version of shadowgraphy enjoyed widespread popularity at the end of the nineteenth century. 'Shadow plays offer a wide and varied field for entertaining children as well as older people,' declared *Harper's Bazar* in 1899. 'With very little preparation and practice a good result may be obtained, and, on the other hand, an elaborate plan can be carried out with little trouble and expense' (Anon 'Shadow Plays' 323). In addition to providing 'innocent amusement for the Home Circle,' as one of the many handbooks of these years promised, shadowgraphy featured regularly in late-Victorian music halls where it shared the billing with other illusion acts by professional prestidigitators (Figure 1).[8]

But even when practised by amateurs shadowgraphy was often technically and narratively ambitious. A contributor named L. Stanley Tree related to readers of *Pearson's Magazine* in April 1897 how his father had built a special, life-sized stage for performing multi-scene shadow plays of which, explained Tree, he was 'at once the manager, the scene-shifter, the decorator, the engineer, and even in most instances the author' (480). Contemporary shadowgraphers did not stop at explaining how to create standard illusions such as 'Girl with the Long Nose' but encouraged novices to develop longer narrative sequences, in the words of one 1903 how-to guide, 'as if the screen were a stage and the entertainment a variety show': 'The ingenious performer cannot only produce the heads as faithfully as if real shadows cast by human beings, but make them appear to live and act

---

[7] For more detail on Henri Rivière's shadow theatre at Le Chat Noir, including illustrations, see Steven Moore Whiting, 'Music on Montmartre,' in *The Spirit of Montmartre: Cabarets, Humor, and the Avant-Garde, 1875-1905*, eds. Phillip Dennis Cate and Mary Shaw (New Brunswick, NJ: Jane Voorhees Zimmerli Art Museum, 1996), 159–98, especially 184–8; Mariel Oberthür, ed., *Le Chat Noir, 1881–1897* (Paris: Editions de la Réunion des musées nationaux, 1992), 40–55; and Armond Fields, *Le Chat Noir: A Montmartre Cabaret and Its Artists in Turn-of-the-Century Paris* (Santa Barbara: Santa Barbara Museum of Art, 1993), 31–6. The relationship between modernism and popular performance arts such as puppetry and shadowgraphy is surveyed in John Bell, 'Puppets, Masks, and Performing Objects at the End of the Century,' *Drama Review* 43.3 (1999): 15–27. See also C. W. Ceram, *Archaeology of the Cinema*, trans. Richard Winston (London: Thames & Hudson), 1965, 47–80.

[8] J. S. Ogilvie, n.p. See also R. D. Chater ('Hercat'), *Chapeaugraphy, Shadowgraphy and Paper-Folding*, London: Dean, 1909, and Winifred H. Mills and Louise M. Dunn, *Marionettes, Masks, and Shadows* (Garden City: Doubleday & Company, 1947), 205–37.

little comedies ...' (Anon 'Silhouette' 41).[9] Popular magazines such as the *Boy's Own Paper* (a journal we know Conrad to have read) supplied amateur shadow-artists with tips on how to reproduce at home the impressive effects achieved by public performers with sophisticated mannequins, stage properties and relays of oxyhydrogen or acetylene gas lamps.[10]

That Conrad should have been drawn to contemporary shadow theatre fits well with what can be inferred of his interest in other visual entertainments such as moving panoramas, dissolving magic lantern views, and waxwork tableaux.[11] His love of scripting and performing in toy theatres was recalled many years later by a childhood friend, and his fiction contains references to entertainments as geographically diverse as Chinese theatres ('Falk'), French carnivals (*The Arrow of Gold*), Polish fairgrounds ('Amy Foster'), and English Punch and Judy shows (*Lord Jim, The Nigger of the 'Narcissus,' The Shadow-Line*), as well as stage hypnotism and blackface minstrelsy (*Chance*) (Dyboski 139). A stanza from the French nursery rhyme 'Les petites marionnettes' provided him with the epigraph for his short story collection *A Set of Six*, and the movements of his fictional protagonists are likened to the stiff gestures of marionettes in 'The Return' and *The Arrow of Gold* as well as in his embellished memoir of the Carlist wars: 'The whole Royalist gang ... appeared to me clear-cut and very small, with affected voices and stiff gestures, like a procession of rigid marionettes upon a toy stage' (*Mirror of the Sea* 176). Indeed, Owen Knowles and Gene Moore have suggested that marionettes held a particular appeal for Conrad as a creative artist by virtue of being 'rigorously controlled creatures who respond to the manipulator's guiding hand' (2000, 367). As he declared to R. B. Cunninghame Graham:

> I love a marionette show. Marionettes are beautiful – especially those of the old kind with wires, thick as my little finger, coming out of the top of the head. Their impassibility in love in crime, in mirth, in sorrow – is heroic, superhuman, fascinating. Their rigid violence when they fall upon one another to embrace or to fight is simply a joy to behold. I never listen to the text mouthed somewhere out of sight by invisible men who are here to day and rotten tomorrow. I love the marionettes that are without life, that come so near to being immortal! (*CL1* 419)

The shadow play is, in fact, invoked explicitly at several points in Conrad's fiction. In *Almayer's Folly*, the union of the lovers Dain Maroola and Nina Almayer

---

[9] See also Tony Denier, *The Great Secret of Shadow Pantomimes; or Harlequin in the Shades. How to Get them Up and How to Act Them* (New York: Duck & Fitzgerald, 1868).

[10] See, for example, 'Shadowgraphs: How to Work Them, by a Drawing-Room Showman,' in *Boy's Own Paper* XX/988/12 (18 December 1897), 190–91, and *Boy's Own Paper* XX/991/15 (8 January 1898), 236–8. Conrad's surreptitious reading of the *B.O.P.* is recorded in John Conrad, 32.

[11] See Donovan 2005, 15–62.

is conveyed metonymically through the prospect of '[t]heir forms melt[ing] in the play of light and shadow at the foot of the big trees' (AF 173), whilst the death of Yankoo Gorall prompts the narrator of 'Amy Foster' to reflect that 'his memory seems to have vanished from [Amy's] dull brain as a shadow passes away upon a white screen' (T 142). The inconsequentiality of Geoffrey Renouard and Felicia Moorsom in 'The Planter of Malata' is underscored by a description of how 'restless myriads of sea-birds rolled and unrolled dark ribbons on the sky, gathered in clouds, soared and stooped like a play of shadows, for they were too far for them to hear their cries' (WT 72–3). In *Victory*, too, Conrad offers shadow theatre as a metaphor of the imperial gaze: 'Both these white men [Schomberg and Ricardo] looked on native life as a mere play of shadows. A play of shadows the dominant race could walk through unaffected and disregarded in the pursuit of its incomprehensible aims and needs' (V 167). And the technique of using black paper to create silhouettes is alluded to at several points in *Nostromo* ('The jagged sierra stood out flat and opaque, as if cut out of paper' [467]), *The Shadow-Line* ('I saw the land profiled flatly as if cut out of black paper' [77]), and *The Arrow of Gold* ('Therese's form appeared flat, without detail, as if cut out of black paper' [154]).

Shadowgraphy was entering a period of rapid transition as Conrad embarked upon his writing career. Despite the shadow theatre's obvious affinities with cinema – Maxim Gorky famously described the silent Lumière feature 'A Street in Paris' as transporting spectators to 'the kingdom of the shadows' – the arrival of projected moving photography marked the beginning of a fatal decline in popularity for the older entertainment.[12] The trend was encapsulated by the pre-eminent hand shadow puppeteer Felicien Trewey's decision to postpone his retirement in the mid-1890s in order to became an exhibitor of the new medium of 'electric shadows'.[13] Shadowgraphy's steady retreat from the sphere of professional performance to that of mere parlour amusement was emblematic of a more general supplanting of traditional visual entertainments by the new communication technologies of the early twentieth century, notably cinema and radio. By the time Conrad's last novel *Suspense* concluded its posthumous serialization in *Hutchinson's Magazine* in August 1925, a cinema advertisement on the facing page was asking readers: 'Have you heard of the tele-vision-scope, the wonderful invention whereby you

---

[12] Reprinted in Colin Harding and Simon Popple, eds., *In the Kingdom of the Shadows: A Companion to Early Cinema* (London: Cygnus Arts, 1996). 5–6, 5.

[13] '[Trewey] became most famous for his virtuosity as *ombromane* or shadowgraphist, telling witty and charming stories while his hands, working in the beam of a magic lantern and manipulating small props, created spell-binding dramas on a screen. He could define a number of characters in vivid detail, returning with precision to each as he led them through moods, actions, and dramatic conflicts' (Barnouw 53). See also Matthew Solomon, 'Twenty-five heads under one hat'.

can see the person to whom you are speaking, even though he or she be hundreds of miles away? Picture the limitless opportunities of such an invention.'[14]

A manual craft that was becoming obsolete as an indirect consequence of advances in technology, shadowgraphy would also have appealed to Conrad by virtue of its role in the evolution of the Victorian magic show. During the professionalization of stage illusion as a theatrical performance in the last decades of the nineteenth century, the shadow show had served both as an inspiration and as an act in its own right. Charles Morritt's 'Afternoon Entertainment,' a matinee billing that opened at London's Empire Theatre in 1893, included hand shadows on its programme of music, sleight of hand, mind reading, and stage illusions, and in the early 1900s Theo Bamberg took his celebrated 'Hand Shadow' act on a tour of the United States with the star magician Harry Kellar (Steinmeyer 123, 212). As Jim Steinmeyer notes, late-nineteenth-century magicians were well aware that their charm derived as much from their imaginative creativity and showmanship as from the technical ingenuity of their illusions, and they saw themselves as competing with the spectacular effects that now accompanied dramatic productions of works such as *Ben-Hur* and *The Tempest* (183–4). As such, late-Victorian shadowgraphy and stage illusionism offer an unexpected parallel with literary production. Increasingly, magicians found themselves called upon to structure their acts around narratives, what Steinmeyer calls 'little work[s] of theatre' (94). As one celebrated creator of theatrical illusions explained in his memoirs: 'I regard a conjurer as a man who can hold the attention of his audience by telling them the most impossible fairy tales, and by persuading them into believing that those stories are true by illustrating them with his hands, or with any objects that may be suitable for the purpose' (quoted in Steinmeyer 93).

Notwithstanding his feigned ignorance of such performances – 'there must be magicians in London' he speculated parenthetically in *A Personal Record* (68) – Conrad was an enthusiastic spectator at magic shows. John Conrad, who was taken regularly to 'Maskelyne's Home of Mystery' in London in the 1910s, recalled his father laughing and clapping in delight as the legendary John Nevil Maskelyne (1839-1917) pretended to find a string of sausages in the boy's sailor suit (103).[15] Maskelyne had risen to fame in the 1870s by demonstrating that magicians could simulate the fraudulent 'summoning' of the dead by spiritualists, and Conrad's own implacable hostility to spiritualism, which serves as a target of his satire on several occasions, can only have strengthened his admiration for the professional magician's integrity and craftsmanship.[16] Echoes of Maskelyne's achievements can be heard in *The Arrow of Gold* when Dominic Cervoni is likened to 'a magician

---

[14] 'Films You Must Not Miss' (advertisement), *Hutchinson's Magazine* XIV (August 1925), 199.

[15] See also *CL*5 518. Presumably John Conrad's identification of the performer as 'Jasper Maskelyne' is a slip since John Nevil Maskelyne's son Jasper was only born in 1902.

[16] See Donovan, 'Pleasant Spectres and Malformed Shades'.

at the end of a successful incantation that had called out a shadow and a voice from the immense space of the sea' (128), and in *Chance* when Marlow describes his own memory as 'a mausoleum of proper names ... awaiting the magic touch – and not very prompt in arising when called' (C 69). Late in life, Conrad praised Sidney Colvin for his masterly evocation of the 'shades' of the past, declaring affectionately: 'You are the most quietly effective of magicians' (*CL6* 447).

Another performer with whose work Conrad would have been acquainted was David Devant (1868–1941), a gifted young magician who was to become even more famous than Maskelyne after the two men joined forces in 1905. A reference in *Chance* to 'that "vanishing girl" trick' (C 51) alludes specifically to 'The Vanishing Lady,' an illusion originally devised by Joseph DeKolta which became synonymous with Devant's name in the decade before World War One (See Steinmeyer, 112, 192–3). And Conrad's quip in the introduction to *Notes on Life and Letters*, an essay collection he deprecatingly called a 'one-man show' (vi), to the effect that the editors of various journals had 'made me perform mainly by kindness' (vi), recalls the slogan of Devant's own one-man show, 'ALL DONE BY KINDNESS,' which had been popularized by John Hassall's classic poster of 1910.[17] Interestingly, Devant had begun his career in the early 1890s by advertising himself as a 'Royal Magician and Shadowgraphist' before emerging as a pioneer of modern magic exclusively. An illusionist who strove to minimize the artificiality and staginess of his act, Devant developed a performance style that became synonymous with grace and imagination. Such was the beauty of his most celebrated illusion, 'The Mascot Moth,' that Edith Nesbit, author of *The Railway Children*, was inspired to make it the centrepiece of a specially-written play, *The Magician's Heart* (1912). In 1905 Devant even produced an elaborate magical science-fiction fantasy titled 'The Coming Race,' which drew upon a novel of the same name by Bulwer-Lytton (Fisher 120–23). In their dazzling use of manual dexterity, dramatic suspense and the play of light to raise the illusionist's craft to new heights, Maskelyne and Devant triumphantly demonstrated the possibility of appealing to an audience's imagination in ways that transcended what Conrad and others saw as the banal verisimilitude of motion photography.[18]

III.

Conrad's marked sensitivity to the visual delights afforded by shadows is evident from his private writings. Thanking John and Ada Galsworthy for their gift of a wrought copper lantern, he related the enjoyment that his family had derived from hanging it in different places. 'The dining room won't do because of the heavy wheelspokes shadows on the walls with a great hub of shade resting on the table,'

---

[17] The poster is reproduced in John Fisher, *Paul Daniels and the Story of Magic*, 132–3.
[18] See Donovan 2003.

he explained. 'The effect is romantically sinister' (*CL3* 512). But shadows were clearly far more than mere ornaments for Conrad. As the frequent references to shadows in his letters indicate, they occupied a central place in his view of the world, a realm he once wearily described to R. B. Cunninghame Graham as a 'jumble of shadows' (*CL2* 155). Thus he told William Rothenstein in 1921 of his desire to collaborate with the painter John Everett on an illustrated edition of *The Mirror of the Sea*. Everett's meticulous paintings of sailing ships 'might be considered studies of sail shadows,' explained Conrad: '[T]hey appeal to me because I have been always alive to the shadow-effects of the sails' (*CL7* 372).

There is, in turn, a strangely overdetermined quality to the shadows of Conrad's novels and short stories. More than just visual traces of material objects, they are often animated by a symbolic force of their own. When Captain Whalley in 'The End of the Tether' walks alone in the darkness, wrestling with despair and the prospect of death, we are told that 'all the time a shadow marched with him, slanting on his left hand – which in the East is a presage of evil' (Y 215). Somewhere between epiphany, theatrical illumination, and Rorschach image, the 'monstrous black shadow' cast by the villainous Ricardo in *Victory* and the anthropomorphized shadows of *Lord Jim*, which Marlow describes as 'possessed of gloomy consciousness' (172) and 'huddled together in corners' (183), operate as nothing less than autonomous agents in the drama.

Conrad's late novel *Chance*, several of whose key scenes take place at night, is particularly creative in its presentation of shadows and the uncanny, as when the hobnailed boots worn by a 'deathly white' porter are presented casting a shadow that is 'enormous and coffinlike' (26). For Marlow, there is something threatening about the feminist Zoe Fyne and her young wards, whom he evokes as a 'shadowy figure' and 'girl-friend shadow[s]' (47–8), and the reader easily detects the tone of disapproval in his repeated observation that John Fyne sees these implicit challenges to his own patriarchal authority as merely 'evanescent shadows' (49) and 'transient shadows' (60). When the sailor shows unwonted compassion towards the motherless Flora de Barral, it is by acknowledging that 'the shadow of the night [was] made more cruelly sombre for her by the very shadow of death' (207).

The complexity of Conrad's treatment of shadows in *Chance* is nicely illustrated by a scene in which the young sailor Charles Powell watches the Thames from the deck of the *Ferndale* in a moment of sublime revelation that apparently confounds the laws of optics: 'Wisps of mist floated like trails of luminous dust, and in the dazzling reflections of water and vapour, the shores had the murky, semi-transparent darkness of shadows cast mysteriously from below' (276). Since a river at mid-morning is no more than a reflector of light, the shoreline cannot, strictly speaking, be darkened by shadows cast, 'mysteriously' or otherwise, from below. Rather, Conrad is engaged in creating two distinct but related effects.

The first is to defamiliarize the river by making it wonderfully strange (literally inverted) in the mind's eye of the reader, a device that parallels Powell's own epiphanic glimpse of a feature he thought he knew well. Indeed, Conrad's work is replete with similarly counterintuitive moments. In *The Nigger of the 'Narcissus,'* his narrator describes the ship as 'seem[ing] to stand resplendent and still' (27–8) while the land recedes from view. In *Heart of Darkness*, Marlow observes two Belgian administrators who 'seemed to be tugging painfully uphill their two ridiculous shadows of unequal length, that trailed behind them slowly over the tall grass without bending a single blade' (Y 92). In 'The End of the Tether,' readers are presented with a conundrum in the ostensibly redundant information that 'periodically [Captain Whalley's] shadow leaped up intense by his side on the trunks of the trees, to lengthen itself, oblique and dim, far over the grass – repeating his stride' (Y 213). And in *Chance*, Marlow recalls how 'By a strange illusion the road appeared to run up against a lot of low stars at no very great distance, but as we advanced new stretches of whitey-brown ribbon seemed to come up from under the black ground' (55).

The second effect is to foreground the seemingly artificial quality of shadows. Just as the narrator of 'The End of the Tether' notes how '[t]he record of the visual world fell through [the serang helmsman's] eyes upon his unspeculating mind as on a sensitized plate through the lens of a camera' (Y 228), Conrad presents vision as embedded in specific viewing situations and technologies rather than as 'natural' apprehension by the visual sense. Even shadows cast from below or behind planar surfaces are depicted in accordance with this performative-spectatorial logic, as when Conrad invites readers of his memoir *The Mirror of the Sea* to visualize the augury of bad weather as 'a mysterious gloom, like the passage of a shadow above the firmament of gray clouds' (86) or the passing of time itself as a 'ceaseless rush of shadows and shades ... like the fantastic forms of clouds cast darkly upon the waters on a windy day' (194).

Any suggestion that the prominence of shadows in Conrad's work is merely a stylistic quirk is further contradicted by his own insistence upon the affinity between shadow and the space of literary creation. 'You know, my life is all stories now, something preoccupied and shadowy' (*CL1* 336), he wrote to Ted Sanderson in 1897, and he reiterated the association in a subsequent letter: 'One's will becomes the slave of hallucinations, responds only to shadowy impulses.... I shall soon come out of my land of mist peopled by shadows, and we shall meet again for another midnight communion – as though we too also had been ghosts, shadows' (*CL2* 205–6). Like D. H. Lawrence's blood-red sunrises and sunsets, Conrad invests light and dark with precise epistemological and aesthetic properties that supply a kind of fugal accompaniment to his narratives as a whole. Thus he describes the 'state of hallucination' in which Mrs Travers in *The Rescue* stands on the deck of the stranded yacht *Lightning* and gazes upon a nocturnal panorama:

> All was unmoving as if the dawn would never come, the stars would never fade, the sun would never rise any more; all was mute, still, dead – as if the shadow of the outer darkness, the shadow of the uninterrupted, of the everlasting night that fills the universe, the shadow of the night so profound and so vast that the blazing suns lost in it are only like sparks, like pin-points of fire, the restless

shadow that like a suspicion of an evil truth darkens everything upon the earth on its passage, had enveloped her, had stood arrested as if to remain with her forever. (151)

With its implicit deconstruction of the imperial metaphors of civilizing light and barbaric darkness, *Heart of Darkness* supplies perhaps the most obvious illustration of this principle. After visiting the Company's Brussels headquarters 'in deep shadow' (Y 55), Marlow ascends the 'broad strip of shadow' (Y 108) that denotes the Congo river, passing 'black shadows of disease and starvation' (Y 66) before finally meeting 'that Shadow' (Y 143), the mysterious Kurtz, whom he describes as a 'shadow [that] looked satiated and calm, as though for the moment it had had its fill of all the emotions' (Y 134–5). The fact that Kurtz can only be apprehended indirectly and in mediated fashion – by reputation, echo and shadows possessed of 'gorgeous eloquence' (Y 155) – epitomizes the uncertainty that runs through every human relationship in the novella. With darkness falling around him, Marlow tells his tale of colonial greed and exploitation to three ex-sailors who have somehow managed to raise themselves to the rank of 'Company Director,' 'Lawyer,' and 'Accountant' (Y 45–6), a degree of social mobility that, as Conrad's ironic capitalizing of their professional titles seems to acknowledge, is remarkable if not actually suspicious. They are, moreover, clearly disturbed by Marlow's narrative. What private darknesses have these men crossed on their own journeys to bourgeois respectability? What shadows lie in their past? What other invisible bonds connect those temporally and spatially removed waterways that Marlow calls 'the dark places of the earth' (48)? Only the reader's imagination can supply the answers.

IV

That Conrad knew the shadow theatre at first hand is not in doubt. Walter Tittle recalled his brisk dismissal of moving pictures in 1922:

> 'They are absolutely the lowest form of amusement. I hate them!' [Conrad] said, with quite a considerable show of heat. 'They are stupid, and can never be of real value. The cinema is not a great medium. It merely affords entertainment for people who enjoy sitting with thought utterly suspended and watching a changing pattern flickering before their eyes. *Shadowgraphs in pantomime are much better*.' (160, emphasis added)

The juxtaposition is a striking one. By 1922 not only had shadowgraphy been eclipsed by cinema but innovative directors such as D. W. Griffith, Cecil B. DeMille and Robert Flaherty had shown the new medium to be capable of complex narrative forms, confirming in the process its status as a major art form in its own right. The release of Robert Wiene's Expressionist masterpiece *The Cabinet of*

Dr. Caligari (1920) had brought the ideogrammatic power of nineteenth-century shadow-theatre to the cinema screen, and shadowgraphy itself was to provide both the subject matter for and a major stylistic influence upon Arthur Robison's Expressionist fantasy *Warning Shadows* (*Schatten*, 1923).

Conrad's stated preference for 'shadowgraphs in pantomime' over cinema is revealing in other ways, too. In addition to confirming his acquaintance with a wide range of visual entertainments, it attests to his willingness to rank them according to his own aesthetic criteria. His comment suggests that he saw this precinematic entertainment as engaging audiences intellectually in ways that motion photography, for all its vaunted fidelity to nature, could not. In an echo of his complaint to the *Boston Evening Telegraph* that 'moving-pictures ... don't show, except in a superficial way, what the characters are thinking,' Conrad implies that true representational 'depth' can only be realized in the viewer's imagination and not through the technological perfecting of some apparatus (Smith 186). As Conrad saw it, the arresting verisimilitude of early cinema effectively denied this principle by encouraging viewers to equate projected shadows with the thing itself. In order to appreciate his own very different view of the representational possibilities that shadows made available to the visual imagination, we need look no further than his extraordinary description of Alvan Hervey, the abandoned husband of 'The Return,' as he falls, figuratively and literally, into shadow:

> He watched the rising tide of impenetrable gloom with impatience, as if anxious for the coming of a darkness black enough to conceal a shameful surrender. It came nearer. The cluster of lights went out. The girl ascended facing him. Behind her the shadow of a colossal woman danced lightly on the wall. He held his breath while she passed by, noiseless and with heavy eyelids. And on her track the flowing tide of a tenebrous sea filled the house, seemed to swirl about his feet, and rising unchecked, closed silently above his head. (TU 182)

In 1894, the Swedish playwright August Strindberg was so impressed by a visit to Henri Rivière's Théâtre d'Ombres in Paris that he considered establishing a shadow theatre of his own (Bergman 59).[19] Although the project eventually came to nothing, Strindberg remained interested enough in the medium to include '*Shapes and shadows*' among the dramatis personae of his mystery play *Advent* (1900) and to script an extended shadowgraph sequence for one of its central scenes.[20]

---

[19] I am indebted to Vreni Hockenjos for this reference.

[20] '*A procession of shadows issues from the Mausoleum, with a distance of five or six paces between every two; they pass noiselessly by: Death, with a sickle and hourglass; the White Lady, fair, tall and slim, wearing a ring on her finger set with a brilliant emerald; the Goldsmith, with the silver-gilt monstrance; the Beheaded Sailor with his head in his hand; the Auctioneer, with hammer and notebook; the Chimney-sweep, with cord, scraper and brush; the Fool bearing his cap with donkey's ears and bells on a pole, with the inscription "the cap of victory"; the Land-surveyor, with plank and tripod; the Judge,*

In Dublin, meanwhile, an adolescent James Joyce was collecting his first literary sketches under the title *Silhouettes*, at least one of which comprised a domestic melodrama seen from the point of view of a shadow-theatre spectator.[21] To be sure, it seems unlikely that Conrad ever considered appropriating the shadow-play as a model or frame for his art in quite so explicit a fashion. And yet, as we have seen in a variety of contexts, his stated affection for marionettes and his preference for 'shadowgraphs in pantomime' over cinema did leave their mark upon his writing, not least in the curiously stylized gestures of his protagonists and the peculiar insistence of his narratives upon the play of light and dark. Like Giorgio di Chirico and Salvador Dalí, in whose paintings shadows serve as visual metaphors of the unconscious, the censored and the unknown, Conrad's relentless pursuit of shadows to the very limits of the communicable reminds us of the resourcefulness of modernist artists in their self-appointed task, as T. S. Eliot memorably defined it, 'to digest and express new objects, new groups of objects, new feelings, new aspects' (327).

---

exactly resembling the Lagman, and dressed like him, with a rope round his neck; his lifted right hand has the index finger missing. As the procession enters, it grows dark; and the stage is empty while it proceeds' (Strindberg 1921, 31–2). Other contemporary instances of literary treatment of shadowgraphs include Ruth McEnery Stuart and Albert Bigelow Paine, *Gobolinks; or, Shadow-Pictures for Young and Old* (New York: Century, 1896), and Edward Shanks, *The Shadowgraph and Other Poems* (London: Collins, 1925).

[21] '*Silhouettes*, like the first three stories of *Dubliners*, was written in the first person singular, and described a row of mean little houses along which the narrator passes after nightfall. His attention is attracted by two figures in violent agitation on a lowered window-blind illuminated from within, the burly figure of a man, staggering and threatening with upraised fist, and the smaller sharp-faced figure of a nagging woman. A blow is struck and the light goes out. The narrator waits to see if anything happens afterwards. Yes, the window-blind is illuminated again dimly, by a candle no doubt, and the woman's sharp profile appears accompanied by two small heads, just above the window-ledge, of children wakened by the noise. The woman's finger is pointed in warning. She is saying, "Don't waken Pa"' (Joyce 90).

Chapter 7
Comedy and Romance:
A New Look at Shakespeare and Conrad

Katherine Isobel Baxter

In an interview on the first night of the staging of *The Secret Agent* at The Ambassadors Theatre, Conrad explained how, 'I had read the whole of Shakespeare by 1880, and I re-read him in the following years' (Mégroz 40–41). Indeed Conrad cites Shakespeare as one of his first memorable experiences of English Literature, in *A Personal Record*:

> That afternoon, instead of going out to play in the large yard which we shared with our landlord, I had lingered in the room in which my father generally wrote. What emboldened me to clamber into his chair I am sure I don't know, but a couple of hours afterwards he discovered me kneeling in it with my elbows on the table and my head held in both hands over the MS. of loose pages. I was greatly confused, expecting to get into trouble. He stood in the doorway looking at me with some surprise, but the only thing he said after a moment of silence was:
> 'Read the page aloud.'
> ... If I do not remember where, how and when I learned to read, I am not likely to forget the process of being trained in the art of reading aloud. My poor father, an admirable reader himself, was the most exacting of masters. I reflect proudly that I must have read that page of 'Two Gentlemen of Verona' tolerably well at the age of eight. (PR 71–2)

It is hardly surprising that of the various topics that fall under the heading, 'Conrad and the Performing Arts,' Conrad and Shakespeare has received more attention than most. It is addressed in the various biographies, and Adam Gillon's *Conrad and Shakespeare; and Other Essays* devotes the majority of its pages to the topic.[1]

The first section of this essay will survey those Shakespearian elements that critics and biographers have noted already as particularly influential in Conrad's work. These are, by and large, drawn from the tragedies, with the exception of *The Tempest*. The second section will consider the ways in which Conrad's reception of Shakespeare was mediated through his father, Apollo Korzeniowski's, works,

---

[1] See Karl 1979; Baines 1986; Batchelor 1994.

and how that mediation invites an interpretative shift of focus from the tragedies to the comedies.

Adam Gillon's work on the influence of Shakespeare on Conrad is certainly the most notable in the field for its extent and detail. His first article on the subject, in what became a series of four, appeared in the first number of *Conradiana* in 1968. Gillon's articles provide the reader with extensive evidence of Conrad's borrowings from Shakespeare predominantly at the verbal level but also at the level of motif. Gillon opens his first article by noting that 'the fairly recent recognition of Conrad as an important tragic novelist has opened a Pandora's box of critical investigations of influences upon Conrad' (19). Indeed prior to Gillon's own work two articles had appeared in *Notes and Queries* during the 1950s, noting specific allusions and commenting on their implications;[2] and in the 1960s Thomas Schultheiss's article, 'Lord Hamlet and Lord Jim' appeared, as well as two illuminating articles on *The Tempest* and *Victory*, to which we shall return.[3] Gillon, writing against this background of interest, comments that 'the quest for analogies ... can become rather pedantic unless the textual evidence ... reveals a clear affinity ... or unless it sheds more light on the meaning of Conrad's own writing' (19). Gillon does not entirely avoid the pedantry he notes in others, nor are all his examples of allusion convincing, yet his exposition of these allusions is convincing enough, and the sheer extent of his examples indicates the critical importance of Shakespeare's presence in Conrad's oeuvre.

Prior to Gillon, Thomas Schultheiss's, 'Lord Hamlet and Lord Jim' presents one of the most commonly noted and strongly argued borrowings from Shakespeare in Conrad's work.[4] He is careful to point out early on that 'Jim ... has a thoroughly recognizable individuality of his own and ... is not simply Conrad's Hamlet' (101). And indeed a good deal of his argument focuses on thematic similarities, particularly notions of dreaming and illusion. Schultheiss pairs Stein's notion of the new born man as one who 'falls into a dream' (LJ 214) with Hamlet's various musings on dreams, in order to consider the extent of Stein's meaning. After this philosophical excursion Schultheiss ends by asking a series of rhetorical questions which in fact point up a good number of practical similarities between Hamlet and Jim, and finally wonders 'whether we may be able to find other manifestations of the plays of Shakespeare in the work of Conrad' (133).

Thomas Schultheiss's case is interestingly complicated by a study of Conrad's letters, which reveals various echoes of *Hamlet*, particularly in relation to himself. Thus, for example, Conrad writes to his Aunt, Marguerite Poradowska:

---

[2] Arthur Sherbo's 'Conrad's "Victory" and "Hamlet"' *Notes and Queries* 198 (1953): 492–3; and William B. Bache's '"Othello" and Conrad's "Chance,"' *Notes and Queries* 200 (1955): 478–9.

[3] Schultheiss; Lodge; Dilke.

[4] Gillon also argues this case at some length; see *Conrad and Shakespeare; and Other Essays* (New York: Astra Books 1976), 53–69.

You are laughing at your nephew in comparing him to the late Hamlet (who was, I believe, mad). Nevertheless, I allow myself to say that apart from his madness he was an altogether estimable person. Thus I am not offended by the comparison. I do not know where you found any signs of my contempt for mankind. (19 October 1892; *CL*1 118-19)

Some six years later he casts himself as Hamlet's father's ghost, when writing to Jane Cobden Unwin, 'some people ... are coming on purpose to have the felicity of beholding me in "my habit, as I live"' (22 February 1898; *CL*2 41–2; see *Hamlet*, III.iv.135). A third example appears in a letter to Edward Garnett in which he explains in some detail his father's literary work, apparently in response to a question from Garnett. At the end of this explanation Conrad says that 'I always intended to write something of the kind [as this letter to Garnett] for Borys, so as to save all this from the abyss a few years longer. And probably he wouldn't care. What's Hecuba to him or he to Hecuba' (20 January 1900; *CL*2 247; see *Hamlet*, II.ii.552). This comes after a vivid description of 'piles of MS. Dramas, verse, prose, burnt after his [Apollo Korseniowski's] death according to his last will'.

All three allusions appear during the period of Conrad's first forays into English letters, and all three are addressed to literary friends. In the first instance the role of Hamlet is given to Conrad, and therefore we cannot read much into this reference, other than that Conrad clearly distances himself from the characteristics for which Hamlet was particularly celebrated in late Victorian culture: his madness and his gloominess. The second two allusions are more revealing, and throw a light back on the first again.

Turning to Conrad's letter to Garnett first, we recall that the quote comes at the end of the very long second scene of the second act. Hamlet is left alone, by Rosencrantz, Guildenstern, Polonius and the players, wondering at the ability of the player to bring tears to his eyes when performing the speech of Priam's slaughter, witnessed by Priam's wife Hecuba. Hamlet rebukes himself for lacking the player's alacrity of emotion, when faced with the knowledge imparted by his father's ghost. The immediate implication of Conrad's quotation is that Borys will not be interested in the second-hand story of someone whom he does not even know: Borys's grandfather is to Borys as Hecuba is to the player, little more than a fiction. But the quotation turns back on Conrad himself, implying a sense of guilt that he like Hamlet is unable to respond with full emotion to the events of his own childhood. Indeed, if one follows this line of interpretation through completely the quotation actually implies that Borys might weep more than Conrad for the facts of Korseniowski's death. In writing to Garnett, Conrad does record these events, but for a literary friend rather than his family. Thus, in encoding and entrusting the memory of his father within a literary circle Conrad honours his father's literary role above his familial role, albeit awkwardly.

In his earlier comic description of himself as spectacle, Conrad's allusion recalls the incident in Gertrude's bedroom, in which Hamlet sees his father's ghost whilst his mother cannot. Gertrude's rejoinder to Hamlet's plea for her to see the ghost runs thus: 'This is the very coinage of your brain. / This bodiless creation ecstasy / Is very cunning in' (III.iv.137–9). Here the implication is that Conrad's audience will see whatever their fancy dreams up, and yet at the same time he will exist ghostlike behind these projections of his audience. Conrad presumably feels his audience will come to observe him as a writer newly burst forth on the literary scene, and in this respect he is his own father's ghost. Indeed, the authorial connection between Conrad and his father lurks behind these two allusions, in which Hamlet responds to the challenge of his father, and furthermore potentially underlies the allusion of Poradowska. Certainly it is notable that of the several Shakespearian allusions that Conrad uses self-reflexively in this early stage of his career those to *Hamlet* are most numerous. Moreover, it is possible to push the argument yet further, if a little tendentiously, and suggest that the very mode of self-reflexive allusion which Conrad uses from time to time in this period served as a model for the allusions that followed in *Lord Jim*. That is to say that Conrad's echoing of *Hamlet* in *Lord Jim* finds its initial development as a literary mode in Conrad's own self-fashioning references to *Hamlet*.

Looking beyond *Hamlet* and tragedy, *The Tempest* is probably the most cited of Shakespeare's plays for having a significant influence on Conrad's work. As early as 1902 an admirer of his work, Miss Capes, read allusions to the play into *Lord Jim*, allusions which Conrad denied: 'Your fancy is most kind but I fear it is a far cry from Prospero's Island to Patusan' (22 March 1902; *CL2* 384). Echoes of *The Tempest* are most commonly noted, as demonstrated by Miss Capes, in the romance elements of Conrad's novels, and in particular the exotic eastern elements. Prospero's Island, as a world elsewhere in which exiled and lost souls from the European world explore their own natures in relation to each other and the indigenous population, is an obvious template for Conrad's ambivalent presentation of the imperial romance. The growth in postcolonial readings of *The Tempest* further augments the apparent resemblances since the critical frameworks applied are often the same as those applied to Conrad's imperial romances. Furthermore, Miss Capes's comments indicate that in Conrad's lifetime *The Tempest* was read, at least by some, as relating to imperial romance narratives.

Of Conrad's novels *Victory* is that which is most commonly associated with *The Tempest*.[5] Jocelyn Baines's biography refers to Pedro as a 'Caliban-like creature' and notes that '*Victory* has several, presumably fortuitous, echoes of *The Tempest*' (475).

---

[5] Although Gillon asserts allusions to the play in *The Shadow-Line* (see *Conrad and Shakespeare* 46–51), Jeffrey Meyers asserts connections with *Heart of Darkness* (see 'Savagery and Civilization in *The Tempest*, *Robinson Crusoe*, and *Heart of Darkness*,' *Conradiana* 2.3 [1969–1970]: 171–9); and Arthur Sherbo draws useful parallels between *Victory* and *Hamlet* (see 'Conrad's "Victory" and "Hamlet"' *Notes and Queries* 198 [1953]: 492–3). It is worth noting here too that coincidentally the recurrence of *Hamlet* references in Conrad's later letters appear in relation to the staging of *Victory*; for Irving ran *Hamlet* earlier that year at the Savoy, and actors from the *Hamlet* production were later used at the Savoy in *Victory*.

His presumption of fortuity is queried by Karl, who comments that, 'it is not accidental that Conrad's interest in Shakespeare's play never appeared stronger than at this time [when he was writing *Victory*]' (1960, 247). Donald A. Dilke took up these hints to explore the similarities more closely. Dilke focuses on the abstract geography of Samburan, Sourabaya and Prospero's island. The argument he develops serves the purpose of later postcolonial approaches without itself adopting such an approach. Dilke argues that 'neither of these places has ... cultural identity ... the kind which Conrad ... gives, in *Nostromo*, to Sulaco. Samburan and Sourabaya are merely views; they can be seen but they cannot be felt' (95). Of Conrad's character's Dilke continues that they are:

> Outcasts not merely from one or another society but from history: the territory of the collective will to progress. Outside this territory Heyst and Lena, like Prospero and Miranda, test a fugitive atmosphere, the laws of cultural gravity tentatively suspended, familiar facts dissolved into fantasy. (96)

Dilke suggests that in such an environment, which he qualifies as essentially pastoral, moral and epistemological problems 'fuse and become one' (113). Dilke does not question the presentation of either island as fantastical, devoid of history and culture. His interest is in the European's behaviour, not in the challenge to their behaviour offered by the other inhabitants of the island. Moral and epistemological problems do not extend, in Dilke's argument, to these other inhabitants outside the Western history and culture from which Prospero and Miranda's, or Heyst and Lena's, problems apparently arise.

Lodge goes further than Dilke, identifying a responsive use of *The Tempest* in *Victory*, whereby Conrad ironises the original text in a characteristically modernist manner: 'The myth of Shakespeare's play asserts the victory of love and forgiveness over hate and revenge; Conrad's novel shows good triumphing over evil only through its own self-destruction and in the admission of its own weakness' (196). Lodge identifies specific borrowings of character in the novel, suggesting Wang echoes Ariel 'in his apparent ability to transcend the laws of physics,' and that Ricardo's relationship with Pedro recalls Prospero's with Caliban, displaying 'the same combination of threats, physical chastisement, accusations of ingratitude and assertions of the creature's unregenerate nature' (196). He notes also ironic echoes, such as the contrasting power and enervation which Prospero and Heyst gain, respectively, from their books (198).

Lodge argues that the modernist irony, which he identifies in Conrad's echoes of *The Tempest*, assists Conrad's creation of 'a drama of conflicting ideologies or value-systems,' in which these echoes 'help the novelist to magnify and universalize the significance of his characters and their actions, and direct the reader to the appropriate level of response' (199). Here, Lodge does present conflicts of ideology in the texts, yet these remain, for him as they did for Dilke, most important for the European protagonists. Although the other inhabitants of the island are acknowledged, their existence is understood in terms of the

Europeans' social structure: 'In the spiritual economy of *The Tempest*, Caliban is the least guilty, because the least rational ... A similar hierarchy is observable in *Victory*' (197).

John Batchelor, more recently, addresses with subtlety the interrelationship between the European and other island inhabitants. In much the same way that Lodge demonstrates Conrad's ironising of Shakespearian tragi-comedy into a comedy of the absurd, Batchelor demonstrates how Conrad's allusions blur the apparent distinctions between European 'civilisation' and the 'primitive other' (Lodge 198; Batchelor 145). Working from Frank Kermode's proposition that Caliban's name derives from 'Carib' and the related 'Cannibal,' Batchelor aligns first Pedro and then Ricardo with the figure of Caliban. He then recalls that Heyst himself mentions his own experience of cannibals, although without ever explaining how they came about:

> a lost episode – Heyst among the Cannibals – lingers in the hinterland of the reader's mind so that when we encounter Pedro and Ricardo, the opposition Heyst-versus-Caliban/Cannibal is one with which we feel familiar without being able to place it. (145)

This easing of racial alignments, that had seen Jones, Ricardo and Pedro simply as the Milanese castaways, and Heyst, however ironically, solely as Prospero, begins to acknowledge the potential for cultural slippage in both the play and the novel.

Batchelor's article is in part structured by his interpretation of where *Hamlet* and *Lord Jim*, *The Tempest* and *Victory* fall in their authors' oeuvres. Of *Hamlet* and *Lord Jim* he says that:

> Both are written at the ends of their respective centuries ... both take an existing form – revenge tragedy and the story of imperial adventure – and adapt it so drastically that the mould is broken and a new literary form is created ... In the careers of Shakespeare and Conrad these two early works are consciously innovative, while the two late works, *The Tempest* and *Victory*, occupy similarly parallel positions. (144)

Batchelor's reasoning for paralleling *The Tempest*, Shakespeare's final play and often read as his valediction to the stage, with *Victory*, which Conrad followed with four more novels published in his lifetime, is based on the historical context of *Victory*'s publication: a 'farewell to the world before the Great War' (144). Despite this reasoning, however, there is a danger in applying this parallelism of implying that Conrad's subsequent novels are somehow beyond the canon. This danger is reinforced by the thesis of 'achievement and decline' in Conrad's oeuvre, first put forward to Thomas Moser in 1957 and still influential today. Furthermore there is a presumption inherent in such an argument that this was in some way Conrad's final use of Shakespeare: that having worked his way chronologically through the plays in synchrony with his own novel writing Conrad put down Shakespeare and took up writing Haggardian romance.[6]

Whilst it is true that Shakespearean allusions are infrequent in later romances like *The Rescue* and *The Arrow of Gold*, this does not in itself indicate a setting aside of Shakespeare completely. Indeed, *The Rover* provides an interesting late example of Conrad's use of *The Tempest* in his work. In this novel, although Peyrol does not work magic his careful and secretive manipulation of events is worthy of Prospero. And like Prospero he is unwilling to give up, or acknowledge the limits of, his powers. He tests the valour of Réal and is unwilling to give up Arlette to this young suitor, as Prospero seems loath to give his daughter to Ferdinand.

Michel, who can execute 'an instantaneous sideways leap with all the precision of a wild animal,' is a less complaining Ariel in his silent devotion to Peyrol (Ro 184). Michel almost credits Peyrol with magic when Symons's 'bewitched corpse … [comes] on board flying through the air' (Ro 123), and later wonders at the power of Peyrol's command of a foreign language to calm the now revived and pugnacious Symons (Ro 128). When Peyrol gives Michel his 'last order' to 'let go the foresheet to help the tartane to fly into the wind's eye … Now go forward and fear nothing. Adieu' (Ro 266), we may recall Prospero's final command to Ariel, to provide 'auspicious gales' for the returning Milanese and 'then to the elements/Be free, and fare thou well!' (V.1.314–18).

The cripple provides a benign version of Caliban, for whilst his 'wretched little carcass,' 'a twisted scrap of humanity,' recalls Prospero's description of Caliban as 'a freckl'd whelp … not honour'd with/A human shape' (I.ii.283–4), and whilst Peyrol brings him into the tartane, as Prospero had once lodged Caliban in his own cell, there is no equivalent violation (Ro 93). Indeed whereas Miranda teaches Caliban her language and implicitly her culture, not only does the cripple teach Peyrol the recent savage history of the citoyens, but it is he who arranges the refloating of the tartane and the financial negotiations necessary to do so. Thus the apparent echoes of the Prospero-Caliban relationship are subverted, ignoring the romance trope that associates male disfigurement with evil intent.[7]

More generally we may note a further subversion of the imperial romance trope, for Conrad shows his hero, Peyrol, disoriented in his native land rather than in some exotic setting: 'an utter stranger in his native country the landing on which was perhaps the biggest adventure of his adventurous life' (Ro 13). Peyrol may resemble Prospero, but his activities are conducted in the land of his family, not on some faraway island, not even on the island of Porquerolles, on which Peyrol thinks he was born (Ro 6). Conrad is at pains to underline this point with comparisons between the alien culture of the Giens peninsula and Peyrol's former

---

[6] Batchelor does not go this far, but he does suggest that having apprenticed himself to Shakespeare Conrad gained success with *Chance* and *Victory* and came into his own (151).

[7] See *Cymbeline* for extensive play upon the correlation of physical features with heart's intent.

life as a Brother of the Coast: followed by women and children to the tartane he is 'a phenomenon and a wonder to the natives, as it had happened to him before on more than one island in distant seas' (Ro 84). This subversion of imperial romance structures serves to underline the exoticism of Peyrol's previous life as a Brother of the Coast, and at the same time underlines the terrible strangeness wrought on the peninsula by the violence of the revolution.

Returning to Caliban, if we follow Batchelor and Kermode in reading Caliban as 'cannibal' we are reminded of Michel's comment that 'we are all savages here' and his characterisation of Scevola as 'one of the best' of the 'drinkers of blood' (Ro 20). Indeed Scevola proves a far more convincing Caliban that the cripple, not only because of Michel's cannibalistic hints, but also because of his violation of Arlette's family and her mind, recalling Caliban's attempt on Miranda's honour. Furthermore, Scevola's devotion to the violence of the revolutionary cause is given the lie by Caliban's drunken devotion to the reprobate Stephano: 'I'll Kiss thy foot; I'll swear myself thy subject' ... 'Freedom, high-day! high-day, freedom!' (III.ii.142, 146). The implication of this echo is that the cause to which Scevola devotes himself is no more honourable than the parodic monarchy of Stephano. Here, again, Conrad subverts the paradigmatic narrative security of traditional romance in which good overcomes evil: Scevola takes control of Arlette, until she yells, 'exactly like the others ... the very same words' as those of the bloodstained revolutionaries who had killed her parents (Ro 154). Arlette does not have the power to repulse that Miranda has: 'I let myself go at last. I could no longer resist' (Ro 155).

A final echo of *The Tempest* is to be found in the character of Symons, or 'Testa Dura' as he was known to Peyrol in their days amongst the Brotherhood of the Coast. The fraternity of the Brotherhood clearly allies Symons with Prospero's usurping brother, Antonio, who is washed ashore through the magic worked by Prospero and Ariel. In a similar manner Symons echoes Michel in his attribution of miracle working to Peyrol: 'walking on air behind a fellow's back and felling him like a bullock' (Ro 129). Symons's inability to recognise Peyrol, and his eventual escape, can be read back into Antonio's near silence in the final act. If Antonio refuses to acknowledge his brother through silence, Peyrol also no longer exists for Symons as a 'brother,' as a living man. Symons lack of recognition turns Peyrol into a generic old man, whose place is outside their shared history, and this too is very much what Antonio had hoped for his brother in usurping him.

However, whilst Antonio and Symons fall silent and do not acknowledge their 'brothers' lives, both Prospero and Peyrol are revivified in tales of exploits. Prospero gives up the art of magic for the art of narration: 'delivering all' 'the story of my life, / And the particular accidents gone by / Since I came to this isle' (V.1.313, 304–6).[8] Peyrol goes further than Prospero's 'every third thought shall be my grave' and gives up his life entirely (V.i.311). However, the discovery of the

---

[8] For an early example of Prospero's ability to narrate his own and others' history see I.ii.1–371.

fairytale gold, planted by Peyrol in the Escampabor well, prompts Real and Arlette to talk of Peyrol 'openly, as though he had come back to live again amongst them' (Ro 284). Thus both men, in renunciation of their crafts, are able to live on through the power of narrative.

Conrad's free adaptation of *The Tempest*, in structuring *The Rover* and in characterising its protagonists' relationships, can be read in much the same way that Batchelor reads the echoes in *Victory*. However, here Conrad's novel is not a valediction to 'the world before the Great War' but a valediction to the romance genre itself. In this, too, he mirrors Shakespeare. For we can trace in the development of Shakespeare's romance works a movement from the expansive plots of the early romances such as *Pericles* and *Cymbeline*, through the more tightly constructed, *The Winter's Tale*, to the sharply compact *The Tempest*. In this development Shakespeare gradually sheds the tendency to disquisition and the episodic structures that characterise the literary romances, which were his models, whilst keeping the larger-than-life protagonists who people them, so that he is finally left with a near Plautine structure in which to explore the themes of romance, such as the differentiation between illusion and reality, and the nature of honour, through the activities of romance characters.

Conrad's own use of the romance genre runs along similar tracks, starting with the expansive narratives of *Lord Jim*, *Nostromo* and *Romance*, where he makes a very art of the romance tropes of digression and episode that would be criticised in non-romance texts. In his later romances he attempts, not altogether successfully, to martial these tropes: in *Victory* through allusion to *The Tempest*, and in *Chance* through the apparently clear division of the book into 'Knight' and 'Damsel'.

Then, following *The Rescue*, which Conrad characterised as 'the swan song of Romance as a form of literary art,' comes *The Rover* with its tight plotting and romance themes (15 February 1919; *CL6* 362). Conrad's description of *The Rescue* implies that he intended to cut out that fruitful mode for his fiction, near the end of his career, and in some ways *The Rover* cannot be considered as completely romance, in the same way that *The Tempest* cannot. Instead Conrad constructs a post-romance landscape, peopled by stock romance characters. These characters live in a world bereft of the romance narratives that had previously given them purpose, these narratives having come to an end: Peyrol has returned from his varied life at sea, a life that echoes some of Conrad's earlier romance heroes; Catherine lives a life of restraint and denial after her early infatuation with a priest; Michel lives on after the death of his only companion, his dog; Scevola, Arlette and Réal are drawn (back in Arlette's case) to the Escampabor farm after the bloodbath of the revolution. Inactive in any way that relates to their more romantic pasts, all that these characters are left with, it seems, is the power of observation, an observation that is apparently no more than a matter of silent purposeless surveillance. Yet to this purposeless surveillance Peyrol gradually gives meaning, even a plot (the deception of the British fleet), and with his death he brings back the art of storytelling, by giving the remaining protagonists a past they can bear to look upon. If *The Rescue* is romance's swan song then *The Rover* is Conrad's valediction.⁹

We noted at the beginning of this paper Conrad's latent anxiety about looking back on his own past, and reconstructing it for Borys, and the future. It is worth turning at this juncture to consider this past and its potential to mediate Conrad's uptake and his use of Shakespeare. Conrad's father was an author and playwright of some repute in Poland. Although not now valued for the brilliance of their literary expertise, his works were, as Andrzez Busza puts it, 'motivated less by a powerful creative urge than by a passionate desire to teach and edify' (118). This didactic urge was nationalist and to some extent socialist. Korzeniowski heroises the worker whilst frequently keeping him in a pastoral setting. In a poem called "Dzisiezszym" (To the Contempories) he writes, 'I will remain alone, for I prefer / O truth, your hard holy bread! / Noblemen-pedlers, Noblemen-sugarmongers, / Sheepfarmers, chapmen, merchants, beermongers' (Busza 120). This is closer to the romance of *The Winter's Tale* than the romanticism of Wordsworth for whom the peasant is best appreciated as an artefact signifying a world from which the author is utterly alienated. Korzeniowski rather appreciates the innocent animation of the peasant and wants to join in, like an Arcadian prince-shepherd.

Korzeniowski's play, *Komedia*, a free adaptation of Gribojedov's *Goré ot Uma* (*The Mischief of Being Clever*), runs along similar themes. The hero, Henryk, having tricked his well-to-do sweetheart into thinking he is unworthy of her, rejects her and her world as hypocritical, when she eventually realises her mistake. The play's plotting, drawn though it is from Gribojedov, is not dissimilar to that found in early Shakespeare comedies, yet the ends to which the plot is put are far more political and satirical. Busza comments that Act III contains 'some of the most open and bitter social criticism that was written in Poland in the 1850s' (122). Indeed Conrad himself, in the last years of his father's life, turned his hand to political playwriting. As Najder explains, quoting the recollection of one of Conrad's childhood playmates, these plays were 'usually on the subject of the insurgents fighting against the Muscovites ... "his most spectacular drama was called *The Eyes of King Jan Sobieski*"' (33).

Korzeniowski, besides writing his own plays, translated five of Shakespeare's: *Othello, Two Gentlemen of Verona, Much Ado About Nothing, Comedy of Errors* and *As You Like It*. It is worth noting that of these five, four are comedies, indicating something of the value that Korzeniowski placed on the genre. *Comedy of Errors* was the first he translated, and a letter Korzeniowski wrote to Kazimierz

---

⁹ The appropriately named *Suspense* is the clear anomaly here. And the only defence that can be made is that its sprawling nature meant that Conrad left it incomplete and unpublished at his death. Whilst critics argue over the extent of its incompletion the implications leave us in suspense: did Conrad intend to publish a sprawling romance narrative, and thus mar future critics readings of his creative development as following Shakespeare's? Or did he intend to revise the text dramatically, creating a pared down, and restrained narrative in the vein of *The Rover*?

Kaszewski at the time indicates his aesthetic programme in translating: 'The comedy is excellent and ready for the stage. I have tried to preserve not only the thought but in certain respect the literary meaning and shape of the verse'.[10] Korzeniowski indicates its readiness for the stage here, but it was also published in serial form in the weekly *Kłosy* in 1866 (no. 36–41) as *Komedia Obędów*.

In addition to translating Shakespeare Korzeniwski also published an essay, 'Studia nad Dramatycznością w Utworach Szekspira' ('Studies on the Dramatic Elements in Shakespeare's Works') in *Biblioteka Warszawska* (April 1868). In this article he expounds his view that 'drama is essentially a social art form ... [achieving] fullness of expression only in the theatre'; moreover, 'dramatic art develops and rises to the heights of achievement only when it stands "close to the majority, the masses, the people," and declines and degenerates, when it becomes exclusive and dependent solely on "the upper classes"' (Busza 131). Korzeniowski saw in Shakespeare this ability to appeal to 'the taste, the customs, the whole life of the people' (Busza 131). Indeed, Shakespeare's interest and power, according to Korzeniowski, is in his insight into 'the essence of man' (Busza 131):

> The Bard's genius was moved and inspired by a universal spectacle; a spectacle of almost daily recurrence and yet one which goes unperceived by mankind, in spite of the fact that man is in it both the author and the spectator. This spectacle is the deadly struggle of the might of *man* with the powers of fate.... (Busza 131)
>
> .... in this struggle, finally when his life is smashed to pieces, man perishes – but with that quality, with which God has endowed him for all time in the act of creation, still *intact*. (*Conrad Under Familial Eyes* xvi)

Given this interpretation of Shakespeare it may at first seem surprising that Korzeniowski turned his hand primarily to the translation of comedies. Whilst they are more inclusive in their representations of society than the tragedies, they are no more so than the histories. Furthermore, both the nobility and the non-nobility of the comedies are far more romanticised that those of the histories. Nor did Korzeniowski see them otherwise; for him they are Shakespeare's 'escape into the world of illusions from the terrors of reality' (Busza 131). However, the comedies themselves are often filled with terrors for the protagonists, and it is only for the audience, who have been prompted by an indicative title, that most of the proceedings are amusing.[11] *The Comedy of Errors*, for example, is nightmarish in the maddening confusion of masters, mistresses and slaves. Moreover, it opens

---

[10] 6/18 September 1865. *Conrad Under Familial Eyes*, ed. Zszisław Najder, trans. Halina Carroll-Najder (Cambridge: Cambridge University Press 1983), 98. 'Kazimierz Kaszewski (1825–1910), was a fellow author and Polish patriot.

[11] Whilst the histories, tragedies and two earliest romances use proper names in their titles, the comedies and the two later romances (whose tighter structure brings them closest to comedy) have descriptive, riddling titles.

with a man about to be put to death for apparently breaching an international trade embargo, whilst in fact searching for one of two lost sons. The error seems hardly comic. In the context of Poland's recent history, one in which international boundaries were constantly being redrawn, carving up Poland in the process, Korzeniowski's translation must have had particular pertinence. Indeed, one appeal of the comedies for Korzeniowski may well have been the fact that they lack overt political subject matter, thus making them acceptable to the censor, whilst allowing for topical allusion.

Korzeniowski's interpretation of Shakespeare, whereby Shakespeare's genius is moved by a 'universal spectacle' of 'the deadly struggle' of man and fate, needs no adaptation to apply equally well to Conrad's own oeuvre. And this prompts us to think again about the mediation of Conrad's reception of Shakespeare through the literary influence of his father. In particular we may consider what impact if any the comedies had on Conrad's work, an area which has been left virtually untouched by the various critics who have broached the topic of Shakespeare's presence in Conrad's oeuvre.

The first thing that must be admitted is that the verbal evidence of Conrad's free adaptation of or borrowing from Shakespeare's comedies is negligible. In proceeding then we must turn to thematics and schematics. The one novel of Conrad's which wears its comedy most readily on its sleeve is *Chance*. The whole of the first section 'The Damsel' is pervaded by suppressed laughter, and we shall return to this laughter in due course. But let us initially turn to the structural and thematic Shakespearian echoes. The first is the motif of doubling. In *Chance* the motif is used most clearly for the male characters and is pointed up early in the novel by the 'chance' encounter of the two Powells. This initial doubling alerts us to others, and we find in the second section of the novel, 'The Knight,' that we are confronted with a choice of at least two possible chivalrous heroes, Anthony and Powell. Furthermore, Marlow clearly feels he too is in contention for the title, believing, despite Flora's flat denial, that he had in some way saved her life on their first meeting by the quarry (C 213).

Doubling is used most famously by Shakespeare in *Comedy of Errors* but appears elsewhere with doubled lovers, such as we find in *A Midsummer Night's Dream*, *As You Like It* and *Two Gentlemen of Verona*. It is also a schema used in *Measure for Measure*, a play whose uneasy tone matches that of *Chance* in certain ways. In *Chance* the initial doubling of the Powells acts as a comic symbol, indicating a mode of narrative. The second doubling, of the chivalrous heroes, is more complex, confusing the reader rather than helping them out. It embroils the reader in the same problem that embroils the protagonists: what is the most appropriate and chivalrous action to take as a man when faced with the plight of Flora de Barral. Conrad, here, transforms the Shakespearian doubling motif, which normally indicates an 'escape into the world of illusions,' in order to explore the romance problems afflicting reality.

The second thematic similarity is the prominence given to female characters in both *Chance* and Shakespeare's comedies. These comedies contain intelligent, ingenious, witty and courageous women whose narrative importance is equal at least to the men's. In this respect they come close to the Polish tradition of female figures in romantic drama 'whose roles often function as a reminder of the inadequacy of the male hero or the futility of his pursuit of an idealist quest' (Susan Jones 53). Whilst Flora is rarely witty, and readily admits of herself that she is 'not a very plucky girl' (C 213), she demonstrates a certain kind of ingenuity and intelligence, which is underwritten by her determination to provide for her father.[12] The problem that Susan Jones identifies as besetting Flora, namely the imposition by others of inappropriate roles for her, which hamper her ability to be herself, is also that of many Shakespearian comic heroines, including the troubled Isabella in *Measure for Measure*. Susan Jones writes of 'the disparity between what a woman is, or might be, and the roles that have been prescribed for her' (102).[13] Whilst Flora may seem an unlikely Beatrice or Rosalind she is able by the end of the novel to turn other people's impressions of her to her own advantage: She recalls Mrs. Fyne's characterisation of her as 'a heartless adventuress' and comments, 'So be it. I have had a fine adventure' (C 404).

Finally in its multiple tellings and framings *Chance* draws upon the implications of *A Midsummer Night's Dream*'s play within a play. The similarity is most noticeable in the suppressed and inappropriate laughter which runs throughout the first section, but which mellows in the second. This laughter and its complexities are well exemplified by Mrs Fyne's interview with Marlow. Mrs Fyne's narrative in all its 'comic exasperation' draws 'jocular' responses from her amused audience Marlow (C 177). In turn Mrs Fyne is at pains in her story of Flora to point out: 'Don't conclude, though, that I think she was playing a comedy then,' echoing Marlow's earlier comment: 'That girl is no comedian' (C 178, 177). However, whilst Marlow's amused detachment extends to Mrs Fyne, he appreciates at least in part the pathos of Flora's story, which Mrs Fyne presents. Again this appreciation is framed in comic terms:

> It would be enough to drive a fine nature into the madness of universal suspicion – into any sort of madness. I don't know how far a sense of humour will stand by one. To the foot of the gallows, perhaps. But from my recollection of Flora de Barral I feared that she hadn't much of a sense of humour (C 175).

The comic echoes here are threefold. Firstly the 'universal suspicion' recalls Helena in *A Midsummer Night's Dream*, who feels herself born to 'keen mockery' (II.ii.123). Secondly there is a reminder of the first scene of *Comedy of Errors*, mentioned before, where the opening error at the foot of the gallows seems far from comic, despite the implication of the play's title. Thirdly there is an echo of

---

[12] Incidentally we may note that an overbearing father is another regular feature of Shakespearian comedy.

[13] This is, of course, a problem besetting a good many female heroines throughout European nineteenth century literature.

Korzeniowski's own creation, Henryk, who reappeared after *Komedia* in a sequel, *Dla Miłego Grosza* (*For the Beloved Penny*). This sequel was less lighthearted than the first, and was criticised, by Adam Pług in *Tygodnik Illustrowany* (*The Illustrated Weekly*), for the lack of a sympathetic heroine (Busza 123).[14] In the play Henryk explains that 'I have turned into a perpetual jester, otherwise I would be lost. Here, you must either laugh at everything or despair' (Busza 123). For Marlow, the perpetual jester, Flora's chances look bleak at this point. And indeed Marlow's show of appreciation here, despite the risibility he finds in Mrs Fyne's narration, echoes Theseus's ability to imagine the rude mechanicals as they imagine themselves whilst acting, so that 'they may pass for excellent men' (V.i.214).

Indeed, it is this ability to empathise which converts Marlow's inappropriate and jeering laughter of 'The Damsel' section into sympathetic interest in 'The Knight' section. Moreover, the very nature of this contrast is highlighted by instances of suppressed laughter falling at the ends of each section. In the first, Marlow 'coughs down the beginning of a most improper fit of laughter' when he hears for the first time from Flora of her meeting with Anthony on her way to commit suicide (C 215). This is echoed by Fyne, whose laughter at the thought of Flora, Captain Anthony and de Barral 'crowded into a four-wheeler, and Anthony sitting deferentially opposite that astonished old jail-bird,' sounds 'improper' (C 247). The cynicism of both Marlow and Fyne is directed against romance and melodrama because it is in hackneyed forms of these genres that they read Flora's situation.

In the second instance laughter shares in the romance of Flora's life. Flora and Marlow, 'laughed a little' when they meet at her garden gate for his final interview with her (C 442); 'wreathed in perpetual blushes' from the rosy shade of her light she reflects on her marriage to Anthony 'with a shy half-laugh' (C 443). But most significantly the cynical laughter, which had accompanied Marlow's earlier audiences with Flora, is finally turned on Marlow by his own audience: 'What on earth are you grinning at in this sarcastic manner? I am not afraid to go to church with a friend,' exclaims Marlow to his companion (C 447). Yet this final laughter is also an absolving one, given by the frame narrator whose responses to Marlow's speech have directed, and chimed in with, our own responses. The laughter of the frame narrator is the signal to the reader to laugh with him too, to see Marlow transformed, as Falstaff is in *The Merry Wives of Windsor*, without malice, accepting the comic and unified ending.[15] In this respect the frame narrator's laughter forms the briefest of epilogues, of the kind in which a Puck, a Rosalind, or even a Prospero, address the audience and in doing so draw them into the magic circle of dramatic art and at the same instant dissolve the circle by acknowledging that art.

---

[14] A criticism also made of several Conrad novels.

[15] This is of course the Falstaff of *The Merry Wives of Windsor* rather than of *Henry IV. Part 2*.

Conrad's relationship to Shakespeare is complex, as we have seen. It is mediated by his own artistic practice and by his reception of Shakespeare, most significantly through his father. His borrowings were at a verbal, thematic, and structural level. Whilst these borrowings are most clear in relation to the tragedies and *The Tempest* the comedies lurk significantly behind *Chance*, in particular. John Batchelor, in his article on Conrad and Shakespeare, concludes that by 1915 Conrad 'certainly felt more confident with his English-speaking audience. It could be said that he had taken his chance and secured a kind of victory' (151). As we have seen Batchelor reaches this conclusion by considering Conrad's oeuvre in comparison to Shakespeare's and placing at their apex *The Tempest* and *Victory*. I would like to suggest that the victory comes primarily with *Chance*, and its successful appeal to an English audience as an English novel.[16] *Chance* had been a long time in the making, a time during which he composed the strongly European *Under Western Eyes* and *The Secret Agent*. Conrad had hoped for success with *The Secret Agent*, and his London setting may have been, in part, an attempt to engage with his national audience. However, writing to John Galsworthy at the beginning of 1908 he was 'cast down':

> The *Secret Agent* may be pronounced an honourable failure. It brought me neither love nor promise of literary success. I suppose I am a fool to have expected anything else. I suppose there is something in me that is unsympathetic to the general public – because the novels of Hardy, for instance, are generally tragic enough and gloomily written too – and yet they have sold in their time and are selling to the present day.
> Foreignness I suppose. (*CL4* 9)

Conrad's associates his foreignness and gloominess here, and sees in their fusion a reason for his lack of success. Whilst this did not stop him from writing *Under Western Eyes* we can surmise at least that Conrad, however subconsciously, turned to Shakespeare – the paragon of English letters, whose ability to reach the people his father had celebrated, and whose comedies his father had translated – for models and modes of native and cheerful narrative that would bring him success.

---

[16] My use of the term English here is specific and to be differentiated from British.

Chapter 8
Conrad in the Operatic Mode

Laurence Davies
In memoriam Steven Paul Scher[1]

I.

Operatic composers turn verbal compression into musical fullness. Verdi, for example, asked Francesco Maria Piave, one of his librettists for 'poche parole, stile conciso' (201).[2] Wagner, who wrote his own libretti, may be an exception here, but in general, the book is short, the score is long. A similar tautness prevails in short fiction, yet novels work quite differently, challenging any musical adaptor not only with their complexity and range but their looser texture. Except in Beckett's later work, *novel* and *compression* are not words that go together. On the grounds that 'the core of their artistry is descriptive and analytical rather than lyrical and expressive,' Gary Schmidgall cites a group of authors 'for whom the idea of operatic translation is virtually inconceivable'. Conrad does not feature in this list of such novelists as Sterne, Austen, Dickens and Woolf (14),[3] but, at first glance, he would seem a likely candidate; hardly a man of few words, his verbal flights are lengthy, demanding and vertiginous.[4] Yet, in the manner of opera's most dramatic moments, he is also pungently concise. Kurtz's 'the horror, the horror' echoes Verdi's *Simon Boccanegra*[5]; Linda Viola's desperate cry, 'Never! Gian' Battista,' followed only by one brief statement of a key motif, could have been (but isn't) a borrowing from Leoncavallo or Mascagni. '*Giammai! Gian' Battista!*' … plangent chords, and curtain. In fact there have been several operatic versions of Conrad

---

[1] Although sadly lacking the benefit of his wisdom, this essay is dedicated to the fond memory of Steve Scher, who wrote so thoughtfully about literature and music. Whether 'in grauen Stunden' or in brighter hours, he delighted friends and colleagues with his wit and generosity.

[2] 'Few words, concise style'. Piave's libretti included *Rigoletto, Macbeth, La traviata, La forza del destino* and the 1857 version of *Simon Boccanegra* quoted below.

[3] A counter-argument might begin with Britten's *Death in Venice* and *The Turn of the Screw* or, if novellas seem easier to adapt than novels, Prokofiev's *War and Peace*.

[4] As one, regrettably unidentified, critic put it, 'I have just been listening to a performance on the Conrad.'

[5] The words *orror* and *orrore* were as indispensable to Italian librettists as *vendetta* and *addio*, but even so, their frequency here is noteworthy. In Act I of the 1881 version, they occur three times, and in Act III, as Paolo is dragged away to the gallows, he first cries 'Ah! orrore!!' then 'Orrore! Orror!' In the 1857 version of the third act, there is yet another occurrence, Fiesco's 'Orror! … va … fuggi!'

stories, and he himself thought that '*Victory* may make a libretto for a Puccini opera anyhow' (To J. B. Pinker [March 1915]; CL5 452).'[6] His oeuvre is that of a writer who loved opera, drew upon it as a model and an inspiration, and inspired librettists and composers in his turn.

The references to composers in his letters place him in a distinctive triangulation of old and new. On the side of the old, he responded warmly to the Parisian tradition of grand opera. In 'A Portrait,' a brief memoir of his father's later years, John Galsworthy recalled Galsworthy Senior's respect for the operas of Giacomo Meyerbeer, the most extravagant representative of what had become a thoroughly unfashionable tradition. Though forty years younger, Conrad had shared the same respect.

> I suppose that I am now the only human being in these Isles who thinks Meyerbeer a great composer; and I am an alien at that and not to be wholly trusted. I remember well you telling me of Your father's liking for Turgueniev. It seemed always a very mysterious thing till you enlightened me. Yes, it must have been that – the common worship of beauty. (18 June 1910; *CL*4 338)

The combination of names is remarkable. In Conrad's circle, Turgenev epitomised artistic scrupulousness; indeed he was the only Russian author Conrad could bring himself to admire. If they paid him any attention at all, most of Conrad's contemporaries found Meyerbeer to be frivolous as well as turgid. Equally fascinating is Conrad's reference to being an alien: though driven by a different motive from Conrad's, the need for more hospitable management and audiences, Meyberbeer too had chosen exile. Conrad heard at least some of the operas in Marseilles during the 1870s, and may have heard more in Australia.[7] Jean-Aubry records that 'Although 50 years, or very nearly, had elapsed since then, he had kept of that time most accurate recollections and he retained a very correct impression of Meyerbeer's or Verdi's operas, as well as of Offenbach's operettas' (1924, 39).[8]

---

[6] Among the works adapted have been 'To-morrow,' *Under Western Eyes*, *Lord Jim* and *Victory*, this last in a version by Richard Rodney Bennett with a libretto by Beverley Cross. For details, see Knowles and Moore 2000, 262–3. Tarik O'Regan and Tom Phillips, his librettist, are working on an operatic 'Heart of Darkness,' which has had workshop productions in London, Princeton, and New York.

[7] Frank Baldanza lists the operas performed in Marseilles during the relevant period: among the Meyerbeers were *Les Huguenots*, *L'Africaine*, *Le prophète* and *Robert-le-diable* (1–16). In Australia, *Les Huguenots* was among the most popular works staged by the Lyster Company, which toured to Melbourne (where Tom Lingard made his single, never-forgotten visit to the opera) and Sydney: *New Grove Dictionary of Music and Musicians*, ed. Sadie Stanley (Oxford: Grove, 2001), s.v. Australia, 216.

[8] For the significance of Conrad's opera-going in Marseilles, see also Pamela Bickley and Robert Hampson, '"Lips That Have Been Kissed": Boccaccio, Verdi, and *The Arrow of Gold*,' *L'Epoque Conradienne* (1988): 75–91. In addition, the authors note a possible echo of Verdi's *Falstaff*, staged at Covent Garden in 1894, while Conrad was in London.

To Conrad's seriously musical contemporaries, even in the Nineties, Meyerbeer was a shameless monger of artistic sensation, responsible for such extraordinarily inopportune stunts as staging a skaters' ballet in the middle of *Le prophète*, a supposedly serious opera about the Münster Anabaptists,[9] or, in *Robert-le-diable*, composing a bacchanale for an orgy of spectral nuns conjured up by necromantic powers. To the less serious, he was just ridiculously quaint, the favourite of a dying generations. Supreme among the composers who had replaced him was Wagner.[10] Here, with reservations, Conrad took sides with the new.

According to Galsworthy, 'The blare of Wagner left him as cold as it leaves me' (82). Yet, in describing the last chapter of *Almayer's Folly* as if it were an operatic scene, Conrad imagines it as a combination of the older operatic manner with the newer. 'Il commence avec un *trio* Nina. Dain. Almayer. et il finit dans un long *solo* pour Almayer qui est presque aussi long que le Tristan-solo de Wagner' (2 May 1894; *CL1* 155–6). He knew what he was talking about, for he had just heard the Belgian première of *Tristan und Isolde*, sung in French.[11] Since he probably attended the performance with the recipient of this letter, Marguerite Poradowska, this may be an allusion to shared experience; in any case, it is a finely two-edged irony, a joke at his own expense and, at the same time, a link between an apprentice author and the most famous, the most daring and the most demanding composer of the day. When, eight years later, Conrad defended his fictional practice to William Blackwood, he put such nineteenth century figures as Thackeray, Scott and Eliot behind him and turned to experimentalists in other arts:

> I am long in my development. What of that? ... G. Elliot [sic] – is she as swift as the present public (incapable of fixing its attention for five consecutive minutes) requires us to be at the cost of all honesty, of all truth, and even the most elementary conception of art? But these are great names. I don't compare

---

[9] Conrad and Ford thought of collaborating on a historical novel about John of Leiden's disastrously failed utopia (*CL9* 73–4). Jeffrey Meyers connects the spectacular explosion in the final scene of *Le prophète*, set off by John himself, with Jörgenson's suicidal destruction of the *Emma* in *The Rescue* (339).

[10] Wagner loathed the older composer for being Jewish and thus, according to him, inadequately rooted in the ground of German purity, spiritual and artistic. 'Meyerbeer ... wanted a monstrous piebald, historico-romantic, diabolico-religious, fanatico-libidinous, sacro-frivolous ... dramatic hotch-potch, therein to find material for a curious chimeric music, – a want which, owing to the indomitable buckram of his musical temperament, could never be quite suitably supplied' (94).

[11] At the Théâtre de la Monnaie, Brussels, in March 1894. According to the source of this information, a letter to Christopher Sandeman of 11 July 1917, this was his only experience of Wagner in performance. The same letter insists upon his ignorance of Germanic mythology (*CL9* 208). Whether or not Conrad had ever seen *Der fliegende holländer*, Mario Curreli detects its presence in the fiction: 'Leitmotifs from Coleridge and Wagner in *Nostromo* and Beyond,' in *Nostromo: Centennial Essays*, eds. Allan H. Simmons and J. H. Stape (Amsterdam: Rodopi, 2004), 96–109.

myself with them. I am *modern*, and I would rather recall Wagner the musician and Rodin the Sculptor who both had to starve a little in their day – and Whistler the painter who made Ruskin the critic foam at the mouth with scorn and indignation. (31 May 1902; *CL*2 418)

Apart from James, and perhaps Crane, no English-language novelist would have suited Conrad's argument, but in any case, to cite a musician, a sculptor and a painter in a synaesthetic unity of artistic purpose was an avant-garde statement in its own right.[12] Moreover, the example of Wagner was peculiarly apposite. Whistler took Ruskin to court for claiming that he painted hastily, but no one ever made the equivalent complaint about Wagner's music. By calling himself 'long in my development,' Conrad appears to mean both that he is a serious artist whose time is yet to come, and the kind of serious artist who, like Wagner, takes his time within each work. As the publisher of *Lord Jim*, Blackwood knew the latter tendency very well.

Strict and consistent taste is the prerogative of critics naming great traditions.[13] Wagner, Verdi, Donizetti, Meyerbeer, Gounod, Mascagni, Bizet:[14] Conrad's taste was heterogeneous. No Gluck, no Mozart, everyone belonging to the nineteenth century, but within those bounds, the variety is fascinating, as is the affection for unexpected composers. By pursuing the links to individuals, though, it is easy to lose sight of opera as an institution. After discussing the possibility of formal influence, I shall pursue the general question not so much of why Conrad liked opera (why not, and who could presume to know in any case?) but of what it might have signified to him as a venturesome yet deeply-rooted artist, and what, in turn, one might make of this significance.

---

[12] George Eliot often cited painting as an analogue of what she was doing, but her examples came from the seventeenth century Dutch rather than the present-day.

[13] Joseph Kerman's *Opera as Drama* does to Puccini what the younger F. R. Leavis did to Dickens.

[14] According to Galsworthy, *Carmen* was Conrad's favourite. When they heard it at Covent Garden after the voyage in the *Torrens*, 'It was already his fourteenth time of seeing that really dramatic opera' (82). E. C. Bufkin sees a possible link between the crowd scene at the end of *Nostromo*, Part 1, and the opening scene of the opera (211).

Conrad's attitude to Mascagni (perhaps to *verismo* in general) is debatable. As he sat in his Pimlico lodgings writing up the death of Willems, a barrel organ in the street played 'the abominable Intermezzo of the ghastly Cavalleria' (to Garnett, 17 September 1895; *CL*1 245), but he liked the opera well enough to whistle tunes from it (Borys Conrad 34). In a letter to Cunninghame Graham (16 February 1905; *CL*3 218), Conrad quotes the last words of Leoncavallo's *Pagliacci*, inverting the word order as Chekhov does in *Uncle Vanya*.

II.

There is a curious two-page passage in *An Outcast of the Islands* (OI 5) where the narration abruptly shifts into the present tense, even as the narrative perspective grows more distanced. The prose reads like a set of stage directions or, even more, the detailed synopsis of an 'oriental' opera. This is one of those experimental moments, frequent in the early fiction, where Conrad tries out something new only to discard it. In contrast with the face-to-face dialogue that precedes and the deeply novelistic passage in indirect discourse that follows, this particular experiment reflects a fondness for the lavish theatrical effects common in opera. For example:

> By the riverside indistinct forms leap into a noisy and disorderly activity. There are cries, orders, banter, abuse. Torches blaze sending out much more smoke than light, and in their red glare Babalatchi comes up to say that the boats are ready. (OI 135)

An operatic vocabulary also characterises the letter quoted earlier in which Conrad describes the ending (or finale?) of *Almayer's Folly* as a trio followed by a lengthy solo.

In terms of the published version, that description is incomplete. It omits the scenes with Ford and the concluding paragraphs, yet this conclusion offers further operatic touches:

> 'Is he dead?' – he asked.
> 'May you live!' – answered the crowd in one shout, and then there succeeded a breathless silence. (AF 155)[15]

Given the fascination of nineteenth century librettists with religions of all kinds (Bellini's Puritans and Druids, Meyerbeer's Huguenots and Hindus, Spontini's Vestal Virgins, Rossini's and Donizetti's Muslims), even the last, pious blessing in the name of Allah evokes the vicariously ritual world of opera. In fact, at the time when Conrad sketched the ending out for Mme. Poradowska, the last two chapters were not written – or so he told T. Fisher Unwin later in the year (*CL*1 176).[16] Yet whatever the difference between intention and completion, the trio-solo pairing cries out for attention; not only is it operatic, it combines two modes

---

[15] Floyd Eugene Eddleman and David Leon Higdon, ed. (Cambridge: Cambridge University Press, 1994). All following references are to this edition.

[16] The Cambridge editors note that revision to the MS 'is rather limited in scope. There is no evidence of any major changes in the plot, characterization, or the general conception of the novel' (163). It is quite possible, though, that Conrad began his literary life in the way he continued, and, as modern creative writing teachers would put it, wrote beyond the original ending.

of opera and two ways of speaking about the relation of literature and music. In the first part of Chapter 12, Nina, Dain and Almayer wait on an islet at the mouth of the Pantai for the canoe that will take Almayer's daughter and her lover away from him for ever. The dialogue is broken up with pictured landscape and psychological analysis, the former akin to an elaborate mise-en-scène (as in the seaboard vistas of *Tristan*), the latter thickening the narrative in a way typical of prose fiction. This second feature is especially evident in the paragraph preceding the final, intensely operatic repetition of 'I will never forgive you, Nina' (144–5). Here, Almayer's morose brooding comes in the form of interior monologue rather than stage dominating solo, as the desire to reject and to forget are deflected by a sense of his own grandeur into a transitory dream of magnanimity. For the rest, this is indeed a trio, the movements of the speakers towards and away from each other carefully blocked as if in an opera house. The imagery reinforces the musical associations: from this moment on, 'the last time in his life that he was heard to raise his voice,' the father will 'whisper like an instrument of which all the strings, but one, are broken' (AF 145); the light shining on the scene is 'violent and vibrating, like a triumphal flourish of brazen trumpets' (AF 146). Part of a dynamic of passion and impassivity, speech and silence,[17] the body language is expansive, suited to a large-scale setting: '"Here is the boat coming now"—said Dain, his arm outstretched towards a black speck on the water between the coast and the islet' (AF 145). Vocal ensembles – trios, quartets and even larger groups – frequently sing past each other, not only because its members must project their voices, but because, despite the harmonies they create, their obsessions do not chime together.[18] No one in the trio of Nina, Dain, and Almayer entirely understands the other two. This is a scene devoted to the making and breaking of bonds, bonds of duty, bonds of passion, and the delusory bonds of race, and each of these bonds joins or separates the characters, even as they speak. At the same time, language does the work of music, echoing, amplifying, meaning something different for each speaker. Echoes and variations of 'life,' 'love,' 'forgive,' and 'forget' resonate throughout this episode, as in: '"Could you give me happiness without life? Life" she repeated with sudden energy that sent the word ringing over the sea. "Life that means power and love"—she added in a low voice' (AF 143), and 'I will never forgive you Nina – and to morrow I shall forget you! I shall never forgive you' (AF 144). In all, 'forgive' or its derivatives occur four times in the dialogue and twice more in the narrative links, and 'forget' runs to the same total.

Conrad describes what follows as 'un long *solo* pour Almayer qui est presque aussi long que le Tristan-solo de Wagner.' Unless he had originally given his character a direct speech whose traces he later eliminated, this description comes

---

[17] While typically regarded as *loud*, grand opera in the Franco-Italian tradition also relies upon mutely expressive gesture. As its title indicates, the founding work in this subgenre, Auber's *La muette de Portici* (1828), has as one of its principal characters a heroine who cannot speak.

[18] For a luminous discussion of this point, see Abel 28–30.

closer to metaphor than the allusion to a trio does. The trio has much of the formal quality and the performance characteristics of pre-Wagnerian opera, albeit translated into literary terms; again as in pre-Wagnerian opera, the solo makes a dramatic contrast with what has gone before, one that in terms of pace and diction is audible as well as legible. It is not clear which 'Tristan-solo' Conrad had in mind: it might be King Mark's in Act II, scene 3, which resembles Almayer's in its sense of grievance, or Tristan's in Act III, scene 1, which is more than twice as long.[19] Neither is continuous; Tristan briefly interrupts the first, Kurwenal makes several interpolations in the second. Yet, thanks to the presence of musical and verbal leitmotifs and the absence of those pauses necessary to the introduction of each number in the old tradition, the whole is *durchcomponiert* (through-composed). In a less thoroughgoing way, one could say the same of *Almayer's Folly*. In the course of his otherwise silent monologue, Almayer does utter two words, 'forget' and 'eternity,' words forceful in their singularity, their gravamen, and their echoing of key moments in the trio.[20] Yet however 'novelistic' Wagner may be, his Total Work of Art is not a novel; the scene of Almayer returning to his Folly has more in common with a stage soliloquy than with an operatic solo, even one of Wagner's, and most in common with Flaubertian *syle indirect libre*.[21] In the case of the trio, one may argue that Conrad's mode of composition owes a debt to musical example, while, in the case of the solo, the analogy is suggestive, but a little less exact.

In any event, Conrad knew enough about nineteenth century opera to refer to its techniques, and even to adapt them to his own purposes. Whether this conscious knowledge extended to the leitmotif, we have no way of telling. Perhaps, like Thomas Mann, he followed Wagner's lead deliberately, but even if he didn't, the leitmotifs are audible, especially in such works as *Heart of Darkness* and *Nostromo*. They are the verbal equivalents of musical phrases. Joseph Kerman defines them as 'short flexible fragments recurring many times, associated with a person, an idea, or a mood' (185). Any one of them amounts to 'nothing less [...] than the whole complex of all the associations, dramatic and musical, that attach to its every appearance' (187). In Wagner's mature work, 'They are always present, always busy, recombined, reorchestrated, reharmonized, rephrased, developed' (208–9).[22]

---

[19] In Karajan's 1971–72 recording, one lasts twelve minutes, the other, thirty-three.

[20] And, by the way, embodying concepts essential to the opera. Any intertextual speculation about this similarity, though, needs to acknowledge the ironic tinge of Conrad's narrative, and the presence of Schopenhauer in both artists.

[21] For Wagner's links to modern fiction, see Peter Conrad, *Romantic Opera and Literary Form*, especially, 26–8. The author's contention that opera shares more with novels than with plays works best when the plays are bound by late nineteenth and twentieth-century naturalism; in a broader view of time and space, opera has much in common with theatre inflected by ritual, stylized acting, and other conventions that are non- or anti-'realistic'.

[22] The word originated not with Wagner, but his commentators: *The New Grove Dictionary of Opera*, vol.2 (1137).

Here, the question of equivalence is a vexed one. Within the ambit of literature, there is the difficulty that writers were using creative repetition centuries before *Tristan und Isolde* or *Der Ring des Nibelungen*. What about the epithets of epic poetry? The image clusters in Shakespeare? The indentifying tics and quirks of Dickensian characters? When one brings in music, the difficulties multiply. Aren't words more explicit than musical phrases? And in a certain way more limited, so that any text becomes a resonator? Without resorting to the strained or the archaic, how many synonyms could a writer find for light or darkness? And why invoke Wagner or Debussy when, for many years, their elders had been moving audiences with poignant echoes – for example the reprise of happier moments as Violetta dies in the last act of *La Traviata*? One answer lies in the complexity of what Wagner – and Conrad – was doing, their density of texture.[23] Another lies in a convergence of the arts. Although some musicologists might balk at this claim, the poetry of Wagner's libretti is also dense with motifs, and the full effect of every one of Conrad's major works depends on the reader's willingness to hear as well as see.

Here is the Intended, in a passage from the extraordinary duet that always seems to be on the point of bringing *Heart of Darkness* to its close:

> '…Who was not his friend who had heard him speak once?' she was saying. 'He drew men towards him by what was best in them.' She looked at me with intensity. 'It is is the gift of the great,' she went on, and the sound of her low voice seemed to have the accompaniment of all the other sounds, full of mystery, desolation, and sorrow, I had ever heard – the ripple of the river, the soughing of the trees swayed by the wind, the murmurs of wild crowds, the faint ring of incomprehensible words cried from afar, the whisper of a voice speaking from beyond the threshold of an eternal darkness. 'But you have heard him! You know!' she cried. (Y 159)[24]

Even in a first encounter with this passage, much here would seem familiar: for instance, wilderness, the river, mystery, sorrow, whispers, charisma, speech's power to enchant or baffle. In the last two of these examples, I have deployed an expression that does not occur in the text but represents a recurrent idea, in others, the word itself: as noun or verb, *whisper* appears more than twenty times; it is associated with ivory, public opinion, the coastline of West Africa; the wilderness has whispered to Kurtz, Kurtz whispers his dying words, the memory of that literally dreadful moment pervades the scene with the Intended. In its present

---

[23] Baldanza discusses the presence of Wagner in Conrad's plots, especially those of 'Falk' and 'Freya of the Seven Isles' (the only story to mention Wagner's name). The resemblances are intriguing, but in cases like this, the *hows* of borrowing require as much attention as the possible *whats*.

[24] Doubleday, and Dent Uniform following, omits 'wild,' which appears in the British first edition.

place, *ripple* looks quite harmless, but earlier it has been a sign of snags dangerous to navigation. The rhetorical question that begins this extract gives yet another resonance to *friend*: in an ironic spirit, Marlow has previously applied this word to the steamer, its Congolese crew, the sort of person who can help one's career, and his opinion of the Intended's intended, saying, as usual equivocally, 'I am Mr. Kurtz's friend – in a way' (Y 138); now it comes from the mouth of an idealist. A few paragraphs earlier, Marlow has given a fine description of overlaid motifs: 'I saw her and him in the same instant of time – his death and her sorrow – I saw her sorrow in the very moment of his death. Do you understand? I saw them together – I heard them together' (Y 157). As in a musical treatment, the effect is cumulative yet enriched by variation, binding and differentiating; like a trickster constantly assuming new identities, the idea or word itself becomes a protean force. In Conrad, the most easily recognised of these mutating terms are light and darkness, white and black. In Wagner's *Tristan*, the terms are night and day.

Placing the literature of Conrad's time in its relation to the other arts required, and still requires a pliable vocabulary. His own reference in a letter to Cunninghame Graham (19 January 1900; *CL2* 242) to 'mere Crane-like impressionism' touched on what was a long-running debate about the influence of contemporary painting upon poetry and fiction. Twelve years earlier, Henry James had analysed Maupassant's technique in the language of photography (1968, 119). What was the nature of this pairing of the verbal with the visual or musical: a metaphor, an analogy, a call to try out new techniques, or an attempt to dish up chalk with cheese? If, as Pater claimed, all art aspired towards the condition of music, music, in the minds of Wagner and Debussy, aspired towards the condition of poetry. The arts were becoming not so much interchangeable as permeable, part of a continuum. When he smuggled himself across artistic borders, Conrad did so in the best of company.

III.

So far, I have dwelt on Conrad's engagement with the operatic avant-garde. He was also well-versed in longer standing traditions, many of them less radical artistically yet politically bolder. The history of opera is rife with struggles against censorship: the attempts to ban or hobble adaptations of the Figaro plays; the pressure on Auber and Scribe to rewrite *Masaniello*, the seventeenth century story of a Neapolitan revolt against their Spanish overlords which the Royalist authorities in nineteenth century Paris considered an incitement to treason; in post-Conradian times, Stalin's hysteria over the frank sexuality and adventurous harmonies of Shostakovich's *Lady Macbeth of Mtsensk*.[25] Opera is costly yet often popular, sometimes populist, national and international.

---

[25] The toned down version of *Masaniello* (*La muette de Portici*) is credited with starting the Belgian revolution of 1830, and at Verdi's state funeral in Milan, mourners

In nineteenth century opera, composers and librettists showed off their national roots by staging picturesque customs, indigenous music, distinctive histories of suffering nobly borne, and their corollary, the promotion of national unity and independence. The names of Balfe in Ireland, Antônio Carlos Gomes in Brazil, Verdi in what would become Italy, Weber and Wagner in what would become Germany suggest the geographical and stylistic range. Polish opera nourished similar longings. The principal houses, both of them on the international circuit of famous singers, were in Warsaw and Lemberg (Lwów / Lviv), with others in such centres as Cracow and Breslau (Wrocław). The most popular composer was Stanisław Moniuszko; in his *Halka* (first performed in Wilna, 1848) the gentry or *szlachta* dance the polonaise, and *górali* (Carpathian highlanders), the mazurka. In the next generation, Władysław Żeleński set *Konrad Wallenrod* (Lemberg, 1885), Mickiewicz's poem of duplicity in the cause of national revenge. Yet, as the last example with its Poles and Lithuanians ranged against the Teutonic Knights shows, opera also thrived on international or intercultural turmoil. Conflicts of allegiance, especially when they brought in lovers from opposite sides of national, racial, political, or religious frontiers feature in plot after plot: there are the Cavaliers and Roundheads in Bellini's *I Puritani*, Gauls and Romans in his *Norma*, English and Indians in Delibes's *Lakmé*, Normans and Sicilians in Verdi's *I vespri siciliani*, Ethiopians and Egyptians in *Aïda*, Catholic Portuguese and (with a touch of operatic licence) Malagasy Hindus in Meyerbeer's *L'Africaine*. Although such divided loyalties occur in prose fiction – Christians and Jews in *Ivanhoe*, for instance, Asians and Europeans in Loti – they are not as frequent as in opera, and, in this sense, the interracial loves of *Lord Jim*, *Almayer's Folly*, and *An Outcast of the Islands* are operatic.[26]

Opera's audience, too, was international. Successful French, German and Italian operas travelled round the world. Meyerbeer's *L'Africaine*, set variously at sea, and in Portugal and Madagascar, made its début in Paris, in 1865. By the end of 1869, there had been productions in 25 other cities, among them London, Algiers, Madrid, New York, St. Petersburg, Sydney, Lemberg, Montevideo, Riga, New Orleans and Havana. Verdi's *Il trovatore* premièred in Rome in 1853; over the next two years, local or touring companies performed it in twenty-four other venues, including Warsaw, Valetta, Temesvar, Rio do Janeiro, Alexandria, Constantinople and Odessa. By the end of 1866, twenty more had joined the list. From a Conradian point of view, the most interesting of the latter places are Lemberg / Lwów, Melbourne, Sydney and (closer to the world of Babalatchi and

---

lining the streets broke into a spontaneous rendering of 'Va pensiero,' remembering full well that *Nabucco* had identified the Babylonians with the Austrian occupiers and the Israelites with suffering Italians.

[26] But never in the mode of another kind of international work, the totally exotic, such as Bizet's *Les pêcheurs de perles* with its purely Sinhalese characters, or the large array of Italian operas set in Scotland. Even in 'The Lagoon,' his most exotic story, Conrad always deals in ethnic multiples.

his hand-organ set to play the *Miserere*) Batavia, capital of the Dutch East Indies, where the company sang the French translation.[27]

We know from the letters to his agent J. B. Pinker and his collaborator Ford Madox Ford that Conrad gave much thought to questions of audience. How many readers and of what sort, what experience, what level of sophistication? Although Conrad's surviving correspondence does not mention opera in such terms, it offered a model that fitted as nearly as the difference in medium allowed his situation as an artist. In its concerns with duty, honour, solidarity and outlawry – and in its acknowledgment of suffering and atrocity as enduring facts of life rather than aberrations – opera came closer than any current English fiction to embodying the major themes of Polish literature. Yet although often rooted in nationalism, opera was cosmopolitan, virtually a global art. Its plots negotiated turbulent, yet often poignant encounters of culture against culture, creed against creed, pitting sexual desire against the loyalties of custom, family, or nation; such encounters could be heard and seen in local terms, so that one kind of oppression or self-sacrifice stood in for another. For its stories as well as its music, opera was, in the nineteenth century at least, genuinely and widely popular. Moreover, it was extravagant, even absurd enough to appeal to the sardonic humourist in Conrad, and intense enough to mirror his own 'un-English' fierceness. It spoke, in other words, to his artistic doubleness.

IV.

Questions of what is real in art and life dominate the most notable discussion of opera in Conrad's fiction. It occurs in Part V, Section 3 of *The Rescue* as one passage of an exchange between Edith Travers and Tom Lingard. In language echoing her unspoken thoughts in Section 2, Mrs. Travers recalls what was a very public display of coolness in the face of danger:

---

[27] For the full lists, see Loewenberg. A list of names chosen to show geographical range also brings out the political variety: some of these cities, such as London, Paris, Constantinople and Madrid, were imperial capitals, some, such as Batavia, Sydney, Lemberg, Warsaw, Valetta, Riga, Havana and Algiers were cities within large, multicultural empires, others, such as Montevideo and New York, were in former colonies. Whatever the ethnic make-up of particular audiences, most of their members lived in places where questions of loyalty, freedom and identity were both intricate and urgent, sometimes to the point of bloodshed: Warsaw was, so to speak, between insurrections; just a few years earlier than the presentation of Verdi's opera about Spaniards, Basques and Gypsies, New York had seen the worst rioting in its history, which started with protests over the conscription of Irish immigrants, and turned into a massacre of African-Americans, some of whom, like Azucena's mother, were burned alive.

> I mean the morning when I walked out of Belarab's stockade on your arm, Captain Lingard, at the head of the procession. It seemed to me that I was walking on a splendid stage in a scene from an opera, in a gorgeous show fit to make an audience hold its breath. You can't guess how unreal all this seemed, and how artificial I felt myself. An opera, you know … (Res 300).

Since he once went to the opera in Melbourne with a group of fellow diggers from the goldfields, Lingard does know.

> 'How it must have have jarred on your sense of reality,' said Mrs. Travers, still not looking at him. 'You don't remember the name of the opera?'
> 'No. I never troubled my head about it. We – our lot never did.'
> 'I won't ask you what the story was like. It must have appeared to you like the very defiance of all truth. Would real people go singing through their life anywhere except in a fairy tale?' (Res 301)

Lingard retorts:

> 'Fairy tales are for children, I believe […] But that story with music I am telling you of, Mrs. Travers, was not a tale for children. I assure you that of the few shows I have seen that one was the most real to me. More real than anything in life.'
> Mrs. Travers, remembering the fatal inanity of most opera librettos, was touched by these words as if there had been something pathetic in this readiness of response; as if she had heard a starved man talking of the delight of a crust of dry bread. (Res 301)

This is an erotically-charged scene, tense with inarticulate desire, not entirely a debate, not entirely a revelation of character but something of both. Neither of them 'wins'; neither speaks incontestably on Conrad's behalf. Mrs. Travers inverts the orthodox notion that women melt at any show of passion and men stay rational and cool. When Lingard says that his one exposure to opera 'carried me away. But I suppose you know the feeling,' she replies, 'No. I never knew anything of the kind, not even when I was a chit of a girl' (Res 302). The scene also inverts the associations of culture and social standing. She belongs to a class that is said to be the mainstay of the cultural amenities, opera prominent among them, while Lingard is a grizzled outsider whom her husband thinks to be a rogue. The case she makes against the artificiality of opera is the standard, no-nonsense one popular among English-speakers. His case is more challenging: not only does it come from a surprising source, it is also unfamiliar, and, in spite of Lingard's bluffness, enigmatic. What does make an opera 'more real than anything in life'? Is it life without the tedious bits, blood and passion all the way? Or a call to wake up from the dream that Conrad's narrators so often take to be the nature of existence? What if the 'inanity' of opera, the coincidences, the readiness to burst out singing, everything that Mrs. Travers thinks ridiculous, could render life more vividly and powerfully than anything more sensible and humdrum? What if opera's many cruelties – the tortures, the betrayals, the acts of desperate revenge, the massacres, the martyrdoms, the abrupt insanities – were closer to Lingard's (and to Conrad's) experience than, say, domestic melodrama or the comedies of Sheridan? The show that Lingard saw 'was not a tale for children'.[28]

The lay-out of the scene offers a third view of opera, one where Lingard's total surrender to its power and Mrs. Travers's patronising rejection are framed by performance, or rather a series of performances. At one end is the stylised extravagance of opera, at the other, an edgy conversation between two English characters in a novel. It is the middle, however, that makes this series a continuum. Here, they are not simply English; they have performed their Englishness to an audience of native Borneans, and expatriate Malays and Arabs. Lingard congratulates Mrs. Travers on her display of poise: 'You carried yourself first rate' (Res 302). To say that they were performing Englishness oversimplifies, however. Lingard has made a speech in Malay whose command of voice and idiom show his perfect understanding of the role of mediator. Originally at his prompting and now by her own inclination, Edith Travers has been dressing up:

> 'Yes, I was absurdly self-conscious,' continued Mrs. Travers in a conversational tone. 'And it was the effect of these clothes that you made me put on over some of my European – I almost said disguise; because you know in the present more perfect costume I feel curiously at home; and yet I can't say that these things really fit me. The sleeves of this silk under-jacket are rather tight. My shoulders feel bound, too, and as to the *sarong* it is scandalously short.' (Res 303)

Indeed, it is scandalous four times over. For a woman of her place and time, short skirts are the costume of young girls and ballet-dancers in grand opera; to the outrage of her bigoted and pompous husband, she has adopted 'native' dress; by Malay just as much as English standards, the *sarong* is shamelessly revealing; and the infatuated captain is, as she must know, acutely conscious of her body. Later in the scene, as if referring to a character in a script, they will discuss the implications of the name King Tom. In short, they are performing not only to others but to each other.[29] The procession out of Belarab's stockade has not been the only 'gorgeous show'. If operatic characters are, as she implies, 'artificial,' so are we all in the regular way of living, acting out our parts as women, men,

---

[28] Cf. Conrad's remark that 'The Idiots' was 'Not for babies' (to Unwin, 22 May 1896; *CL*1 279). Contrasting the emphasis on mercy in *opera seria* with the cruelty embodied in its Romantic successors, Mladen Dolar writes: 'Opera found itself in a merciless world – though neither is it quite a tragic one' (Žižek and Dolar 17).

[29] The opportunity for a spirited duet between Lingard and Mrs. Travers encouraged Jean-Aubry and Gide to imagine *The Rescue* as an opera; Jean-Aubry saw similar possibilities in *Almayer's Folly* (1924, 41).

beggars, sailors, teachers, politicians, saints, rajahs, ranees and philanthropists. The difference lies not in the action but the muteness. It may, however, take an exotic setting such as the west coast of Borneo or the seaboard of a fictitious Latin American republic to remind us of all this.

V.

Shortly after the coronation of George V, carried off with all the appropriate rituals and splendours, Conrad wrote to congratulate Sir Hugh Clifford on *The Downfall of the Gods* (1911). Set principally in Angkor Wat at the zenith of Khmer power, this is a novel of empire on the brink of decadence.

> What a tremendous subject for a great a really great Opera! And pray don't think it mean praise! No great poem for music has been written yet; subjects of course are lying about. What I mean to say is that here is a subject, the subject of *the* Great Oriental Opera, worked out. Absolutely done! The simplicity of the highly dramatic action, the picturesquely imposing background, the irresistible blind movements of the crowds and the tragic fatality of the 'passion charnelle' – all is there to inspire some musician of the future great enough to express the very spirit of the East in the music of the West. ([22 June] 1911; *CL*4 451–2)

Whatever Conrad did with opera in his novels was not as picturesque or simple. He was not expressing the very spirit of the 'East' (or those other sites of exotic opera, Africa and the Americas) in the fictional idiom of the 'West' but creating an overlay of attitudes and cultures that drastically refracts the very idea of a place's spirit. Marlow's first experience of the east is as the grimy survivor of a shipwreck being, literally, looked down upon.

Yet his unhappy experience as a playwright suggests that Conrad found the grandeur of opera more congenial than the blandness of straight theatre. As a dramatist, he lived in the wrong place and the wrong time. The requirements of naturalism as practised on the London stage under the stern and philistine eye of the Examiner of Plays left him miserably cramped, the result being a mannered combination of verbosity and forced melodrama. It is not surprising, then, that he wrote so disparagingly of the theatre and, except when prospecting for actors (particularly leading ladies) or directors, spent little time there. He needed something less costive, something more like French or Polish Romantic drama – or indeed like Shakespeare. Whether carried out by him alone or in collaboration, dramatisations of Conrad's novels and stories never seem to have touched their audiences at all deeply. Films were another matter. Conrad, the first English writer to try his hand at a scenario (of 'Gaspar Ruiz'), seemed happy to see his fiction transposed onto the screen, and not only because production companies paid handsomely for the rights.³⁰ In the silent cinema, sets and acting tended to be less naturalistic than they were in contemporary theatre, closer to the operatic.³¹ Silence (or the accompaniment of pit band or piano) required a style of acting characterised by sweeping moves, well-suited to the body language to be found, especially, in his early fiction. This, for example, is Willems insisting on his whiteness: 'He shouted, his head thrown up, his arms swinging about wildly; lean, ragged, disfigured; a tall madman' (OI 271); this is Aïssa meeting his wife: 'She tore the belt off and threw it at Joanna's feet. She flung down with haste the armlets, the gold pins, the flowers; and the long hair, released, fell scattered over her shoulders, framing in its blackness the wild exaltation of her face' (OI 358); and this is the Intended, yearning after Kurtz: 'She put out her arms as if after a retreating figure, stretching them black and with clasped pale hands across the fading and narrow sheen of the window' (Y 160). Gestures like these do not easily translate into the dramatic idioms of Galsworthy or Ibsen.

Nor do his moments of sardonic humour. Conrad often wrote in dual modes; among these pairings were the operatic and the ironic, the one playing off the other.³² He also liked to rework the conventions of popular forms, such as the imperial romance or the novel of revolutionary mayhem and intrigue. As Žižek puts it: 'A truly creative act not only restructures the field of future possibilities but also restructures the past, resignifying the previous contingent traces as pointing toward the present' (Žižek and Dolar 103–4). Conrad's work with opera resignifies the traces of his operatic kinsmen. Not only does he set up a force-field between the ironic and the operatic, he ironises opera without throwing it away; he treats it irreverently with the confidence of a believer.

In this regard, he is the opposite of the 'provincial Excellency' in *Nostromo* (90) who makes such a production of his exquisite taste while attributing Donizetti's *Lucia* to Mozart. As in his sometime master Flaubert, milieu and juxtaposition

---

³⁰ In the late nineties, he and Crane had 'earnestly fantastic discussions' about collaborating on a play. Looking back in 1923, he thought that they 'must have been unconsciously penetrated by a prophetic sense of the technique and of the very spirit of film-plays, of which even the name was then unknown to the world' (*Last Essays* 116 [New York: Doubleday, 1926]). The scene described bears some resemblance to the ending of Puccini's *Manon Lescaut* (1893).

³¹ For extensive discussions of Conradian cinema, see Gene M. Moore, ed., *Conrad on Film* (Cambridge: Cambridge University Press, 1997). Lesley Stern distinguishes between two styles of acting in silent films, the naturalistic and the histrionic: 'in more histrionic cinema, the gestural tends more to the abstract, expressive, and stylized ... and ... is more likely to be articulated according to a cinematic logic' (43).

³² I have argued the ironic side of this claim in '"The Thing Which Was Not" and the Thing That Is Also: Conrad's Ironic Shadowing'. Herbert Lindenberger discusses the treatment of opera in fiction as a layering of 'higher' and 'lower' narrative, offering many valuable examples (145–9). Using *ironic* and *operatic* as complementary rather than hierarchical terms, I prefer the horizontal axis.

count. In *A Personal Record*, Conrad remembers a berth in Rouen, where, through his port-hole, he could see a café:

> [...] the very one where the worthy Bovary and his wife, the romantic daughter of old Pere Renault, had some refreshment after the memorable performance of an opera which was the tragic story of Lucia di Lammermoor in a setting of light music. (PR 5)[33]

In such passages as the seduction carried out against a serenade of bleats, grunts, and boosterism from the agricultural show, Flaubert alternates grandeur and banality at a faster pace than Conrad. What seems tragic in a whole chapter of Conrad, though, may yet be darkly comic in a broader context. *An Outcast of the Islands*, II, 6, the scene where Willems catches up with Aïssa at Lakamba's compound and her blind father tries to kill him, makes a good example. It is exotic to the point of hallucination (as with the 'long perspective of fantastic trees,' [OI 145], and the appearance of Omar's disembodied head); rich in large gesture ('she listened, one hand still behind her back, the other arm stretched out with the hand half open as if to catch the fleeting words that rang around her, passionate, menacing, imploring' [OI 152]), and even uses a theatrical simile ('the solid blackness seemed to wave before his eyes like a curtain disclosing movements but hiding forms,' [OI 156]). The long unvoiced passages are broken with dialogue that would translate very satisfactorily into Italian:

> 'And now you want to take me far away where I would lose you, lose my life; because your love is my life now. What else is there? Do not move,' she cried violently, as he stirred a little – 'do not speak! Take this! Sleep in peace!' (OI 155)

At this point, deliberately missing, but only just, she throws a *kris* at him. Like so many operas, *An Outcast* stages a conflict of loyalty, possessiveness, hatred and mistrust. Willems loathes 'that race which is not his race ... out of all that abhorred crowd he wanted this one woman, but wanted her away from them, away from that race of slaves and cut-throats from which she sprang' (OI 152). Aïssa feels just as vehemently; the fierceness is dramatically balanced, as it would need to be on stage. 'Instead of thinking of her caresses, instead of forgetting all the world in her embrace, he was thinking yet of his people; of that people that steals every land, masters every sea, than knows no mercy and no truth ... She must put between him and other white men a barrier of hate' (OI 153). These moments of hostility, though, are interspersed with love passages sounding like abbreviated Wagner: 'he experienced a sense of peace, of rest, of happiness, and of soothing delight. His hands strayed upwards about her neck, and he drew her down so as to have her face above his. Then he whispered – "I wish I could die like this—now!"' (OI 141).

---

[33]   For relevant discussions of the *Lucia* scene in Madame Bovary, see Abel (29), and Lindenberger (159–62).

Yet this man who hankers after *Liebestod* is Mr. Peter Willems of Macassar, ship-jumper and embezzler.

Parody would be the wrong word for what goes on here,[34] and there is no evidence that Willems is under the influence of opera as Emma Bovary is under the influence of romantic novels or Lord Jim, tales of daring deeds. Indeed, Conrad's prose subjects him to several outbursts of narratorial indignation unlike anything in Flaubert. By pushing the analogy with Wagner, perhaps too glibly, one could claim that these outbursts correspond to leitmotifs; for example, not as a phrase but as an idea, 'the horror of bewildered life' (OI 149) appears again and again in this chapter and elsewhere. Here it encapsulates the derangement of Willems's senses as well as the bewilderment and sheer angst, frequent in Conrad, at the seemingly uncontrollable fecundity and wildness of the tropical forest. In its sudden shifts of tone and point of view, his own prose can be bewildering, yet, to step around the marshy terrain of authorial intention, the mercurial sense of life it renders, its manic quality, its many voices are among the best of reasons for encountering it at all. Although its voices contradict each other, this is a prose where no one voice is adequate. This, too, is a prose able to express the unexpected: Willems's adventures in romantic delusion; Aïssa's denunciation of European civilisation as she knows it in sharp, tight language. Without the operatic mode, this expressiveness would be choked off.

Chapter 6 of *Almayer's Folly* ends with another such moment of unexpectedness. Lakamba, Rajah of Sambir, is so excited by his stratagem of poisoning Almayer's coffee that he cannot sleep. He tells the 'exhausted statesman' Babalatchi to 'fetch the box of music the white captain gave me' (AF 67), the captain being the same Captain Lingard who, in *The Rescue*, will come to opera's defence. The box is a hand-organ, set to play the passage from Act IV of Verdi's *Il trovatore* generally known as the *Miserere*. The troubadour Manrico is to be beheaded on the orders of the Conte de Luna, his rival in love; although neither of them knows this, they are brothers. Off stage, a chorus of monks intones the prayer for the condemned. On stage, Leonora waits at the foot of the tower where Manrico, her lover, is incarcerated. The chorus terrifies her, but then she hears Manrico singing from above. Without a knowledge of plot or libretto, one might imagine that he's wooing Leonora with a theatrically heartfelt serenade, accompanied in 3 / 4 time by a lute. What he actually sings is his farewell to her, even as she insists that her love is stronger than death. Musically speaking, theirs is a duet interspersed with passages by the chorus; but spatially they are far apart, and Manrico does not realise her presence. With its multiple musics, its blithe lyricism, its religiosity and its dark, gothic setting, the whole scene is one of the most extravagant in a particularly extravagant opera whose plot originates in an event both abominable and absurd: as her mother, condemned for witchcraft, burned at the stake, the Gypsy Azucena

---

[34] Though Conrad's early fiction itself invited parody, as in Max Beerbohm's *A Christmas Garland*, which shrewdly achieves its goal by rendering the exotic without the accompanying irony.

hurled a baby into the flames, thinking it was the son of their persecutor, but it was indeed her own.

From a bizarre episode, Conrad makes something still more bizarre. Faltering with exhaustion as his master falls asleep, Babalatchi cranks away.

> Nature slept in an exhausted repose after the fierce turmoil, while under the unsteady hand of the Statesman of Sambir the Trovatore fitfully wept, wailed, and bade good-bye to his Leonore again and again in a mournful round of tearful and endless iteration. (AF 68)[35]

For technical reasons, it would have been difficult to set all three strands of music on a hand-worked organ; the wording here points to Manrico's part rather than the chorus that gives the scene the name by which it is usually known.[36] Although, when occasion suits, Babalatchi assumes the role of pious Muslim, he will do all kinds of things to succeed, whether it be poisoning an inconvenient trader or grinding out a tune associated (unknown to him, of course) with the shameless and unsanctioned passion of two infidels set against a background of the Christian liturgy. In its depiction of a ruthless toady at his work, the scene comes close to burlesque; here is a Malay, and a rootless one at that, who cannot hope to do justice to the splendours and the codes of European statesmanship and culture – bearing out the assumptions of the essayist (Alice Meynell) who found fault with writers who wasted their gifts on the 'de-civilized'.[37] Yet, as an advertisement for Christian, or any kind of civilisation, *Trovatore* falls a little short: witch-burning, racial persecution, torture, the unjust use of absolute power – Lakamba would be hard-pressed to keep up with the Conte di Luna. In a scene like this, which appears at first so ridiculous and so patronising, no one has the final laugh.

Sometimes Conrad works with the grain of opera, sometimes against. Holding no one, stable sense of its powers, he treats it as passionate and compelling, absurd, and indispensable. This instability, this lack of commitment to a cultural hierarchy broadened his sense of what was possible, of what might be said, and how. The opinions he expresses, and the specific borrowings he may have made

---

[35] Chamber barrel organs were popular from the eighteenth century on, and in the nineteenth, Imhof and Mukle of London 'made handsome hand-worked barrel pianos' (*The New Grove Dictionary of Musical Instruments* vol.1. 163). In this context, common usage made no distinction between *piano* and *organ* (*OED*).

[36] Wayne Koestenbaum cites this scene, which is something of a test of how much outrageousness an opera-goer can take, in his 'Pocket Guide to Queer Moments in Opera': *The Queen's Throat: Opera, Homosexuality and the Mystery of Desire* (223–4). In 1991, Christie's, New York, sold a first edition of *Almayer's Folly* with a tipped-in pen and ink drawing (8 October, lot 43). Bearing a pencilled note, 'Done by Joseph Conrad in Paris about 1893,' it shows a minstrel singing to a lady, and perhaps illustrates a moment from Act I.

[37] See Conrad's Author's Note (1895) and the Cambridge edition, xxxviii–xli.

reinforce one's sense of his engagement with opera. Yet in chasing the individual examples, it is easy to lose sight of the way in which an artist takes ideas from one form to another. The analogy, the attempt to find equivalence or common ground, will often be more stimulating than the echo or the mirror image. Such is the case with Conrad and opera. Opera is a mode both of experiencing the world and representing it; it is not the only one, but one he could not do without.

Bibliography

Abel, Sam. *Opera in the Flesh: Sexuality in Opera Performance*, Boulder, CO: Westview, 1996.
Andreas, Osborn. *Joseph Conrad: A Study in Non-Conformity*, Hamden, CT: Archon, 1959.
Anon ['Silhouette'], *Modern Shadowgraphy*, London: Hamley Bros, 1903.
Anon, 'Shadow Plays,' *Harper's Bazaar* 32.15 15 April 1899: 323.
Armstrong, Tim. *Modernism, Technology and the Body: A Cultural Study*, Cambridge: Cambridge University Press, 1998.
Baines, Jocelyn. *Joseph Conrad: A Critical Biography*, Harmondsworth: Penguin, 1986.
Baldanza, Frank. 'Opera in Conrad: "More Real Than Anything in Life,"' *Studies in the Literary Imagination* 13 (1980): 1–16.
Barnouw, Erik. *The Magician and the Cinema*, New York: Oxford University Press, 1981.
Batchelor, John. 'Conrad and Shakespeare,' *L'Epoque Conradienne* 18 (1992): 125–51.
Baxter, Katherine Isobel. 'The Strange Spaces of *The Rescue*,' *The Conradian* 29.1 (2004): 64–83.
Beckett, Samuel. *The Complete Dramatic Works*, London: Faber, 1986.
Beerbohm, Max. 'The Feast' (1912), *A Christmas Garland*, London: Heinemann, 1950. 127–34.
Bender, Todd K. *Literary Impressionism in Jean Rhys, Ford Madox Ford, Joseph Conrad, and Charlotte Brontë*, New York and London: Garland, 1997.
Benjamin, Walter. 'The Work of Art in the Age of Mechanical Production,' in *Illuminations*, ed. Hannah Arendt 1968, trans. Harry Zohn, London: Pimlico, 1999. 211–44.
Bergman, Gösta M. *Den moderna teaterns genombrott 1890–1925*, Stockholm: Bonnier, 1966.
Betts, Ernest. *Heraclitus: of the Future of Films*, London: Kegan Paul, Trench & Trubner, 1928.
Bhabha, Homi K. *The Location of Culture*, London: Routledge, 1995.
Bluestone, George. *Novels into Film*, Berkeley and Los Angeles: University of California Press, 1957.
Bond, Edward. *Two Post-Modern Plays: Jackets and In the Company of Men*, London: Methuen, 1990.
Bordwell, David, and Kristin Thompson. *Film History: An Introduction*, New York: McGraw-Hill (7th ed.), 1994.

Bratton, Jacky, Jim Cook, and Christine Gledhill, ed. *Melodrama: Stage, Picture, Screen*, London: British Film Institute, 1994.

Brewster, Ben, and Lea Jacobs, *Theatre to Cinema*, Oxford: Oxford University Press, 1997.

Bufkin, E.C. 'Conrad, Grand Opera, and *Nostromo*,' *Nineteenth Century Fiction* 30 (1975–1976): 206–14.

Busza, Andrzej. 'Conrad's Polish Literary Background and Some Illustrations of the Influence of Polish Literature on His Work,' *Antemurale* 10 (1966): 109–256.

Chanan, Michael. *The Dream That Kicks: The Prehistory and Early Years of Cinema in Britain*, London: Routledge & Kegan Paul, 1980.

Chance Newton, H. *Crime and the Drama or Dark Deeds Dramatized*, London: Stanley Paul, 1927.

Clifford, Hugh. 'The Trail of the Bookworm: Mr Joseph Conrad at Home and Abroad,' *Singapore Free Press* 1 September 1898.

——. 'Some Notes and Theories Concerning Lâtah,' *Studies in Brown Humanity* (1898), London: The Richards Press, 1927. 186–201.

——. *In Court and Kampung*, Singapore: Graham Brash, 1989.

Clifford, James. 'On Ethnographic Allegory,' in *Writing Culture: The Poetics and Politics and Politics of Ethnography*, ed. James Clifford and George E. Marcus, California: University of California Press, 1986. 98–121.

——. *The Predicament of Culture: Twentieth Century Ethnography, Literature, and Art*, Cambridge: Harvard University Press, 1988.

Conrad, Borys. *My Father Joseph Conrad*, New York: Coward-McCann, 1970.

Conrad, John. *Joseph Conrad: Times Remembered*, Cambridge: Cambridge University Press, 1981.

Conrad, Joseph. *Conrad to a Friend: 150 Selected Letters from Joseph Conrad to Richard Curle*, ed. Richard Curle, London: Samson Low, Marston, 1928.

Conrad, Joseph, and Ford Madox Ford. *The Inheritors*, Stroud, Gloucestershire: Allan Sutton, 1991.

Conrad, Peter. *Romantic Opera and Literary Form*, Berkeley and Los Angeles: University of California Press, 1977.

Cook, Olive. *Movement in Two Dimensions: A Study of the Animated and Projected Pictures Which Preceded the Invention of Cinematography*, London: Hutchinson, 1963.

Cox, C.B. *Joseph Conrad: The Modern Imagination*, London: Dent, 1974.

Craig, Mike. *Cultural Geography,* London: Routledge, 1998.

Curle, Richard. *The Last Twelve Years of Joseph Conrad*, London: Sampson Low, Marston, 1928.

Danius, Sara. *The Senses of Modernism: Technology, Perception, and Aesthetics*, Ithaca: Cornell University Press, 2002.

Davies, Laurence. '"The Thing Which Was Not" and the Thing That Is Also: Conrad's Ironic Shadowing,' in *Conrad in the Twenty-first Century*, ed. Carola Kaplan, Peter Mallios, and Andrea White, London: Routledge, 2004. 223–37.

Deleuze, Gilles. *Masochism: An Interpretation of Coldness and Cruelty together with the entire text of Venus in Furs by Leopold von Sacher-Masoch*, trans. Jean McNeil, New York: Zone Books, 1991.

Dilke, Donald A. 'The Tempest of Axel Heyst,' *Nineteenth Century Fiction* 17.2 (1962): 95–113.

Donald, James, Anne Freidberg, and Laura Marcus, eds. *Close Up 1927–1933: Cinema and Modernism*, London: Cassell, 1998.

Donovan, Stephen. *Joseph Conrad and Popular Culture*, Basingstoke: Palgrave Macmillan, 2005.

——. 'Pleasant Spectres and Malformed Shades: Stevenson, Conrad, and Spiritualism,' in *Stevenson and Conrad: Writers of Land and Sea*, ed. Stephen Arata, Linda Dryden, and Eric Massie (forthcoming), Lubbock: Texas Tech University Press.

——.'Sunshine and Shadows: Conrad and Early Cinema,' *Conradiana* 35.3 (Fall 2003): 237–56.

Dryden, Linda. 'Conrad and Hugh Clifford: an "Irreproachable Player on the Flute and A Ruler of Men,"' *The Conradian* 23.1 (Spring 1998): 51–73.

——. *Joseph Conrad and the Imperial Romance*, Basingstoke: Macmillan, 2000.

Dyboski, Roman. 'From Conrad's Youth,' in *Conrad Under Familial Eyes*, ed. Zdzisław Najder, trans. Halina Carroll-Najder, Cambridge: Cambridge University Press, 1983. 137–42.

Elbert, Monika. 'Possession and Self-Possession: the "Dialectic of Desire" in *Twixt Land and Sea*,' in *The Conradian: Conrad and Gender* (17.2), ed. Andrew Michael Roberts, Amsterdam: Rodopi, 1993. 123–46.

Eliot, T.S. 'Swinburne as Poet' (1920), in *Selected Essays*, London: Faber, 1986. 323–7.

Erdinast-Vulcan, Daphna. *The Short Fiction of Joseph Conrad: Writing, Culture and Subjectivity*, Oxford: Oxford University Press, 1999.

Fisher, John. *Paul Daniels and the Story of Magic*, London: Jonathan Cape, 1987.

Ford, Ford Madox. *Joseph Conrad: A Personal Remembrance*, London: Duckworth, 1924.

——. *Henry James: A Critical Study* (1913), New York: Octagon Books, 1964.

Fraser, Gail. "The Short Fiction," in *The Cambridge Companion to Joseph Conrad*, ed. J.H. Stape, Cambridge: Cambridge University Press, 1996. 25–44.

Galsworthy, John. *Castles in Spain and Other Screeds*, London: Heinemann, 1927.

Geertz, Clifford. *The Interpretation of Cultures*, London: Hutchinson & Co Ltd, 1975.

Gillon, Adam. 'Joseph Conrad and Shakespeare: Part 1,' *Conradiana* 1.1 (1968): 19–25.

Gish, Lillian, with Ann Pinchot. *The Movies, Mr Griffith and Me*, London: W.H. Allen, 1969.

Goffman, Erving. *The Presentation of Self in Everyday Life*, Harmondsworth: Penguin 1990.

Gogwilt, Christopher. *The Invention of the West: Joseph Conrad and the Double-Mapping of Europe and Empire*, Stanford: Stanford University Press, 1995.

Gordon, Mel. *Lazzi*, New York: PAJ, 1983.

Graver, Lawrence. *Conrad's Short Fiction*, Berkeley: University of California Press, 1969.

Greenblatt, Stephen. *Marvelous Possessions: The Wonder of the New World*, Oxford: Clarendon Press, 1991.

Greenlees, T. Duncan. 'Insanity among the Natives of South Africa,' *Journal of Mental Science* 41.172 (1895): 71–8.

Griffith, D.W. 'D.W. Griffith Speaks,' *New York Dramatic Mirror* 71.1830 14 January 1914: 49, 54.

Guerard, Albert J. *Conrad the Novelist*, Cambridge: Harvard University Press, 1958.

Gullick, J.M. *Malay Society in the Late Nineteenth Century: The Beginnings of Change,* Singapore, Oxford & New York: Oxford University Press, 1987.

Gunning, Tom. 'The Cinema of Attractions: Early Film, Its Spectator and the Avant-Garde,' in *Early Cinema: Space, Frame, Narrative*, ed. Thomas Elsaesser, London: BFI, 1990. 56–62.

Guy, John. *Woven Cargoes: Indian Textiles in the East*, London: Thames and Hudson, 1998.

Haggard, H. Rider. *She*, Oxford: Oxford World Classics, 1991.

Hammond, William A. 'Miryachit: a Newly described disease of the Nervous System and its Analogues,' *British Medical Journal* 1.19 (April 1884): 758–9.

Hampson, Robert. 'Introduction,' *Victory*, London: Penguin, 1989. 9–32.

——. *Joseph Conrad: Betrayal and Identity*, Basingstoke: Macmillan, 1992.

——. *Cross Cultural Encounters in Conrad's Malay Fiction*, Basingstoke: Palgrave, 2000.

Hand, Richard J. (2001a) 'Staging an "unbearable spectacle": Joseph Conrad's *Laughing Anne*,' *Studies in Theatre and Performance* 21.2 (2001): 109–17.

——. (2001b) 'Conrad and the Reviewers: *The Secret Agent* on stage,' *The Conradian* 26:2 (Autumn 2001): 1–67.

——. 'Producing *Laughing Anne*,' *Conradiana* 34.1–2 (Spring–Summer 2002): 43–62.

——. *The Theatre of Joseph Conrad: Reconstructed Fictions*, London: Palgrave, 2005.

——, and Michael Wilson. *Grand-Guignol: The French Theatre of Horror*, Exeter: University of Exeter Press, 2002.

Hansen, Miriam. *Babel and Babylon: Spectatorship in American Silent Film*, Cambridge: Harvard University Press, 1991.

Harding Colin, and Simon Popple, eds. *In the Kingdom of the Shadows: A Companion to Early Cinema*, London: Cygnus Arts, 1996.

Hepworth, Cecil M. *Animated Photography: The ABC of the Cinematograph*, London: Newman & Guardia, 1897.
——. *Came The Dawn: Memories of a Film Pioneer*, London: Phoenix House, 1951.
Hepworth, T.C. *The Book of the Lantern, Being a Practical Guide to the Working of the Optical (or Magic) Lantern*, London: Hazell, Watson, and Viney, 1894.
Hervouet, Yves. *The French Face of Joseph Conrad*, Cambridge: Cambridge University Press, 1990.
Hewitt, Douglas. *Conrad: A Reassessment*, London: Bowes (3rd ed.), 1975.
Hutchinson's Magazine XIV August 1925.
Ibsen, Henrik. *Hedda Gabler and Other Plays*, Harmondsworth: Penguin, 1961.
——. *A Doll's House and Other Plays*, Harmondsworth: Penguin, 1965.
Innes, Christopher, ed. *A Sourcebook on Naturalist Theatre*, London: Routledge, 2000.
James, Henry. *The Art of the Novel: Critical Prefaces with an Introduction by R. P. Blackmur*, New York: Charles Scribner's Sons, 1934.
——. *The Scenic Art*, London: Rupert Hart-Davis, 1949.
——. *Selected Literary Criticism*, ed. Morris Shapiro, Harmondsworth: Penguin, 1968.
Jean-Aubry, G. 'Joseph Conrad and Music,' *The Chesterian* 6.42 (November 1924): 37–42.
——. *Joseph Conrad: Life and Letters Vol II*, London: Heinemann, 1927.
Jones, Henry Arthur. *Saints and Sinners: A New and Original Drama of Modern English Middle-Class Life*, London: Macmillan, 1891.
Jones, Susan. *Conrad and Women*, Oxford: Clarendon, 1999.
Joy, Neill R. 'The Conrad-Hastings Correspondence and the Staging of *Victory*,' *Conradiana* 35:3 (Fall 2003): 184–225.
Joyce, Stanislaus. *My Brother's Keeper: James Joyce's Early Years*, New York: Viking Press, 1958.
Karl, Frederick R. *A Reader's Guide to Joseph Conrad*, London: Thames and Hudson, 1960.
Karl, Frederick R. *Joseph Conrad: The Three Lives*, London: Faber and Faber, 1979.
Keating, Peter. 'Conrad's *Doll's House*,' in *Papers on Language and Literature Presented to Alvar Ellegard and Erik Frykman*, ed. Sven Backman and Goran Kjellmer, Goteberg: ACTA Universitatis Gothoburgensis, 1985. 221–31.
Kerman, Joseph. *Opera as Drama*, New York: Knopf, 1956.
Kierkegaard, Søren. *Either/Or* (1843), trans. David F. Swenson and Lillian Marvin Swenson, with revision and foreword by Howard A. Johnson, vol. 1. New York: Anchor Books, 1959.
Kirschner, Paul. 'Conrad, Ibsen and the Description of Humanity,' *Conradiana* 25.3 (Autumn 1993): 178–206.
Knowles, Owen. *A Conrad Chronology*, Basingstoke: Macmillan, 1989.

Knowles, Owen, and Gene M. Moore. *Oxford Reader's Companion to Conrad*, Oxford: Oxford University Press, 2001.
Koestenbaum, Wayne. *The Queen's Throat: Opera, Homosexuality and the Mystery of Desire*, London: GMP, 1991.
Krafft-Ebing, R. von. *Psychopathia Sexualis,* trans. F. J. Rebman, London: Rebman, 1901.
Leavis, F.R. *The Great Tradition* (1948), Harmondsworth: Penguin, 1974.
Lewis, I. M. *Ecstatic Religion: An Anthropological Study of Spirit Possession and Shamanism*, Harmondsworth: Penguin, 1971.
Lindenberger, Herbert. *Opera The Extravagant Art*, Ithaca: Cornell University Press, 1984.
Lodge, David. 'Conrad's "Victory" and "The Tempest": an Amplification,' *Modern Languages Review* 59.2 (1964): 195–9.
Loewenberg, Alfred. *Annals of Opera, 1597–1940*, 2 vols. Geneva: Societas Bibliographica, 1955.
Low, Hugh. *Sarawak; Its Inhabitants and Produtions: Being Notes During a Residence in the country with H. H. The Rajah Brooke*, London: Richard Bentley, 1848.
MacCarthy, Desmond. *Drama*, London: Putnam, 1940.
MacKenzie, John M. *Propaganda & Empire: The Manipulation of British Public Opinion 1880–1960*, Manchester: Manchester University Press, 1984.
Mallios, Peter. 'Declaring Victory: Towards Conrad's Poetics of Democracy,' *Conradiana* 35: 3 (Fall 2003): 145–83.
Mamet, David. *Oleanna*, London: Methuen, 1993.
Mangan, J. A. *Athleticism in the Victorian & Edwardian Public School: The emergence & consolidation of the educational ideology*, Cambridge: Cambridge University Press, 1981.
Mashman, Valerie. 'Warriors & Weavers: A Study of Gender Relations Among the Iban of Sarawak,' in *Female & Male in Borneo: Contributions & Challenges to Gender Studies*, ed. Vinson H. Sutlive Jr., vol. 1. Williamsburg, VA: Borneo Research Council 1993. 231–70.
McFarlane, Brian. *Novel to Film: An Introduction to the Theory of Adaptation*, Oxford: Clarendon, 1996.
Mégroz, R. C. *A Talk with Joseph Conrad and a Criticism of his Mind and Method*, London: Elkin Matthews, 1926.
Meyer, Bernard C. *Joseph Conrad: A Psychoanalytical Biography*, Princeton: Princeton University Press, 1970.
Meyers, Jeffrey. *Joseph Conrad*, London: John Murray, 1991.
Moi, Toril. *Sexual/Textual Politics: Feminist Literary Theory*, London: Methuen, 1985.
Money, Tony. *Manly & Muscular Diversions: Public Schools & the Nineteenth-Century Sporting Revival*, London: Duckworth, 1997.
Monod, Sylvère. 'Heemskirk, the Dutch Lieutenant,' *The Conradian* 31.2 (2006): 85–91.

Moore, Gene M. 'Conrad's "film-play" *Gaspar the Strong Man*,' in *Conrad on Film*, ed. Gene M. Moore, Cambridge: Cambridge University Press, 1997. 31–47.
Morf, Gustav. *The Polish Shades and Ghosts of Joseph Conrad*, New York: Astra Books, 1976.
Moser, Thomas. *Joseph Conrad: Achievement and Decline*, Cambridge: Harvard University Press, 1957.
Mulvey, Laura. *Visual and Other Pleasures*, Basingstoke: Macmillan, 1989.
Najder, Zdzisław. *Joseph Conrad: A Life*, Rochester, NY: Camden House, 2007.
Naremore, James. *Acting in the Cinema*, Berkeley: University of California Press, 1988.
New Grove Dictionary of Music and Musicians, ed. Stanley Sadie, 2nd ed. London: Macmillan, 2001.
New Grove Dictionary of Musical Instruments, ed. Stanley Sadie, vol. 1. London: Macmillan, 1984.
New Grove Dictionary of Opera, ed. Stanley Sadie, vol. 2. London: Macmillan, 1992.
O'Brien, H.A. 'Latah,' *Journal of the Straits Branch of the Royal Asiatic Society* (June 1883): 143–53.
Ogilvie, J.S. *Hand Shadows on the Wall; Comprising Amusing & Novel Figures to be Formed by the Hands*, New York: Ogilvie, 1889.
Pearson, Roberta. *Eloquent Gestures: The Transformation of Performance Style in the Griffith Biograph Films*, Berkeley: University of California Press, 1992.
Postacioglu-Banon, Sema. '"Gaspar Ruiz": A Vitagraph of Desire,' *The Conradian* 28.2 (Autumn 2003): 29–44.
Pratt, Mary Louise. *Imperial Eyes: Travel Writing & Transculturation*, London: Routledge, 1992.
Proust, Marcel. *Remembrance of Things Past*, trans. C.K. Scott Moncrieff and Terence Kilmartin, vol. 2. New York: Vintage, 1982.
Ray, Martin, ed. *Joseph Conrad: Interviews and Recollections*, Basingstoke: Macmillan, 1990.
Rees, A.L. 'Cinema and the Avant-Garde,' in *The Oxford History of World Cinema*, ed. Geoffrey Nowell-Smith, Oxford: Oxford University Press, 1997. 95–105.
Roberts, Andrew Michael. 'What else could I tell him?: Confessing to Women and Lying to Men in Conrad's Fiction,' *L'Epoque Conradienne* 19 (1993): 7–23.
———. *Conrad and Masculinity*, Basingstoke: Palgrave, 2000.
Rudlin, John. *Commedia dell'arte*, London: Routledge, 1994.
Sacher-Masoch, Leopold. 'Venus in Furs,' in Gilles Deleuze, *Masochism: An Interpretation of Coldness and Cruelty*, trans. Jean McNeil, New York: Zone Books 1991. 143–276.
Said, Edward. *Orientalism: Western Conceptions of the Orient*, London: Penguin, 1978.
Salt, Barry. 'Film Form 1900–1906,' in *Early Cinema: Space, Frame, Narrative*, ed. Thomas Elsaesser, London: BFI, 1990. 31–44.

——. *Film Style and Technology: History and Analysis*, London: Starword, 1992.
Schmidgall, Gary. *Literature as Opera*, Oxford: Oxford University Press, 1977.
Schultheiss, Thomas. 'Lord Hamlet and Lord Jim,' *Polish Review* 11.4 (1966): 101–33.
Schwab, Arnold T. 'Conrad's American Speeches and His Reading from Victory,' *Modern Philology* 62.4 (May 1965): 342–47.
Scott, James C. *Domination & the Arts of Resistance: Hidden Transcripts*, New Haven & London: Yale University Press, 1990.
Shaw, George Bernard. *Complete Works of Bernard Shaw Volumes 25: Our Theatres in the Nineties Volume 3*, London: Constable, 1931.
——. *Plays Unpleasant*, Harmondsworth: Penguin, 1977.
Sherry, Norman, ed. *Conrad: The Critical Heritage*, London: Routledge & Kegan Paul, 1973.
Showalter, Elaine. *The Female Malady: Women, Madness & English Culture, 1830–1980,* London: Virago Press, 1995.
Simmons, Allan. '"Conflicting Impulses": Focalization and the Presentation of Culture in *Almayer's Folly*,' *Conradiana* 29.3 (1997): 163–72.
Skeat, William Walter. *Malay Magic, being an Introduction to the folk-lore & popular religion of the Malay Peninsula*, Singapore: Oxford University Press 1984.
Smith, James Walter. 'Joseph Conrad – Master Mariner and Novelist,' *Boston Evening Transcript* 12 May 1923, reprinted in *Joseph Conrad: Interviews and Recollections*, ed. Martin Ray, Basingstoke: Macmillan, 1990. 181–9.
Solomon, Matthew. '"Twenty-five heads under one hat": Quick-Change in the 1890s,' in *Meta-Morphing: Visual Transformation and the Culture of Quick-Change*, ed. Vivian Carol Sobchack, Minneapolis: University of Minnesota Press, 2000. 3–20.
Staiger, Janet. 'The Eyes Are Really the Focus: Photoplay Acting and Film Form and Style,' *Wide Angle* 6.4 (1985): 14–23.
Stape, John. *The Several Lives of Joseph Conrad*, London: Heinemann, 2007.
Steiner, George. *The Death of Tragedy*, London: Faber, 1961.
Steinmeyer, Jim. *Hiding the Elephant: How Magicians Invented the Impossible and Learned to Disappear*, New York: Carroll & Graf, 2004.
Stern, Lesley. '*The Tales of Hoffman*: An Instance of Operality,' in *Between Opera and Cinema*, ed. Jeongwon Joe and Rose Theresa, New York: Routledge, 2002. 39–57.
Stewart, Heather, ed. *Early and Silent Cinema: A Source Book*, London: British Film Institute, 1996.
Strindberg, August. *Advent: A Play in Five Acts*, trans. Claud Field, London: Holden & Hardingham, 1921.
——. *Plays: 1*, London: Methuen, 1982.
——. *Plays: 2*, London: Methuen, 1982.
——. *Plays: 3*, London: Methuen, 1993.

Sutlive Jr., Vinson H. *The Iban of Sarawak*, Prospect Heights, IL: Waveland Press, 1988.
Swinburne, Algernon Charles. *A Study of Shakespeare*, London: Chatto and Windus, 1880.
Thompson, Bill. *Sadomasochism: Painful Perversion or Pleasurable Play?*, London: Cassell, 1994.
Tittle, Walter. 'The Conrad Who Sat For Me,' in *Joseph Conrad: Interviews and Recollections*, ed. Martin Ray, Basingstoke: Macmillan, 1990. 153–63.
Tree, L. Stanley. 'The Shadow Play,' *Pearson's Magazine* 3.16 April 1897: 480–84.
Verdi, Giuseppe. *Lettere 1835–1900*, ed. M. Porzio, Milan: Mondadori, 2000.
Wagner, Richard. *Opera and Drama*, trans. William Ashton Ellis, Lincoln: University of Nebraska Press, 1995.
Watt, Ian. *Conrad in the Nineteenth Century*, Berkeley: University of California Press, 1979.
Watts, Cedric. 'Introduction and Notes,' *Victory*, London: Everyman, 1994. xv–xxxiv.
——. '*The Ebb-Tide* and *Victory*,' *Conradiana* 28.2 (1996): 133–7.
——. *A Preface to Conrad*, Harlow: Longman 1993.
Wheatley, Alison E. 'Conrad's *One Day More*: Challenging Social and Dramatic Convention,' *The Conradian* 24.1 (Spring 1999): 1–17.
——. 'Laughing Anne: an Almost Unbearable Spectacle,' in *Conradiana* 34.1–2 (Spring/Summer 2002): 63–76.
White, Andrea. *Joseph Conrad and the Adventure Tradition*, Cambridge: Cambridge University Press, 1993.
Winzeler, Robert L. '*Latah* in Sarawak with Special Reference to the Iban,' in *Female & Male in Borneo: Contributions & Challenges to Gender Studies*, ed. Vinson H. Sutlive Jr., vol. 1. Williamsburg, VA: Borneo Research Council 1993. 317–33.
Žižek, Slavoj, and Mladen Dolar. *Opera's Second Death*, New York: Routledge, 2002.

Index

Works by Joseph Conrad appear under their titles; works by others appear under the author's name.

Acres, Birt 69
acting 1, 88–9, 90, 141, 141n31
aesthetic modernism 76
alliteration 50
Almayer's Folly (1895) 17, 18, 19–20, 31, 32, 34–8, 102–3, 144n36
    'Author's Note' 11, 18, 19, 23
    behaviour from cultural programming and stereotyping 18
    frontstage performance and backstage contradictions 34–5
    frontstage performance and spirit possession 31, 37–8
    importance and writing of 1, 2, 13, 13n3, 14
    interracial marriage in 136
    Mrs Almayer as "acting a mask" 35
    Nina and Dain 13, 19–20
    opera's influences 129, 131–3, 143–4, 144n36
    'look, the' 39
American cinema 67–8, 94–5, 108–9
Andreas, Osborn 50, 54, 57
animals 36–7, 50
anthropology 5, 12
Archer, William 1, 2
Armstrong, Tim 74
Arrow of Gold, The (1919) 103, 104–5
the arts 89, 99, 110, 129–30, 135
audience cinema 69
    Conrad on 14–15, 81, 94, 125, 137, 140
    opera 136–7, 137n27
    shadowgraphy, Conrad on 109
    theatre 1, 104, 105
'Author and Cinematograph' (1923 lecture) 72, 79, 80–81, 83

Baines, Jocelyn 46, 47, 54, 55, 114
Baker, Josephine 5

Batchelor, John 116, 117, 118, 125
'Because of the Dollars' (1915) 3, 46, 59, 83, 83n8
Beckett, Samuel *Endgame* 51
Beerbohm, Max parody of 'The Lagoon' (1912), 98, 98n2
Bender, Todd K. 78, 80
Benjamin, Walter 'The Work of Art in an Age of Mechanical Reproduction' 75–6
Berthoud, Jacques 35
Betts, Ernest *Heraclitus: of the Future of Films* 68n6
Bhabha, Homi K. 33, 42
'Black Mate, The' (1908), 13n3
Blackmur, R.P. 63, 63n2
Bluestone, George 77, 80
body language 64, 132, 141
Bond, Edward 58
    'The Village School' and 'The City' in *Jackets* (1989) 58
bourgeois culture 6, 7, 11–12, 55, 56, 61
Brewster, Ben 88–9
British cinema 68–70
Busza, Andrzez 120

'Censor of Plays: An Appreciation, The' (1907) 3
censorship of British theatre 3
    of opera 135–6, 136n25
    Poland and Korzeniowski's Shakespeare translation 122
Chanan, Michael 69, 70n9, 71
Chance (1913) 6, 7, 59, 72–5, 83, 105, 122–4, 124n14, 125
    and Korzeniowski's work 123–4, 124n14
    light and dark motif, and shadows in 105, 106, 107

Shakespeare and doubling motif 122
character development, and action to
    clarify a theme 9
  appearance to fit role and type 49–51
  behaviours from cultural programming
    and stereotyping 18
  characters as actors, in *Victory* 66
  and *commedia dell'arte* 48
  Conrad and female characters 6–7
  Conrad on, for *Almayer's Folly* 4,
    13–14
  of Europeans imperialist adventurers, 16
  influenced by racial and cultural
    studies 5
  as voices both polyphonic and
    heterogeneous 4, 9, 12, 14, 27
cinema; *see also* film visual image
    techniques
  aesthetics and technology 75–6
  avant-garde and cinema writing
    (1912–1914) 82–3, 83n7
  cinematic narration, in *Victory* 85–6,
    86n11, 86n13
  and Conrad 66, 68, 70–74, 72n12,
    78–9, 80–83, 85–9, 92–4, 140–41,
    141n31
  cross influences with fiction 77, 78, 94,
    94n22
  documentary 'human interest' films 69
  early film 67–8, 69, 79–80, 87–8
  effects of camera 75–6
  first public screening 1
  influence on Conrad's fiction 66–7
  magic-lantern tradition in 69
  melodrama and 68n5, 68n6
  and middle class attraction to 93–4
  'moving pictures', Conrad and double
    meaning 79
  narrative cinema 82, 85–6, 86n11,
    886n13, 88–9, 88n18, 93–5
  peeping Tom films 67, 68
  pre-narrative films 87–8, 90, 90n19,
    141, 141n31
  quality and acceptance of 93–4, 94n22
  as replacing shadowgraphy 103
  and romanticised masculinity 90
  self-image productions and 79–80,
    87–8

successive scenes, in Conrad's fiction
    70–71
  and technology for visual pleasures, in
    Chance 72–5
  and voyeurism 67–8
Cinematographe 68
Cinematographe-Lumière 70; *see also*
    Lumière, Auguste and Louis
Clifford, James 11–12, 15, 15n6
Clifford, Sir Hugh 13n4, 16, 16n8
  life and author 15
  The Downfall of the Gods (1911), 140
Close Up journal (Macpherson Bryher and
    H.D.) 75
cloth industry and trade 33–4
colonialism 30–31, 42–3, 115–16; *see also*
    imperialism
comedy, classical performance comedy in
    'Freya of the Seven Isles' 47, 49
comedy and tragedy 58, 116
  and Conrad 57–8
commedia dell'arte 6, 45, 48–53
Conrad, Borys (son) 113, 120
Conrad, John (son) 104, 104n15
Conrad, Joseph
  on audience 14–15, 77, 78–9, 80, 81,
    91, 94, 113–14, 125, 137, 140
  on characters 4–5, 13–14, 63–6
  collaborations of 59
  and criticism 3, 47, 54, 97, 98
  early fiction 13, 20, 131
  and Hamlet 113–14
  and his father (Korzeniowski) 113
  Hugh Clifford on 13n4, 15, 15n4, 16,
    16n8, 140
  on imperial genre of the East 5, 11,
    11n1, 19–20
  legacy 4, 6, 54, 57–8, 81, 84–5, 97,
    98, 140
  on literary endings 52
  and Malaysia 15–16, 15n5, 17–18
  on narratives 79, 143
  and nationalism 3
  and new imperialist genre 5–6, 9, 11,
    12, 14, 16–17, 19–20, 27
  novels after *Victory* 116–17, 117n6
  personal life of 8–9, 14, 15, 100, 102,
    104, 105–6, 111, 113–14, 120

on photography 78, 79
popular literary genres and 45, 52
on shadowgraphaphy 100, 108–9, 110
on shadows 105–8
and success 80–81, 80n3, 83
on theatre 3, 4, 45–7, 58, 59, 66
'theatrical imagination' 3, 45, 54, 59, 60, 66
on Wagner 129, 129n11, 130
on writing 13, 14–15, 125, 129–31, 141, 141n32
Cook, Olive 100
Cox, C.B., 47, 54
Crane, Stephen 66, 78, 130, 141n30
Cunninghame Graham, R.B. 59, 102, 106, 135
Curle, Richard 46, 67
curtains 20, 34, 34n8, 35, 38, 52, 73

Danius, Sara *The Senses of Modernism* 76
Davies, Laurence 15n5
death, and dark and light motif 98–9
and sexual relationships 39, 40
Deleuze, Gilles 40
Demeny, Georges 68
Devant, David 105
dialogue 55, 60, 63, 64
Dilke, Donald A. 115
Donovan, Stephen 46–7, 66–7, 70, 71, 72, 78
'Sunshine and Shadows: Conrad and Early Cinema' 78
drama and dramatic art, Korzeniowski on 121
dress, Conrad and character introduction 24
as cultural markers of status 23–4
as expression of resentment 33–4
of imperial adventurers, in *Lord Jim* 26
of Malay nobility 23–4
and Mrs Travers' Malay dress 5, 13, 23, 24–6, 139
the red dressing-gown, in *An Outcast of the Islands* 33
'Duel, The' (1908) 45

Elbert, Monika 47, 52, 53
Eliot, George 129, 130

Eliot, T.S. 110
emotions, and conflict between class and real feelings 62–3
crying/laughing 57–8
'Freya of the Seven Isles' 52–3
metaphorically represented by interior décor, in 'The Return' 61–2
'End of the Tether, The' (1902) 97, 106, 107
endings of Conrad fiction 6, 52–3
'English Literary Theatre' 1
English 'Literary Tradition' 2
English novel in late nineteenth century 77
Erdinast-Vulcan, Daphna 45, 46, 47, 53
eroticism 38–9, 40, 67–8, 74
ethnography 11–12, 15, 15n6
European film industry 68, 94–5
European theatre 2
Everett, John 106
Expressionist drama, and Strindberg 56
in *The Secret Agent* and *Victory* 56–7

Famous Players-Lasky 81, 94
female characters 6–8; *see also* women
colonised female 31–8
melodrama and clichés of femininity 6–7, 46, 53, 58
as object of male desire 6–7, 47
victimization 68, 74, 74n16, 75
and voyeurism in early film 67–8
film distribution 82
film, visual image techniques 68–71, 74, 75–6
abstract animation and hand-printing 83, 83n7
alternating close-ups and long shots 70, 73
angle of view, in *Chance* 72–3
cinematic projection of flickering 70, 70n10, 71–2, 72n11
close-ups 68, 69–70, 73, 74, 88
continuity cinema (film editing) 82, 82n6, 93, 94n22
cross-cutting for parallel action 82
fade out 71, 86
fragmenting of the body 71, 73
keyhole peeping, 68, 86
long shot and street-filming, 71

medium shots 89
parallel editing to create suspense 82, 92, 92n21
peep-show 67, 73
of screen direction 82, 82n6
slowing and speeding of time 72, 72n12
sound 73–4
split-screen 68
Flaubert, Gustave 133, 142
Ford, Ford Madox 59, 77, 129n9
Henry James: A Critical Study 63, 63n2
Fordian impressionism 77
French cinema 68, 71, 94–5
Freud, Sigmund 70n10
Freudian symbolism, in 'The Return' 54
Freudian undercurrents, in *She* 38–9
'Freya of the Seven Isles: A Story of Shallow Waters' (1912) 6, 47–53, 58
futurists 83n7

Galsworthy John 105, 125, 129, 130n14
'A Portrait' 128
Garnett, Edward 59–60, 98, 113
Garrick, David 2
'Gaspar Ruiz' (1906), 3, 67
Gaspar the Strong Man (film-script) 3, 4, 59, 66, 81
Geertz, Clifford 12, 14, 16, 17, 21, 27
gender, gendered behaviour, in *Victory* 89, 90, 91
inverted gender roles in *The Rescue* 138
ghosts 46, 47
Gish, Lillian 67, 68
Goffman, Erving 30
Presentation of Self in Everyday Life, the (Goffman) 30
Gogwilt, Christopher 15
Gorky, Maxim 103
Gosse, Edmund 2
Grand-Guignol 4, 45–7
Graver, Lawrence 45, 46, 48, 54
Greenblatt, Stephen 12
Greenlees, T. Duncan 5
Greiffenhagen, Maurice 'Typhoon' 98

Griffith, D.W. 82, 88, 88n18, 92
Guerard, Albert J. 54, 83–4
Conrad the Novelist (1958), 98
Gullick, J.M. 31–2

Haggard, H. Rider 13
She 38–9
Hampson, Robert 11, 16, 23, 24, 27n13
Betrayal and Identity 90
on 'Freya of the Seven Isles' 52
on 'The Return' 55
on *Victory* 45, 83, 84, 90, 91
Hand, Richard 66, 99
The Theatre of Joseph Conrad 66
Hardy, Thomas
Tess of the D'Urbervilles (1891 play), 3
Hastings, Basil Macdonald 4, 59, 63
Heart of Darkness (1899) 1, 77, 86, 97, 98–9, 107, 108, 114n5, 133, 134–5
Heart of Darkness (opera) 128n6
Hepworth, Cecil
Animated Photography: The ABC of the Cinematograph (1897) 69, 69n7, 72n11
Hepworth Films 69
Explosion of a Motor Car (1900) 71
Hepworth, T.C. *The Book of the Lantern* (1894), 69, 69n7
Hewitt, Douglas 45
horror in Conrad's fiction 46

Ibsen, Henrik, *A Doll's House* (1879) 55–6
Conrad's knowledge of 59–60
Ghosts 60
Hedda Gabler 55
Realist plays of 55
'Idiots, The' (1896) 46–7
illusion, stage illusion and magic 101, 104–5
imperial literature 12, 16–18
imperial romance literature 13, 14, 20, 21, 26, 114, 117, 141
imperialism, Conrad on 5–6, 41, 41n17
European/native hierarchies of
The Tempest and *Victory* 115–16
imperial encounter 12

impression management of colonial
power 30
and power and performance 30–31
'impression management' 30
individuality and photography, Conrad on
78–9
'Informer, The' (1906) 45
international film-making 94–5; *see also
under separate countries*
irony 91
and Conrad 4, 23, 115
Italian comedy 47–53

Jacobs, Lea 88–9
James, Henry 1, 2–3, 63, 130, 135
Daisy Miller (1879), adaptation to play
in 1882 3, 52
Preface for *Henry James: A Critical
Study* 63
on 'scenic method' 63
The American (1877), adaptation to
play in 1891 3
Javanese shadow theatre 100
Jones, Henry Arthur 1, 2
Saints and Sinners (play) 1
Joyce, James 'mythic method' 84
Silhouettes 110, 110n21

'Karain' (1897) 13, 22–3, 26–7, 46
Karl, Frederick 3, 115
Kaszewski, Kazimierz 120–21, 121n10
Kellar, Harry 104
Kenyon, Sagar 87, 87n15, 88
Kermode, Frank 116, 118
Kierkegaard, Søren, *Either/Or* 97
Knowles, Owen 55, 102
Koestenbaum, Wayne
'Pocket Guide to Queer Moments in
Opera' 144n36
Korzeniowski, Apollo (father) 111, 113,
120–22, 123–4, 124n14
"Dzisiezszym" ("To the
Contempories") (poem) 120
and influencing Conrad on Shakespeare
8–9, 111–12, 113–14, 122
Komedia (play) 120
'Studia nad Dramatycznością w
Utworach Szekspira' ('Studies
on the Dramatic Elements in
Shakespeare's Works') (essay) 121
translations of Shakespeare comedies
120–21
Krafft-Ebing, R. von
Psychopathia Sexualis 40, 41

'Lagoon, The' (1896) 13, 98, 98n2
language; *see also* dialogue
non-verbal language of movement
49–50, 64, 132, 141
latah (possessed by spirits) 5, 31, 36, 37,
41
Laughing Anne (1920), play adaptation of
'Because of the Dollars' 4, 46, 59,
83, 83n8, 99
Laughter, crying/laughing as commonplace
in melodrama 57–8
laughter motif 123–4
lazzi 51, 58
Leavis, F.R. 98
Leitmotif 133–4 134n22, 143
Les Misérables (film version by Frank
Lloyd 1918) 4, 66
light and dark motif, Conrad and 97, 98–9,
102–3
Lindenberger, Herbert 141n32
literary fiction of late nineteenth century 1,
12, 17, 80, 135, 141, 141n32
literary impressionism 77–8
'Literary Theatre' 1–2
'look, the' 39, 74, 75
Lord Jim (1900) 5, 13, 20–23, 26, 68, 90,
112, 114, 116, 119, 136
Lumière Auguste and Louis 1, 68, 87, 88
Cinematographe-Lumière 70
'Street in Paris' (feature) 103
Workers Leaving the Factory (1895) 88

magic shows and stage illusion 104–5
'make us see', Conrad and 14–15, 49, 77,
78–9, 81–2, 85, 91, 93, 94
Malay society 4, 26, 32, 38
Malay voices, 4–5, 19
Malaysia 11–27
Conrad and 15, 16
Malay Magic (Skeat) and Hugh Low
and Rajah Brooke 37

Sir Hugh Clifford and 15, 16
male characters, and abandonment 57
   emasculation of 38–9, 52
   and European view of males who 'went native' 41
   and Mrs Travers's Malay costume 24–5, 139
   in pre-narrative cinema genre 90
   and role reversal in *An Outcast of the Islands* 41
   and the woman as object of desire and rage 38, 39–40, 52
male/female relationship; *see also* female characters; male characters; sexuality
   and gender role reversal 38–9, 138
   and learned gendered behaviours 89, 90, 91
   Malay females and frontstage performance 37–9
   and male secret brutality 32, 33, 61, 70–71
   male role in 34–6, 60–61
Mallios, Peter 83, 84, 85, 91
Mamet, David 55
marionette performance 48, 53, 102
Mascou 27
Maskelyne, John Nevil 104–5, 104n15
masks "acting a mask" 32, 35, 37
   in *commedia dell'arte* 48, 49, 50, 51
   in melodrama main characters, Chiyo and Matsuo 58
McHale, Brian 84
melodrama; *see also* Grand-Guignol 1, 45, 46, 53, 55, 58, 68, 68n5, 84, 92, 94, 110
   and Conrad 6–7, 45–6, 52, 140
Meyer, Bernard C. 41
Meyerbeer, Giacomo 128, 128n7, 129, 131, 136
mimicry 33
Mirror of the Sea, The (1906) 102, 106, 107
Mitchell, James 87, 87n15, 88
modernism 77
   and postmodernism in Conrad 84–5
Moi, Toril 75
Monod, Sylvère 6

Moore, Gene M. 55, 66, 67, 80, 80n3, 92n21, 102
Moser, Thomas
   Joseph Conrad: Achievement and Decline (1957), 98, 116
movie theatres 67, 82, 93
'moving pictures' 79
Mulvey, Laura 75
music halls 1, 45–6, 79
Mutascope 67

Najder, Zdzislaw 3, 120
naked eye 76
narration, Conrad on 17, 26, 53, 77, 79, 85, 86
   role of 104, 124
narrative cinema 82, 85–6, 86n11, 86n13, 88–9, 88n18, 92, 93
narrative, in shadowgraphy and stage illusionism 104
nationalism, Korzeniowski's writings and Poland 120, 122
   and opera, 136
nickelodeons 67, 82
Nigger of the 'Narcissus', The (1897), 1, 15, 98, 100–101, 107
   Preface, 14–15, 77, 78–9
Nostromo (1904) 103, 130n14, 133, 141
Notes on Life and Letters (1921) (essay collection), 105

One Day More (1905 play), 3, 57–8
opera, and conflicts of allegiance 136
   Conrad on, 127–9, 127n4, 128n6, 129n9, 130, 130n14, 131–3, 136, 136n26, 141–2, 145
   and fiction 127, 141, 141n32
   historical censorship of 135–6, 136n25
   and nationalism 136
   nineteenth-century and religions 131
   popularity and world audience, 136–7, 137n27
   realty of 47, 138–9, 139n28
   as tragedy and comedy 142, 144n36
   unsuitable authors for 117, 117n3
Orientalism 12, 12n2, 19
'Orientalist' fictions 16

'other' 12, 22–3, 25; *see also* colonialism; imperialism
Outcast of the Islands, An (1896) 13, 31, 38–42, 70, 131, 136
  Aïssa's performance 38–41
  Joanna's behaviour and frontstage performance 32–3, 34, 37, 37n13
  as opera narrative 131, 131n16, 133, 141, 142–3

panorama 70–71, 102, 107
Paramount (formerly Famous Players-Lasky) 94
Paul, R.W., *The Countryman and the Cinematograph* (1901 film), 69, 87–8
Pavilion 66
peep-shows 67, 73
perception, investigation of perception as literary impressionism in Conrad 77
performance, and colonialism 4–5, 19, 31, 39–40, 41, 42–3
  of Conrad as writer 13
  as continuum between opera and display of Englishness, in *The Rescue* 138
  culture as (Geertz and Clifford) 12
  declaration of love as, in 'The Return' 60
  dialogue as function of 60
  as display of culture and stereotyping 42
  of imperial encounter 5, 12, 16, 21–2, 26, 29–30
  and *lazzi* in *commedia dell'arte* 51
  in pre-narrative cinema 88
  roles shaped by, in *Victory* 66, 90–91
  as stage performance, Edith Travers and the Malay dress 5, 13, 23, 24–6, 119, 139
  stage soliloquy as 133
  and writing as 13, 14–15, 16
performing arts and Conrad 3, 4, 10
Personal Record, A (1912) 8, 13–14, 17, 104, 111, 142
photography 11, 76
  Conrad on 78–9, 99

Pinker, Eric 72, 81
Pinker, J.B. 66, 67, 81
Pinter, Harold 55
'Planter of Malata, The' (1914) 103
Plato, *Republic* 100
Poland, nationalism 120, 123
Polish opera 136
popular performance genre 45–7
Poradowska, Marguerite (Aunt) 112, 129, 131
postmodernism 58, 84–5, 94
Pratt, Mary Louise 40
Proust, Marcel, *The Guermantes Way* 76
psychology 5
Punch and Judy puppets 48, 102

racial and cultural interests of the late nineteenth century 5, 14
reader, Conrad on 'to see' and 'made to see' 14–15, 49, 77–8, 81–2, 85, 91, 93, 94
realism, Conrad and 17
  post-Realist plays (Strindberg) 56
reality 137–40
  and truth 16, 19
redemption, in *Victory* 66
repetition, leitmotif and 133–4, 134n22
rescue genre 93; *see also Rescue*; *Victory*
rescue motif 91, 92
Rescue, The (1920) 21–2, 107–8, 129n29–30, 137–40, 139n29–30
  Edith Travers and Malay dress 5, 13, 23, 24–6, 119, 139
  and inverted gender roles 138
'Return, The' (1898) 6, 7, 53–8, 60–63, 109
Roberts, Michael 74n16
Romance (1915 film) 67
romance, and adventure 17–18
  and anti-romance 53
  imperial romance 1, 16, 20, 21, 22, 114, 117, 118, 141
  and male disfigurement 117
  post-romance, in *The Rover* 119
romantic fiction 47
The Rover (1923) 98, 117–20

Sacher-Masoch, Leopold von, *Venus in Furs* (1870) 41
sadomasochism 40–41, 40n15
Said, Edward 12, 18
Schmidgall, Gary 127
Schultheiss, Thomas, 'Lord Hamlet and Lord Jim' 112
Scott, James C. 30–31, 38
Secret Agent, The (1907) 3, 6, 46, 53, 57, 59, 70–71, 72, 98, 125
'see' and 'made to see' 14–15, 49, 77–8, 81, 85–6, 91, 93, 94
self 14, 78
self-image 13, 79, 79n1, 87–8
Set of Six, A (1908) 45, 102
sexual harassment in early film 68
    in pre-narrative cinema 90
    and sadomasochism 40–41
shadow theatre 100–102
Shadow-Line, The (1917) 103, 114n5
shadowgraphy; *see also* light and dark motif; shadow theatre
    and Conrad 8, 97, 103–4
    'electric shadows' 103, 103n13
    hand shadows and stage illusion performance 104
    literary treatment of 109–10, 109n20
    professional prestidigitators 101
    shadow-theatre in cinema 108–9
    as silhouettes 100–101, 101n7, 103
shadows 71–2, 106–8
Shakespeare, William 2, 27, 45
    A Midsummer Night's Dream 123
    The Comedy of Errors 121–2, 123
    Hamlet 112–14
    Korzeniowski on 120, 121
    The Tempest 111, 114–16, 114n5
    Translations, *see* Korzeniowski, Apollo
Shakespeare's influence on Conrad 8–9, 55, 121–4, 123n12, 125
    character figures 122–3, 123n12
    influence in later Conrad, 116–17
    as mediated through father, Apollo Korzeniowski 8–9, 111–12, 122
    multiple tellings and framings, in *Chance* 123–4
    and romance genre 119

    The Tempest and *Hamlet*, and *Lord Jim* and *Victory* similarities 116
    thematic similarities in Hamlet and *Lord Jim* (Schultheiss) 112
    and tragedies 111
Shaw, George Bernard 1, 62–3
Sidis, Boris *Multiple personality* (1905) 70
Simmons, Alan 15, 20
slapstick comedy 51
spectacle 12n2, 16, 19, 29, 46, 68, 68n5, 121
Spectator 16
spectator 49, 53, 79–80, 85, 86, 91
    voyeurism in early American film 67–8, 69
spirit possession 36–7; *see also latah*
Stape, John 3
Steiner, George 2
stereotype, Conrad on 17–18, 19–20
    Eastern sterotype 11, 21, 24
Stevenson, Robert Louis, *The Ebb-Tide* 17, 84
Stewart, Heather 67–8
story-telling 38
Strindberg, August 56
    Shapes and Shadows in *Advent* (1900 play) 109, 109n20–21
Survage, Leopold 83n7
Suspense (1925) 103, 120n9
Swinburne, Algernon Charles 2

tele-vision-scope 103–4
Théâtre des Ombres in Chat Noir cabaret (Paris) 100, 109
theatre of late nineteenth century; *see also* Grand-Guignol
    British censorship 3, 140
    magic shows and stage illusion 104–5
    relationship to early cinema in acting 88–9
    Shaw's 'theatrical method' citation 62–3
    'theatrical imagination', in 'The Return' 54, 59–63
Thompson, Bill 40, 41
'To-morrow' (1902) 3, 57, 128n6
Tourneur, Maurice 66
Trewey, Felicien 103, 103n13

Under Western Eyes (1911) 63, 125
Under Western Eyes (opera) 128n6
United States 72, 79, 83; *see also* American cinema

Victory (1915) 45–6, 63–6, 82–7, 89–91, 92–3, 94, 95, 114–16
   allusions and narrative antecedents of 84, 84n10, 92, 114–16, 114n5
   and anonymous narrator 86, 87
   and 'made to see' 85–6, 91, 93, 94
   reader and 87, 93
   and rescue motif 91, 93
   and shadow motif 97, 98, 103
Victory (film version by Tourneur 1919) 66, 84, 87, 90
Victory (opera) 128, 128n6
Victory stage production (Basil Macdonald Hastings) 46, 59, 114n5
Vidocq, Eugène François 46
violence in Conrad's work 46
visual technologies 70, 72, 102
voice equal voices in Conrad's Malay fiction 4, 14, 19, 20
   female voice 37

voyeurism 67–8, 69

Wagner, Richard 129n10, 129n11, 133–4, 134n22, 134n23, 135
Watt, Ian 77
Watts, Cedric 84n10
Wheatley, Alison E. 57, 58
Winzeler, Robert L. 36
women, female voice 37
   and hysteria 32, 33
   and interest in boxing films 90, 90n19
   as judged by appearance 74–5
   laughter and weeping 57
writing, Conrad and making the reader 'see' and 'made to see' 14–15, 77–8, 81, 85, 91, 93, 94

Youth: A Narrative, and Two Other Stories (1902) 141

Žižek, Slavoj 141
Zola, Émile 2–3
   Thérèse Raquin (1873 play adaptation), 2

For Product Safety Concerns and Information please contact our EU representative GPSR@taylorandfrancis.com
Taylor & Francis Verlag GmbH, Kaufingerstraße 24, 80331 München, Germany

www.ingramcontent.com/pod-product-compliance
Lightning Source LLC
Chambersburg PA
CBHW051646230426
43669CB00013B/2462